VALUING NATURE?

The state of the environment is now widely acknowledged as a serious cause for concern. *Valuing Nature?* argues that responding to this concern by economic valuation of the environment as a consumer good only makes matters worse. The book brings together philosophers, economists and sociologists to put the case for a new and more creative approach to environmental policy. The discussion covers:

- the structure of environmental policy-making
- the current orthodoxy in environmental economics and its deficiencies
- the deeper problems with contingent valuation surveys and cost-benefit analysis for environmental decisions
- alternative valuation methods

Embracing three disciplines, this book is nevertheless written in a clear, accessible style. It includes chapters by Geoff Hodgson, Clive Spash, Michael Jacobs, Brian Wynne and John O'Neill. Its ground-breaking critique and suggestions will be of great interest both to specialists in the field and to students of the disciplines concerned; it has important messages for anyone concerned with how decisions about the environment are made.

John Foster has worked in teaching, public sector management and green politics as well as academic research. He is a research fellow at the Centre for the Study of Environmental Change, Lancaster University.

VALUING NATURE?

Ethics, economics and
the environment

Edited and
with an introduction
by John Foster

London and New York

First published 1997
by Routledge
11 New Fetter Lane, London EC4P 4EE

Simultaneously published in the USA and Canada
by Routledge
29 West 35th Street, New York, NY 10001

Typeset in Garamond by J&L Composition Ltd, Filey, North Yorkshire

Printed and bound in Great Britain by
Creative Print and Design (Wales), Ebbw Vale

British Library Cataloging in Publication Data
A catalogue record for this book is available from the British Library.

Library of Congress Cataloging-in-Publication Data
Valuing nature? Ethics, economics and the environment/edited by
John Foster.
Includes bibliographical references and index.
1. Environmental policy—Cost effectiveness.   2. Environmental
economics.   3. Environmental ethics.   I. Foster, John (John
Michael), 1949–   .
GE180.V35   1997
363.7—dc20   96–41517
CIP

ISBN 0–415–12978–8 (hbk)
ISBN 0–415–14875–8 (pbk)

CONTENTS

CONTENTS

CONTRIBUTORS

Jonathan Aldred has recently lectured in economics at Durham University. His research interests are in welfare economics and its relation to ethics.

Simon Bilsborough is an economist with the Countryside Council for Wales.

John Foster has worked in teaching, management and green politics as well as academic research. He is a Research Fellow at the Centre for the Study of Environmental Change, Lancaster University.

Robin Grove-White is Director of the Centre for the Study of Environmental Change, Lancaster University. Formerly Director of the Council for the Protection of Rural England, he is a Forestry Commissioner and Chairman of Greenpeace UK, and has published a number of articles and reports on environment and policy issues.

Geoffrey Hodgson is at the Judge Institute of Management Studies, Cambridge University. Among his publications on institutional economics are *Economics and Institutions* (1988) and *Economics and Evolution: Bringing Life back into Economics* (1993).

Alan Holland is Senior Lecturer in Philosophy at Lancaster University, and editor of the quarterly journal *Environmental Values*. He has published on ethical, bioethical and economic aspects of environment.

Michael Jacobs is Research Fellow in the Department of Geography at the London School of Economics, and Visiting Research Fellow at the Centre for the Study of Environmental Change, Lancaster University. An economist, his publications include *The Green Economy* (1991) and *The Politics of the Real World* (1996).

Russell Keat is Professor of Political Philosophy in the Department of Politics, Edinburgh University. He is the author of *The Politics of Social Theory* (1981) and co-editor of *Enterprise Culture* (1991) and *The Authority of the Consumer* (1994).

CONTRIBUTORS

John O'Neill is Reader in Philosophy at Lancaster University. He is the author of *Ecology, Policy and Politics: Human Well-being and the Natural World* (1993).

Mark Peacock has recently completed a doctoral thesis in economics at Cambridge University.

Jeremy Roxbee Cox has recently retired as Senior Lecturer in Philosophy at Lancaster University. He has published a number of articles on philosophical issues related to the environment.

Clive Spash is Lecturer in Environmental Economics in the Department of Land Economy at Cambridge University. Formerly with the Environmental Economics Research Group at Stirling, he has published widely on contingent valuation approaches to environmental issues. He is Vice-President of the European branch of the International Society for Ecological Economics.

Andrew Stirling is a Research Fellow at the Science Policy Research Unit, Sussex University, where he has recently completed a doctorate on energy policy option appraisal.

Brian Wynne is Professor of Science Studies and Research Director of the Centre for the Study of Environmental Change, Lancaster University. Among his publications are *Risk Management and Hazardous Wastes: Implementation and the Dialectics of Credibility* (1987) and (with Alan Irwin) *Misunderstanding Science?* (1996).

PREFACE

This book really arose in response to the broad conditions of intellectual, political and economic life sketched in its Introduction. These conditions manifest themselves very plainly in the gathering environmental crisis; but also, more insidiously, in much of the way in which our kind of society tries to address this crisis. As well as the state of the environment, the state of our attention to the state of the environment is now seriously alarming. The drive for our book comes from this level of concern.

Proximately, however, the book arose from a grant made by the Economic and Social Research Council under its Global Environmental Change programme to Lancaster University's Centre for the Study of Environmental Change (CSEC), for a project to explore conceptual problems with the dominant neo-classical orthodoxy of environmental economics. These were problems, as described in the research bid, with the representations of value and human personhood on which this orthodoxy depends. In the background lay the work of writers like the American philosopher Mark Sagoff, who had argued (Sagoff 1988b) that there were logical as well as practical difficulties with capturing environmental value on a model of individual preferences. Our project was designed to suggest how controversies affecting the use of neo-classical environmental valuation methods in policy-making might stem from the deliberately restrictive nature of these representations, and correspondingly how more promising ways of handling environmental value in the policy arena could be developed.

CSEC is an innovative research enterprise based in social science, but with extensive and lively connections across the spectrum of environmental thinking both in and beyond Lancaster. It was therefore natural to set this study up as a series of linked research seminars with a diverse cross-disciplinary membership. Philosophers, economists and sociologists from six universities (ranging in seniority from professors to postgraduates) and from the policy world, met in Lancaster for this purpose on half a dozen occasions between 1993 and 1995. As the vigorous, open and fruitful discussion and writing sparked by these arrangements progressed, it became clear to us that we had the materials and the unifying themes, as well as the incentive, for this collection.

What those themes are, and why the book aspires to be more than the random assemblage that 'collection' often implies, I try to show in introducing it. Here, though, let me emphasise that (perhaps despite initial appearances) it is meant not just for academics and students within its various disciplines, but also for the concerned general reader. It is meant specifically for the reader who sees that issues of environmental value are both important and very difficult, and for the reader who is worried about the way in which unquantifiable considerations are dealt with in the policy-making of a modern complex state; and especially, it is meant for the reader who recognises that these concerns are closely and non-accidentally connected. Although the following chapters are of differing academic density, and some indeed are consciously quite challenging, we have tried at all times to keep in mind, and condition for, an intelligent non-specialist audience. One great virtue of cross-disciplinarity is to keep one alert in this respect: having to be intelligible in the first place to each other, we may at least have more chance of being heard beyond the academy.

But what have we to say there? We offer a thoroughgoing and fundamental critique of the environmental economic orthodoxy – but to have offered only critique would have been to stay in the academy with a vengeance. Yet the pervasive conditions to which we respond certainly do not encourage brisk solutions or easy optimism. Nevertheless, the book as a whole – in particular, Part III – suggests a number of new directions and positive developments in social processes for environmental valuation; and these may offer practical resources for a wider cultural hope. (In this connection, the difference between optimism and hope bears pondering.)

ACKNOWLEDGEMENTS

As editor, I must thank in the first place all the other contributors; I hope they will feel that the result rewards their efforts. My Lancaster colleagues have provided much-needed intellectual and moral support – in particular, Robin Grove-White, the Director of CSEC, who has been a rock throughout; Michael Jacobs, in discussion with whom many of the shaping ideas emerged; and Alan Holland, John O'Neill and Bron Szerszinski, all of whose work has illuminated my own.

I am grateful to Alison Kirk, commissioning editor at Routledge, for her patient encouragement; to Barbara Hickson at CSEC for efficient administrative help with the research project; and to Kate Lamb, also at CSEC, for the meticulous clerical assistance without which this book would have been so very much more onerous a task.

Without Rose Foster, it would simply never have happened at all.

John Foster
Lancaster, July 1996

INTRODUCTION
Environmental value and the scope of economics
John Foster

1. VALUING NATURE?

How do we value nature? How do we, and how should we, express our sense of the worth and practical importance of our natural environment, and the significance of our relations with other living things? How do we include such values within the processes of social decision-making? How, in particular, do we integrate them with the economic considerations which feature so prominently in those processes? Can the demands of that integration help us to understand environment and economics better? And do they have a wider relevance to policy – to the development of a democracy which might attend more intelligently to issues of value in general?

These are the questions with which this book concerns itself. They are urgently pressing questions, and they mix philosophical, sociological and economic themes in ways which refuse to respect the confines of these intellectual disciplines. In response, we have tried to combine all three perspectives – ambitiously, perhaps, but the ambition is an index of the urgency.

Why are these questions now so pressing? A sense of the value and importance of the natural environment looms increasingly large in contemporary consciousness as other, more traditional vocabularies for representing our place in the scheme of things fail. At the same time, our collective activity has been impacting more and more compellingly on that environment. We have (we now recognise) for decades been subjecting its systemic organisation both locally and globally to unprecedentedly rapid, far-reaching and often detrimental changes. Acknowledgement of this state of affairs, confined twenty-five years ago to the intellectual fringes, is now well on its way to common acceptance, and has begun to exert a real influence on the shaping of public policy. But, perhaps inevitably, that influence has been most apparent in the emergence of a recognition that environment and *the economy* are inseparable: not only do we impact

1

adversely on the environment through our economic activities principally, but our dependence on this environment is seen as principally a matter of our needing its resources, assimilative capacities, amenities and life-support systems in order to conduct that activity in the first place. If this is certainly an important part of the truth, focusing on it in that way just as certainly shifts the register of responsible concern towards a discourse of measurement, calculation and prediction. Moreover, the language of public policy choice in modern societies is overwhelmingly one of human welfare, conceived in terms of a sophisticated but still radically utilitarian calculus of comparative satisfactions. In combination, these factors seem to promise a decisive recasting of our sense of nature and its claims.

So, although it cannot be denied that environmental concerns are now being taken with some seriousness by society and government, many who in recent years have contended for those concerns have reason to feel anxiously ambivalent about their success. In expressing that ambivalence, the word 'value' is unavoidable. Does the currently favoured discourse of sustainability and natural capital, dependent as it is on explicit economic valuation of the natural environment, really represent a positive *valuing* of nature? Is this new register of nature's value a genuine recognition of nature as valuable? Or does it constitute a further, more insidious stage in its progressive *de*valuing – a new eco-friendly jargon for licensing our aspirations to technological management and control of nature?

These anxieties are not just about words. For one thing, if they are justified, a very important implication is that we are likely to go on generating, on an ever larger and more dangerous scale, the kind of failure of managerial control represented by such emblematic modern disasters as Chernobyl and BSE. Equally, a politico-technico-administrative consensus built in this way may well lack the social robustness, the roots in what people really feel and fear, to cope adequately with such disasters when they do happen – something which the BSE case, for instance, has demonstrated very clearly. But further: lying beneath these substantively 'environmental' worries is a more general concern, attaching less to actual or imagined hazards than to the whole quality of our common experience (which is quite often what seems to be fundamentally at stake in the various contemporary forms of environmental controversy).[1] People alert to this order of concern find themselves asking: is this translation into an economic mode really the only way we can handle questions of value in a complex democratic polity? And can the inescapably economic context of decisions actually be reconciled in this way with collective acknowledgement of human ends which are, strictly, invaluable?

'Value', however, is a word with all the complexity of life itself. What we value, and the rate at which we value it, depends both on our values and on the value of things in themselves – and there are important differences of meaning distinguishing all these usages. The cynic, notoriously, knows the price of everything and the value of nothing; but economists, who aren't generally cynics (many, indeed, seem rather refreshingly innocent), have to study the realisation of comparative value through price. The value which things have for us varies with our desires and inclinations (the basic truth from which the economist works); these, in turn, may reflect the values variously embodied in our culture (the sociologist's field of insight); but to value something which in itself lacks value is to lay those desires, and perhaps also that cultural grounding, open to criticism (the moralist's *point d'appui*). Again, there are in some people's eyes certain fundamental or ultimate values which seem to matter just because they are in themselves beyond the reach of any deliberate evaluative scrutiny; but at the same time, sincerely to call something 'invaluable' is to value it very highly, a valuation which must translate somehow into practice and comparabilities. The notion of value, in short, eludes our definitional grasp with a supple duplicity characteristic of the really important concepts in human experience; and many of its doublenesses of meaning underlie the specific ambiguity which is put to the question in our title.

We have tried to begin the process of grappling with these complexities in the open-ended, interdisciplinary way which they clearly demand. The following collection comprises contributions by economists, philosophers and social scientists, organised around certain common themes but without seeking too hard to impose any single framework or artificial synthesis. They range in preoccupation from administrative practice through economic, social and political analysis to ethical theory. They exhibit a corresponding and perhaps initially disconcerting diversity of styles. We believe, nevertheless, that a strong commonality of approach manifests itself, and some important shared conclusions emerge; these are sharply critical of the turn represented by recent environmental economic thinking, and in sum support the development of a distinctively different model.

I shall try to indicate the nature of our common themes in the next section of this Introduction, and offer a broad overview of the discussion and its critical conclusions in the third. In the final section, I go on to consider the upshot of positive suggestions emerging from our critique, and to explain why it has, at this stage, a rather exploratory and unresolved character.

2. ECONOMICS AND META-ECONOMICS

In 1974 E. F. Schumacher introduced his richly seminal treatment of environmental issues with a distinction between economics and what he called meta-economics:

> Economics operates legitimately and usefully within a 'given' framework which lies altogether outside the economic calculus. We might say

that economics does not stand on its own feet, or that it is a derived body of thought – derived from meta-economics. If the economist fails to study meta-economics, or, even worse, if he remains unaware of the fact that there are boundaries to the applicability of the economic calculus, he is likely to fall into a similar kind of error to that of certain medieval theologians who tried to settle questions of physics by means of biblical quotations.

(Schumacher 1974: 38)

Economics treats legitimately of how the production of goods and services, the processes of their distribution and exchange, and so forth, are organised: meta-economics as Schumacher conceived of it treats of what gives context, direction and point to all these activities. This includes both the nature of the world in which they are set and from which they draw their resources, and the significance of the fairly extensive subset of human ends to which they conduce.

The fundamental distinction here is not original at the level of theory; its picture of *economics* seems to correspond well enough, for instance, to Robbins's well-known definition of the subject as the study of choice under conditions of scarcity, among alternative means to multiple but given ends (Robbins 1932: 16). Where Schumacher is interesting is in his pointing, in the context (then comparatively novel) of environmental concern, to the strong tendency of economists (and not just economists) to ignore in practice the distinction between attention to means, and attention to the ends and possibilities in relation to which they exist as means. He was disturbed, as an energy economist, about the attitude to natural resources, and as a thoughtfully spiritual man, about the quality of human purposes, in the 'developed' societies; the economic mind-set, preoccupied with means (crudely, money and power) which it is after all a very ancient failing to *take* as self-sufficient ends, seemed to him to be diverting attention from increasingly urgent questions about the material and moral bases of economic activity.

He suggests, it will be noted, two ways in which the importance of meta-economics might be ignored. We might simply think in too narrowly economic a way, concentrating on those matters of production and consumption where the 'economic calculus' (Robbins's 'economic science') at least appears to work, while treating the natural world as essentially a set of free goods, and questions of ends as beyond the purview of scientific concern. But also, and much more insidiously, we might think *economistically*. We might, in Schumacher's terms, fail to recognise the proper scope and limits of that calculus, and try to deal with considerations about the ethical context of economic behaviour, not by ignoring them, but seeking to bring them within the scope of an approach which is itself essentially economic.

Consider, by way of a non-environmental example, how we might think in these various ways about education. To address educational issues in *meta-economic* terms would be to reflect, for instance, on how the development of knowledge and powers of imagination might contribute to a 'becoming existence' (in Schumacher's own phrase) for human beings, given the inevitable material limitations of that existence; and about how these cultural preconditions for proper human flourishing could be promoted in relation to the various economic activities of production and consumption which are necessary for its material support. To think about education in narrowly *economic* terms would be to leave out of account such apparently intractable issues of adjusting right livelihood to its necessary conditions, and to concentrate, instead, on the costs of the process and its actual or potential benefits at the merely economic level: its contribution to improving the literacy or technological aptitude of the workforce, to raising the expectations of consumers, and so forth. But to think about it *economistically* would be to say: 'Of course we must take knowledge, imagination, the promotion of right livelihood and all that into account – these are important components of human welfare; the real problem – and the job with which the economist is best placed to help – is to offset gains in these areas against any concomitant sacrifices in more material production which society must make in order to achieve them, so that we can be sure of pursuing the overall optimal welfare path.'

These useful if rather rough-and-ready distinctions can help us to locate environmental economics. This is a sub-discipline which has in effect developed since Schumacher wrote (and at least partly in response to his strictures and others like them). It represents the recognition that we can no longer think in a narrowly economic way in this domain; we can no longer ignore, when shaping our economic activities, the constraints placed by the environment on practicable modes of human flourishing. But correspondingly, as this recognition has grown, it has only further exposed the dominance of economistic over meta-economic thinking about vital aspects of human–environmental relations.

Now as Schumacher's medieval comparison piquantly insists, either of his ways of failing to attend to meta-economics is actually 'unscientific', and indeed potentially obscurantist. But it is clear enough how, in a climate of positivism, the desire for scientific respectability could come to tell against the narrowly economic view, while still actively conducing to the economistic. The case for ecological limits, applying to raw material resources, waste sinks and ecosystem services, has certainly not become irresistible through the advancement of science *alone* over the period since Schumacher wrote. But accumulating scientific evidence has undoubtedly played a crucial role in moving us from the situation in which he could criticise economics for treating the entire ecological framework as given, to that in which Professor David Pearce can premiss an advocacy of environmental-economic valuation on the position that:

5

environmental scarcity is . . . an ecological fact of life . . . Until the economic value of environmental quality is an everyday feature of the way we compute progress and, more importantly, of the way we make economic decisions . . . the environment will not be given a fair chance.

(Pearce 1993: 3)

Economic thinking, that is, has embraced environmental and ecological limits – and it has done so in a variety of alternative forms, including ecological and steady-state economics, as well as in the mainstream. But it is, overwhelmingly, economistic thinking which has embraced the crucial questions of how environmental value can articulate public policy choices within those limits. That is very clear from the way the mainstream neo-classical version (with which Pearce himself is closely associated in the UK), the only version of green economics with a respectable pedigree in terms of 'economic science', has commanded the field.

Neo-classical economics offers a model of self-interested rational choice to represent how we bring our values to bear on individual and collective decisions. The criterion of value on this model is what people are willing to pay for something, as a measure of what they are prepared to give up to acquire or defend it. Value thus regarded is a function of people's preferences – reflecting differentially-strong desires for goods, which we each seek to gratify optimally given our available resources and the structure of prices. The notion of the allocative efficiency of the market is a corollary of this picture, since the optimal satisfaction of preferences for a number of agents requires the kind of mutual adjustability of demand and supply through the price mechanism which the ideal market situation is supposed to embody. What I am willing, at the margin, to pay for a good and the strength of my preference for it are not, on this model, distinct from one another, nor from the value which I place on it; and the value of the good to people in general is similarly not distinct from its price in a suitably open and competitive market, which can thus be treated for the purposes of analysis as an objective index of value.

It is (at least in the UK) Pearce and his associates who have most persistently developed and advocated the extension of this model to environmental issues. The procedure is, first, to treat desired features of the environment like clean air, unpolluted water, open spaces, climatic stability etc., as if they were variously preferred goods. Correspondingly, environmental harms are treated as *externalities* – damage caused by the inadvertent clumsiness of the 'invisible elbow'[2] attached to Adam Smith's 'Invisible Hand'. This damage can be of different kinds – reduction of the waste-absorption capacities of ecosystems, depletion of the pool of resources, adverse effects on our physical and psychological health – but all its aspects are, in principle anyway, things in regard to the avoidance of which we also have, or could form, preferences. Thus both the goods and

6

the bads, environmentally, are represented as susceptible of having an economic value placed on them. Actual or notional values for these various benefits and costs are to be derived on the basis of our preferences as revealed either in real markets where appropriate, or in hypothetical market situations constructed through social survey techniques (so-called contingent valuation, or CV). Consideration of what course of action might be in our overall best interests can then be informed by an assessment, through cost–benefit analysis (CBA), of how these values in the environmental sphere balance up. In particular, since we now appear to have a means of measuring the net flow of benefit to human beings from the natural environment, the way is open to treating its resources and systemic capacities as a form of capital stock ('natural capital'), and the maintenance of that stock over time as an index of the environmental *sustainability* of human activities.[3]

Claims for this approach have recently been much urged in both official and academic circles, and it has found serious political favour. Although CV, with its requirement for individuals explicitly to *put* a money value on natural objects, remains somewhat controversial (often for essentially methodological reasons), the overall picture of environmental value as expressible and manipulable in money terms may fairly be called the prevailing orthodoxy of the UK policy community on these issues. Robin Grove-White's opening chapter sets the stage for our whole book by tracing the intellectual and institutional history of this orthodoxy in relation to the environment. But, as he also points out, its establishment as an orthodoxy in that domain is symptomatic of much broader trends within 'the dominant "modernist" ontology' – trends towards economistic views of human nature and of the appropriate way to arbitrate its different evaluative commitments right across the board, trends which have now developed an apparently irresistible momentum in our kind of society.

Let us recall Schumacher. He was at least a minor prophet, and if he was even half right, these powerful trends are carrying us into profound and systematic *delusion*. (He concluded the passage already quoted with an even sharper warning: 'Every science is beneficial within its proper limits, but becomes evil and destructive as soon as it transgresses them.') The idea that there are kinds of choice about how we should, as a society, commit our resources, which are simply not addressable in terms of value-for-money – that there are values in pursuit of which we must spend money while unable in principle to capture or prioritise them in those terms – is fast becoming as much of a heresy for modern politics as the idea that the Bible had nothing to say about physics would have been for Aquinas. In education, health care, the defence of the realm, the administration of justice, the prevention of crime, it is increasingly accepted that the economic calculus applies, that value for money is an appropriate overall expectation and audit an appropriate tool. And to call this trend even questionable, never mind

7

'evil and destructive', would now be to meet with widespread blank incomprehension.

So when environmental economics cheerfully carries the banner of the new economistic orthodoxy into the territory of environmental value, the impulse to resistance feels as though it has a more than merely local responsibility. Local resistance is certainly what this book offers: we want to help dislodge this orthodoxy from this particular arena. We are not unduly concerned with methodological or statistical niceties; we want to reveal the whole neo-classical approach to environmental concern for the dangerous misrepresentation which we think it is – and we want to do this in the service of what we take to be more appropriate kinds of regard for nature and for each other. But in the convergence of economics and ethics on environment, we are also confronting a crucial test case. If an argument against economistic orthodoxy cannot be mounted *here*, in relation to something as fundamental as our evaluative experience of the natural context of our lives, then maybe no convincing argument can any longer be mounted. On the other hand, if a convincing argument *can* be mounted, perhaps it may also help us to see how the scope of economics can be more effectively delimited in other areas of our common life.

3. THE CRITIQUE OF ENVIRONMENTAL ECONOMICS

One obvious way of setting up a critique of the economistic orthodoxy as it bears on environmental issues would be to attack its *utilitarianism* in the environmental context. 'Economistic thinking', after all, could be taken as a plausible hostile characterisation of utilitarianism: the unwarranted extension of a calculus of incentives from the economic sphere, to model the processes of rational choice in the sphere of ethics. And in the other two chapters comprising Part I of the book, it is indeed the utilitarian cast of the neo-classical approach which is taken as the principal focus for criticism, from both the economic and the ethical perspectives: Geoffrey Hodgson suggesting some quite general difficulties with an economics thus based, which emerge especially sharply in its attempted application to environment; while Russell Keat argues that cost–benefit analysis fails to engage with key environmental concerns specifically because its utilitarian ethical structure is inappropriate to the kinds of value on which they depend.

This, as I say, offers a good way in; but it might make the target in view seem more limited than actually it is. In fact, it belongs to a cross-disciplinary undertaking like ours to recognise that utilitarianism, the ethical theory or doctrine, can no more be seen as the foundation for a particular habit of attention to value in the area of social policy, than it can be seen as merely a shadow cast over ethics by the economic framework of industrialism. The co-evolution and continuing mutual reinforcement of ideas and social forms is just too intimately complex a matter. Historically, for instance, utilitarianism as a systematic account of the ethical life could hardly have arisen except in a society already in process of reorganising itself through trade, mechanised production and entrepreneurial initiative – but then, these could only have been the dynamic features they were through expressing a sense of the person as moral agent which had already begun to crystallise in the the utilitarian themes of individual satisfaction and its rational optimisation. Correspondingly, what we point to in criticising economistic thinking needs to be seen as something more, or at any rate something other, than either the utilitarian ethic itself, or some large externally identifiable features of the socio-economic formation in which it arose. Perhaps it might better be thought of as the principles on which these ideas and forms configure one another within Grove-White's 'dominant "modernist" ontology', or within what we could alternatively designate, in the cultural analyst Raymond Williams's rather less cognitivist terminology, as the modernist structure of feeling (Williams 1961).

The organising principles of this mutual configuration are a radical individualism and an assumption of the essential commensurability of value. These principles unite to generate the fundamental idea of our engagement with value as a process of *optimising from the perspective of the valuer*. The question for practical choice, whether in individual or social decision-making, is taken to be: how important to me, or to us, is this as against that? How far should we pursue this end or goal as against these others, given that normally we cannot fully achieve all these goals together? And this question is taken to be answerable in terms of an optimal ratio of value among our goals, which will determine the allocation of effort and attention between them which we think will be most beneficial – where 'benefit' is taken in a suitably wide sense, to mean the realisation of the good as it presents itself to me, or to us. (The kinship of this structure with that of economic problems as defined by Robbins – the allocation of limited means as between multiple ends to maximise utility – is clear.)

The chapters in Part II of the book are concerned with exploring different aspects of this economistic configuration as it applies to environmental policy issues. They do this through the further consideration of neoclassical environmental economics, and of the way in which key environmental values seem to challenge and elude its terms. Thus they all follow on thematically from Part I, enriching with more varied detail the argument that the basically utilitarian methodology of CBA cannot accommodate such values. But they also, taken together, begin to map the features which bring environmental concern into *deep* conflict with the structure of modernity. The natural environment is the focus and meeting point for a radical diversity of human practices subtending value; as such, living together as humans sharing a common world, we cannot avoid making practical choices over this diversity; but the world we share is not just there for the benefit of, or with reference to the good as perceived by, human beings.

9

These interconnected general characteristics are sufficient to defeat any economistic modelling of the central environmental concerns.

Recognising the significance of the first of these features depends on our acknowledging, as Mark Peacock reminds us, that our values are rooted in our various practices in a way which necessarily escapes instrumental assessment; any such assessment would still have to take for granted the normatively sanctioned interpretive schemas embodied in at least some of those practices, since only in virtue of these are we able to communicate intelligibly with one another as social beings at all. But then, if we consider just some topic heads from the vast range of different practices within which we engage with the natural world – dwelling in it, sharing it with other living things, cultivating it, conserving it, studying its workings, extracting material resources from it, appreciating its beauty and grandeur, recreating ourselves in it – it is, as John O'Neill suggests, profoundly implausible to suppose that the concerns arising through all these interwoven modes of engagement with what we comprehensively and perhaps too conveniently call 'environment', should be in any substantive sense *commensurable* in themselves – that they should be reducible in principle to the terms of some common basic value.

Moreover, our engagement with environment is not just something which takes place *within* the practices of the various interest groups, associations and communities, with their often widely differing presuppositions, to which we all belong. Of its nature, it provides a principal forum for a great deal of the abrasion, collision, conflict and accommodation *between* these constituencies, which contribute so much colour to life's pageant. Simon Bilsborough shows in an intriguing case-study how the very typical conflicts arising between agriculture and conservation simply cannot be arbitrated in practice through economic valuation; and it is clear that this reflects more than just a specific practical or institutional difficulty. For if the values of farmers and conservationists, for example, are indeed ultimately incommensurable, any offer to align them to a common scale will inevitably become the focus for strategic behaviour of the various kinds which Bilsborough records; there is actually nothing *else* for it to be.

'The environment', in other words, is something upon which very many frames of reference converge.[4] But there is no frame of reference which is as it were 'naturally given', and which does not have to be contended for in environmental debate; no standard or criterion of comparison for environmental value which inherently transcends the perspective of a particular cultural understanding of nature and our relation to it. The importance of Brian Wynne's chapter here lies in the clarity with which it demonstrates, from the closely analogous field of risk studies, how attempts to constitute natural science as such a culture-transcendent knowledge have been self-defeating.

What all this shows is that if we are to make environmental choices which can claim to be rationally optimal, that can only be by annexing these radically diverse values to a structure like preference-satisfaction, which has commensurability and rational optimisation already built into it. The neo-classical model, that is, must be driven by a conception not of what valuing the environment is like, but of what rational practical choice must be like. Given that conception, indeed, irreducible pluralism at the communal or societal level might seem to strengthen the case for the whole approach. For only if this kaleidoscope of concerns could be represented as built up out of the pursuit of perceived benefit, however disparate, to individual valuers (taking benefit in a sufficiently broad sense), and the strengths of preference attaching to values at the individual foci roughly aggregated, should we have enough for an answer to the practical question as economistic thinking envisages it.

But this line of thought is strongly countered by the other two chapters in Part II. Jeremy Roxbee Cox, analysing the intrinsic value attributable to environmental features or objects, shows how this absolutely vital dimension of their significance fails to be captured by the economistic construct of 'existence value' precisely because, while the latter has a beneficial and aggregative structure, the former has not. A species, a forest ecosystem or a wilderness do not matter 'in themselves' for any valuer by supplying benefit to that valuer such as could plausibly be summed across different valuers. Moreover, once we start reflecting in this light on how they do matter to us in themselves, we recognise that we are concerned with them largely *as* not catering to our interests in that way. As Alan Holland develops the point, the very strong impetus behind such concern is actually to defend the natural world 'beyond the call of human interests' – a commitment which the economistic model of our environmental responsibility in terms of sustaining flows of benefit from natural capital, so far from capturing for practical policy-making, renders unintelligible.

This is not of course to deny the obvious truths that things can go better or worse, environmentally speaking, from the human point of view, that humans have an ordinary and entirely natural interest in these things going better rather than worse, and that it makes good sense for them to consult their relevant preferences rationally in any kind of choice or policy-making. (What will constitute rational consultation, if the methodology of neo-classicism is abandoned, is another matter.) Nor is it to claim that such preferences, however articulated, must be in any narrow sense *self*-interested – we can perfectly well have a disinterested common interest in things going better for, say, other species. But there are ranges of environmental value where this story of *our* interest, however disinterested, just cannot be the whole of the story. Sooner or later (and often sooner than we expect) in trying to think about how we should act environmentally, we find ourselves coming up against the recognition that non-human beings and other non-human ordered structures in nature have lives and courses *of their own*,

11

which not only do not belong to us, but simply do not refer to us at all; and we find, too, that our awareness of this non-human-centredness is radically implicated in our sense of nature's worth. Our concern, that is to say, to act in the light of the value of natural existences turns out to be a concern with what matters in large part by virtue of placing our most general perspective of evaluation so firmly beside the point – a concern with it, indeed, precisely because it matters in that way.

Such a concern, it is clear, rebuffs economistic reformulation in its very nature. To model the kind of engagement with value which it represents on the pattern of 'optimising from the perspective of the valuer' would be to involve oneself in deep pragmatic contradiction – for the lives and courses of other things in nature are most characteristically valuable, as it were, just insofar as the acknowledgment of their value disturbs and undercuts that approach from that perspective. To see the natural autonomous life of another species, for instance, as mattering in itself is to yield to a kind of involvement in value – or better, a kind of involvement in the world *through* value – to which the comparative and arbitrative posture that goes with optimising is profoundly alien.

The access which it gives us to that manner of encountering value is at the heart of environmentalism's more general significance, in face of the modernistic drive to annexe and denature Schumacher's meta-economic realm. For if our meta-economic dealings with ends and values are to be genuinely *meta-*, their transcendence of the economic must surely consist in a *radical* incompatibility, a radical difference between ways of asking 'how important . . . ?'. Environmental concern at this level shows us, or reminds us, what it must be like to move in a realm where we encounter value which is not ours to arbitrate. And what the first two parts of this book demonstrate in sum is that there must indeed be a firm boundary line to be drawn around the scope of 'the economic calculus', around the domain in which the economic habit of configuring value can help us think and plan, since such significant elements of our environmental thinking, at any rate, must lie beyond that boundary.

4. PRACTICAL JUDGEMENT AND THE ENVIRONMENT

We might hope, by the same token, that the kind of consideration which environmental concerns seem to demand could show us something of how operating in the meta-economic realm might be organised – and in particular, about how that realm can be respected for itself and at the same time rationally related to the economic.

For it is clear that concerns properly to be called 'environmental' belong in *both* realms. The environmental crisis has an inherently dual aspect, and those who have wanted to see it as grist for an extended economics have been too partial in their vision, rather than wholly mistaken. On the one hand, we are plainly facing a crisis of resources, a crisis in the relation of humankind to the Earth considered in terms of life-support functions (provision of raw materials, waste assimilation and ecological services) which traditional economic categories of land and capital might plausibly be revised to accommodate. On the other hand, however, we are facing (equally plainly, if we care to look at things straight) a crisis of *spirit*: a climacteric in our relations to the world of nature beyond us, at which ultimate questions of human identity, belonging and purpose are being raised. These crises, or aspects of the one crisis, are inextricable: the crisis of spirit is a crisis of the attitude which *takes* the Earth to be basically a set of resources, conservation of which just *as* resources (the economistic model) serves only to lacerate the spirit further. And maybe this, too, is paradigmatic of the situation in other areas of our common life (education, health care . . .) where values demanding meta-economic recognition are just as tangled up with, and just as dangerous in being reduced to, issues requiring specifically economic resolution.

So how might we organise the approach to environmental policy decisions? Methodologically, the alternative to the economistic neo-classical algorithm assumed (with varying degrees of explicitness) throughout this volume is practical judgement, the reasoned consideration of alternatives and resolution of differences within a discursive framework. Although within this framework a use for various measures and algorithmic techniques is bound to be recognised, they will have a role as (in John O'Neill's words) aids to deliberation and reasoned judgement, rather than as what Andy Stirling calls a 'justificationist' substitute for its shared exercise. The essential claim on behalf of such substitutes, as Stirling's account well illustrates, has been their apparent provision of an 'objective', scientific and programmatic way to resolve value conflicts – which in complex modern societies can certainly prove both difficult and deep-seated. But if, as we have argued in relation to environmental economics, this sort of approach is not available at least in key instances of environmental conflict, then there at any rate we are going to be thrown back on the final and inescapable responsibility of the best collective judgement we can muster: a responsibility novel only in that we have for so long supposed that we could have something more.

How, then, is practical judgement best institutionalised in relation to the economic and other explicitly quantitative dimensions of environmental policy-making? The chapters in Part III of the book may all be seen as exploring this question, given both the perceived need to transcend the economistic paradigm, and also the need to exercise such judgement in matters with an inescapable economic aspect.

The difficulties presented by the combination of these two requirements must not be underestimated. They can be illustrated from Pigou's well-known claim that the scope of the economist includes 'that part of social welfare that can be brought directly or indirectly into relation with the measuring-rod of money' (Pigou 1920: 11). On this basis Pigou himself seemed to find no difficulty in ascribing, for example, attunement to the beautiful in nature or in art to the domain of *non*-economic welfare (ibid.: 14). But actually the distinction as he sets it up is unable in principle to prevent economics from extending its purview to embrace all political life. For there are simply no choices which we are called on to make as sharers in a modern polity where monetary considerations do not bear at least indirectly on the goods envisaged. We may choose, say, to protect other living things because a sense of species humility and (however obscurely) of justice demands it; but unless we so choose in the recognition that this option must incur an overall cost, our choice is unlikely to have any practical effect. In choosing to pursue these goods as against others, we must weigh them up as reasons for action within a complex which will include considerations (potential opportunity costs) demanding to be expressed in monetary terms. But then, reasons which can be *weighed* against reasons expressed in terms of the measuring-rod of money are themselves necessarily brought thereby into indirect relation with that measure.

This looks at first blush like the argument that if I won't betray my friend for £1,000, then I must value him at *more* than £1,000 – when of course what one wants to say is that is that I value him in a way to which money values are simply irrelevant. But the point is that while we do have a practice of friendship in which, so long as the practice is well-constituted, money values are indeed irrelevant, we do not have, and plainly could not have, such a practice of social policy choice. Such choice in a complex, highly differentiated and bureaucratically organised society is irredeemably pervaded by money values.

It can, then, seem that the meta-economic mode in social evaluation is inherently defenceless against economistic reduction. How is this problem to be addressed? The approaches considered in Part III range from trying to make room for forms of meta-economic judgement within a more sensitive practice of economic appraisal, through an attempt to give judgement itself something of the quantitative structure which weighing presupposes, to the sketching out of a set of fully deliberative policy-making institutions, in which our collective judgement itself is recognised as ultimate and economic valuation as just a possible means of its exercise.

Thus Jonathan Aldred, reapproaching the issue of 'existence value' as an economist broadly within the mainstream tradition, argues for a distinction between *welfare* and *utility* which could perhaps detach the value we accord to other existents in nature from the optimising perspective of agent-based well-being. This approach, which also allows room for the non-intersubstitutability of money and environmental goods, leads to the interesting suggestion of *in-kind* valuation of environmental damage, based on the costs of what might be judged an appropriate restitution of it (supposing any were available). In complementary vein, Clive Spash demonstrates that quantified benefit-estimation is going to be unavoidable within any approach which sets standards and criteria for effective environmental management from outside economic valuation – since effectiveness here must at least include *cost*-effectiveness. Spash is explicitly concerned with standards (thresholds, carrying capacities and the like) derived from a natural scientific understanding of environmental issues; but his conclusion in favour of 'a new methodology which emphasises choice of a path leading to potential scenarios rather than the selection of a specific equilibrium solution' clearly adumbrates a relation between cost–benefit considerations and the exercise of judgement in applying non-economic standards generally.

One methodology for elaborating scenarios might be the 'multi-criteria mapping' described in Andy Stirling's chapter. This is a development of multi-attribute utility analysis from the perspective of the sociology of science policy, conceived as a way of clarifying systematically the parameters of any policy decision which has to be taken under conditions of indeterminacy of description, factual ignorance, unpredictability of outcome and plurality of values. It might be said to reassemble many of the materials for optimising, but within a framework which emphasises its final impossibility – facilitating only the most fully reflexive assertion, when all the scores have been entered, of some particular perspective against others.

The real question with which multi-criteria mapping leaves one is whether its multiplication of perspectives and option spaces might not tend to neutralise, along with the optimising aspiration, judgement itself – whether it does not make the actual issues for any real judgement unsurveyable. Michael Jacobs's chapter describes an institutional framework for environmental decision-making which certainly does not have this potential drawback. Here, the heart of judgement is not quantified criteria but dialogue: empirical clarification followed by ethical debate. Helpfully summarising the assumptions of the political theory out of which neo-classical environmental valuation comes, Jacobs contrasts those of the theory of deliberative democracy which, as he shows, can much better accommodate the nature of the environment as a 'public good'; and he provides some compelling hints as to how the various institutions generated by this latter theory might work in practice.

Jacobs's focus, however, is so very firmly on institutional design for ethically-mature environmental *management* that one is driven to ask: what is there about the exercise of environmental judgement within a discursive framework which is essentially different from the modernist commitment to optimise in face of policy options? Granted, the shift out of individualistic mode, the recasting of the blunt neo-classical 'What do I prefer?' as the deliberative 'What should we do for the best?', does make a significant difference of tone and style. But does it, of itself, make enough of a difference to the manner of our *engagement in value* for us to be confident that the possibilities of economistic reduction have been decisively left behind? Might not deliberative procedures just be a more effective way of deploying economistic assumptions from a shared perspective – of optimising environmental value from the perspective of a human group? If so, it seems that this alignment of will in collective decision can be reached in just as much of a managerial optimising spirit as any aggregation of preferences; all that has changed is that the machinery of the process has been sophisticated, to the extent that the social construction of preferences through mutual enlightenment, the claims of fraternity and the authority of consensus, has been acknowledged and conditioned for. There seems nothing so far to prevent our *collectively* treating matters of the spirit as though they were matters of resources – albeit resources conceived in terms of public rather than private goods. Indeed, since questions of goods and resources are likely to be so very much easier to *talk* about in any imaginable policy-making forum than deep questions of the kind of value to which we have to yield ourselves, it might be supposed that the widespread extension of deliberative practice could well make the environmental crisis of spirit worse, not better.

My own chapter concluding the volume responds to worries like these. It tries to suggest what there might be in the nature of evaluative dialogue itself, understood as a creative process, which could meet the deep demands of our engagement in environmental value; and it points to the crucial role of education among the social policy institutions which such understanding must inhabit.

The chapters in Part III thus move off in a number of different and not always entirely compatible directions, and raise a great many more questions than they answer. It would be easy enough to claim this as a virtue in itself; in matters environmental, after all, there should surely be a strong presumption in favour of diversity and against the imposition of convergent methodologies. But that would be facile complacency. For one thing, environmental decisions with hard consequences for real people press in upon us now from all sides and at all levels; it is idle to suppose that a society like ours could hope to address such decisions in ways that were not standardised, scientifically informed and bureaucratically rational. One of the main reasons why neo-classical environmental economics demands respect (and this book intends to be, in part, a tribute of the kind of respect due to an honourable adversary) is that it takes so seriously the need for this society to make real practical choices which do give weight to environmental concerns. Valuing nature at the very least requires that we do not systematically *under*value nature by failing to reflect its claims in our day-to-day determination of policy. The crucial challenge, if one rejects an economistic approach to that process on our kind of grounds, is to describe

16

how practical judgement genuinely capable of engaging with environmental value meta-economically can be brought to bear in ways which will make sense on a Tuesday morning in Scunthorpe. This test we certainly have not yet passed.

The other main reason why we cannot rest content with mere open-endedness has to do with an obligation towards the wider themes raised in this Introduction. The attempt to treat our engagement in nature through value by recasting it on an economistic paradigm is symptomatic of a much more general *malaise*. Finally, the over-extension of the scope of economic thinking is the mark in our political life of a pervasive failure of creativity in our collective dealings with value. Correspondingly, articulating the pre-conditions for a satisfactory account of environmental value clears a space where this (literally) vital human power can begin to grow again. But this process is hardly likely to get far without a strong coherence of theory and practice: a continuum from a meta-ethics which makes living sense of how judgement creates value, through to actively creative institutions defending our most basic meta-economic judgements within the mart of political and social life. There is no escape from the responsibility to struggle towards a newly unified picture of economics and ethics – in the first place, on the ground of environmental value.

That struggle will have to contend against still very powerful tendencies of the age, although those undertaking it will be borne up by a gathering intellectual and moral counter-current. In the nature of such an enterprise, nobody yet knows the answers. But what we can claim for this book is to have begun asking the right kinds of question.

NOTES

1 See for instance the essays in Lash *et al.* 1996.
2 This delightful image is due to Michael Jacobs; see Jacobs 1991.
3 The classic texts for this account are Pearce *et al.* 1989, Pearce *et al.* 1991 and Pearce 1993.
4 There is, indeed, a sense of the term 'environment' in which it stands for an intentional concept not wholly distinct from 'frame of reference' – the field of significance which a given community or practice constitutes out of its interaction with its surroundings (see Cooper 1992); but, of course, this process necessarily takes the surroundings in question as really accessible to others.

Part I

ECONOMICS AND ENVIRONMENTAL POLICY

1

THE ENVIRONMENTAL 'VALUATION' CONTROVERSY

Observations on its recent history and significance

Robin Grove-White

1. INTRODUCTION

Modern environmentalism has tended to embody a deep suspicion of economists. It is not hard to see why. At the most obvious level, economic theory has provided – indeed continues to provide – the underpinning for many environmentally destructive practices. Moreover, in the 1970s and 1980s, the environmental movement gained popular strength partly as an implicit counter to political-economy doctrines about the imperatives of undifferentiated economic growth and about the supposedly central role of markets as sources of human welfare.

But these days many economists are on the side of the angels. They are keen to develop new theoretical tools and methods of analysis which can help *solve* environmental problems. They argue that, since it is economic realities which dominate the imperatives of modern government, environmental priorities too need to be expressed in such terms. Only so, it is urged, will these priorities be taken seriously within government. Such economists see themselves, understandably, as friends of the environment. The burgeoning school of economic theorists concerned to develop methods for capturing in monetary terms the 'value' of environmental goods exemplifies this trend. With the most benign of intentions, such individuals have been advancing new concepts and techniques for use within cost–benefit analyses: 'contingent valuation', 'existence value', 'hedonic pricing' and the like. In what follows, I refer to these innovations collectively as 'surrogate valuation' methods.

The chapter considers two issues. First, it discusses some of the recent history of this emerging conceptual toolkit, focusing particularly on the real-world *application* of surrogate valuation methods in selected political contexts in Britain over the past two decades. And second, through this discussion, it tries to throw light on a paradox: that despite their

21

increasingly evident intellectual limitations (a number of which are discussed in subsequent chapters of this volume), the influence of such methods in the policy world continues to grow.

These observations draw on a measure of personal experience, as a participant in a range of environmental-political arguments over the past twenty years.[1] It seems to me that the impetus behind the development of surrogate valuation methods needs to be understood not only as an attempt to advance environmental ends within government. It is driven also by powerful political realities which have been reshaping the requirements of our dominant administrative culture. Thus the drive towards the attempted *quantification* of public values reflected in such methods appears to go with the grain of the new audit culture (Power 1995) now emerging in Whitehall and its equivalents around the world.

Such a suggestion relates in turn to a wider body of recent discussion about the hitherto under-recognised significance of 'cultural' dimensions of the environmental problematique, by sociologists, anthropologists and philosophers.[2] Such commentary pictures environmental concern not only as a response to the physical 'externalities' of industrial exploitation of nature, but also, quite as significantly, as a manifestation of groping wider social reactions to deep cultural tensions in modern complex societies (Lash *et al.* 1996). It points also, more particularly, to the significance of the reductionist tacit representations of human nature employed in neo-classical economics (and hence implicitly within the surrogate valuation methods which are the concern of this chapter), as contributors to the tensions which are tending to find expression in contemporary environmental controversy.[3] My purpose in this chapter is thus to suggest, through some reflections on the emergence of the new valuation methdologies, that the tensions surrounding their development and, more particularly, their application may have a wider signficance for current developments in the polity as a whole.

2. OBSERVATIONS ON RECENT HISTORY

The current wave of interest in and energetic promotion of 'surrogate valuation' methods in the policy world can be dated in Britain to July 1989, with the accession of Chris Patten MP as Secretary of State for the Environment in the third Conservative administration of Mrs Margaret Thatcher. Mr Patten was promoted in the backwash of Mrs Thatcher's landmark speech to the Royal Society in 1988, which had elevated environmental policy to a claimed central concern of her government. In an attempt to underline his ambition to bring environmental concerns to the heart of Cabinet discussion, he announced rapidly that he was appointing a new kind of Special Adviser: Professor David Pearce, then the country's leading protagonist of cost–benefit/surrogate valuation methodologies in the environmental domain.[4] The political symbolism underlying the announcement, in the context of the then-dominance of 'market-economics' idioms in Whitehall, was clear and deliberate. From now on, Patten was understood to be saying, it was to be the Department of the Environment's numbers against the Treasury's. As astute observers such as Tom Burke pointed out, the move was intended to signal an *elevation* of environmental policy. No longer was the latter to be seen by other departments as soft and discretionary; by becoming translated into the grown-up language of economics, environmental priorities would begin to gain the authority they merited at the centre of the concerns of modern government.

Appropriately, Professor Pearce's promotion attracted considerable media interest. A succession of initiatives followed. Pearce's previously unpublicised work for the Department of the Environment (DoE) (commissioned under the tenure of Patten's predecessor, Nicholas Ridley) was published, reinforcing the wave of interest. A sequence of speeches by the Secretary of State consolidated the message.[5] The ripple effects were wide and rapid. The Economic and Social Research Council (ESRC), using Pearce's earlier ESRC-funded work in environmental economics as a standard-bearer, embarked on the development of its Global Environmental Change Programme (its largest-ever single research funding programme), leading in due course to the creation of a designated Research Centre with Professor Pearce and other leading economists of the same neo-classical school at its fulcrum.[6] Within government and its agencies, and within international bodies like OECD, UNEP (United Nations Environment Programme) and the World Bank, intensive activity on the same lines gained extra momentum. Although the September 1990 White Paper *This Common Inheritance* gave a lower profile to the role of such methods than many had anticipated, given the initial expectations aroused by both Patten and Pearce, it was nevertheless the case that within eighteen months, the tools and techniques of environmental valuation, however imperfect, had become established as a mounting preoccupation within many government agencies, and some national non-governmental organisations (NGOs), in Britain. In 1991, the DoE published the manual *Policy Appraisal and the Environment*, which was distributed throughout Whitehall. This highlighted further the officially endorsed significance of economic/surrogate valuation techniques for capturing environmental 'values', in routine administration and decision-making.

These developments were not uncriticised at the time. Whilst the Secretary of State's promotion of the overall significance of economic instruments for future environmental policy was largely welcomed, his more specific endorsement of the potentialities of surrogate valuation methods caused anxiety in the breasts of independent figures in the environmental world, such as Nigel Haigh of the Institute for European Environmental Policy and Fiona Reynolds of the Council for the Protection of Rural

England (CPRE). From their perspective, Patten appeared innocently – and dangerously – to be endorsing approaches to environmental 'valuation' which already had a long and troubled history behind them. This was a history which, they implied, Whitehall had apparently forgotten, or which, if remembered, was being misread or deliberately overridden.

Several previous examples of the use of such methods in environmentally controversial contexts were alive vividly in the minds of such critics. It is useful briefly to recall one or two of these.

First, and furthest back in time, was the case of the third London Airport controversy of the late 1960s and early 1970s. This had crystallised politically in the Roskill Inquiry (Roskill 1971), an official Commission of Inquiry which in 1967–70 explored and evaluated a range of possible sites for London's third airport, relying heavily on techniques of formal cost–benefit analysis, and in particular on surrogate valuation methods, to reach its conclusion in favour of an inland site at Cublington in Buckinghamshire. Famously, the report and its methods attracted derision for the valuation of a Norman church at Stewkley by surrogate means of its commercial insurance value (£50,000), as well as for a variety of other assumptions, particularly about the value of the 'time' of individuals, in particular population groups relevant to the proposed new airport. The case provoked an intervention (the first of many redoubtable challenges in this field over the coming twenty-five years) by Dr John Adams, an academic geographer at London University and subsequently adviser to Friends of the Earth, who challenged the fundamental epistemological pretensions of the methods.

Sir Colin Buchanan's common-sense Minority Report dissented eloquently from the Roskill Commission's conclusions (and methods), and the government opted, albeit only temporarily, for Foulness on the Essex coast, rather than the recommended Cublington site. This outcome led to a brief flurry of exchanges in the broadsheet press, in which economists criticised sceptical lay opinion as emotional and irrational, and non-economists inveighed against the encroachments of economic methodology into domains of moral and philosophical 'value'. It was to be a pattern of exchange which would recur in a number of fields over the next two decades.

A second key arena was the government's motorway construction programme of the 1970s. This programme, flowing from commitments announced officially in 1971, had spawned a succession of local controversies by the middle of the decade, including significant civil disobedience at public inquiries into new road proposals up and down the country, as the social and environmental impacts of new motorways became increasingly familiar (Levin 1979). A key focus for controversy was the cost–benefit appraisal model ('COBA') employed within the Ministry of Transport (at the time under the umbrella of the Department of the Environment), to justify particular schemes. The critiques of Friends of the Earth and others, crystallised by Adams and others (Adams 1979), highlighted the undue significance given to a small number of variables encompassed within COBA as 'benefits'. These imputed economic values to, for example, the projected savings in the cumulative driving times of individuals using the new motorway, and to the accident 'reductions' claimed likely to result from construction. The dominant emphasis on such selective surrogate representations of 'value', and the effective marginalisation of other less readily quantifiable environmental and social 'costs' in the official justifications for new motorways, fanned the flames of controversy – particularly when coupled to the mechanistic traffic forecasting methods then employed by the ministry.

Cumulatively, these various developments came rapidly to threaten a crisis of legitimacy for the motorways programme overall. In 1974–5, to defuse the situation, the government found itself forced to set up two parallel committees of inquiry: the Leitch Committee into 'Trunk Road Assessment', and an inquiry into 'Highways Inquiry Procedures'. The first of these led directly to the creation of the permanent Standing Committee on Trunk Road Assessment (SACTRA), which exists to this day. This was read at the time as a tacit acknowledgement that quantified cost–benefit analytical methods – and, in particular, reliance on surrogate valuation of a small range of variables – in this sphere had backfired politically.

It is crucial to recall that the controversies surrounding COBA and the surrogate valuation methods it employed were far from simply *technical*. The methods were a focus of contention because they became seen by objectors (local and national) as having been developed by technical experts as biased contributors to the intellectual rationale for an unbalanced national transport policy.[7] Increasingly, innovative national NGOs such as Friends of the Earth, the Conservation Society and CPRE linked with local objectors and amenity societies to highlight the potential cumulative consequences of ever greater commitment to road transport – consequences which, they claimed, the methods in question were acting to *obscure*, rather than to clarify. It has to be said that, twenty years later, these arguments appear broadly vindicated. Indeed, the 1994 report of the Royal Commission on Environmental Pollution, 'Transport and the Environment',[8] can properly be read as an authoritative update of precisely the critique of trends in transport policy underpinning the 1970s' NGO challenges to COBA and its unbalanced surrogate valuation methods.[9] Yet there is disconcertingly little sign of recognition of this continuity, or its implications, within government.[10]

The third London Airport and the motorways programme were far from being the only arenas in which 'environmental' controversies about surrogate valuation methods took hold in the 1970s and 1980s. Both the Ministry of Agriculture's land drainage programmes, and the National Radiological Protection Board's cost–benefit approaches to public

25

exposures to low-level radiation from nuclear power stations, generated analogous criticisms. In all of these various cases, apparently technical methodological challenges reflected deeper tensions of mounting social and environmental significance.

What insights might Chris Patten and his advisers properly have distilled from this history, before embarking on the government's promotion of surrogate valuation methods in the early 1990s?

In the first place, he might have noted the significance of the particular *patterns* of 'lay' dissent that had been provoked by the methods. The sporadic brouhahas surrounding surrogate valuation had been brought alive not by economists, but rather for the most part by lay individuals peering into official methodological thickets, in attempts, as citizens, to understand how contentious new schemes were being justified by government. These processes generated powerful and durable insights. However, what was also striking was how little the resulting critiques disturbed, or were even acknowledged seriously by, the economists favouring such methods.[11] After a burst of controversy in each case, and a response from government aimed at displacing it (the rejection of an airport at Cublington, the creation of the Leitch Committee, etc.), NGO and government attention moved elsewhere. Like most administrators in government, the NGO *non*-economists who had crystallised the controversies had little interest in economic methodology *per se*. One consequence was that, as particular storms blew themselves out, economists interested in new methodological refinements simply continued down their specialist paths, unperturbed. When the political climate towards environmental concerns changed in the late 1980s, the same surrogate valuation approaches, albeit refined technically in ways significant for economists themselves, were available to be taken up.

All of this points to a further significant feature of these historical disputes: the particular *moral* intensity which had characterised the arguments. On the lay NGO side, what appeared to be at stake was more than simply an intellectual critique of a technical methodology. Central to the passions aroused were unarticulated feelings of acute *threat* and *moral resentment* at the way in which issues of wide normative public significance were being converted into a Procrustean and trivialising technical language, by official fiat. In other words, the idioms of surrogate valuation were experienced as *imposed*, with no discussion about whether or not they were socially appropriate,[12] and minimal negotiation about which variables or specific valuations, if any, might be appropriate for inclusion.

Equally, on the economists' side too, there were strong normative commitments. The key protagonists inside and outside government saw themselves as having a mission to develop and employ techniques of economic appraisal, techniques which were not only more 'rational' but also more likely to have purchase on government behaviour than less quantified forms of evaluation. Moreover, few environmental economists would endorse the picture I have drawn above of surrogate valuation as in some respects hegemonic. Rather they saw (and continue to see) themselves as embattled standard-bearers for clearer headed, more 'objective' approaches to questions of environmental value than the supposedly 'emotional', even Luddite, approaches of 'conventional' environmental campaigners. The intensity of the resulting disputes continues to surface publicly from time to time.

The above historical reflections illustrate that surrogate valuation methods had already had a bumpy history of their own in the environmental sphere, well before Chris Patten's period as Secretary of State. However, the significance of these past controversies appears to have been unappreciated, or at least discounted, at the time of the 1989 announcements. Since then, an overriding political concern to elevate environmental issues in the pecking order of UK public policies has led to the methods gaining, in principle at least, an enhanced political credibility.

In the UK, this tendency has been reinforced in the early to mid-1990s by parallel developments within government, wholly unrelated to environmental concerns. New doctrines of political accountability, reflected in the increased 'marketisation' of many public sector activities, through the creation of arm's-length executive agencies, contracting-out of hitherto civil service functions, and the like, have been generating a new 'audit' mentality in much of the public sphere (Power 1995).[13] One effect of this has been to enhance the role of the Treasury as *de facto* arbiter of public priorities in domains formerly governed by less exclusively economistic articulations of the public interest, frequently exercised through administrative discretion. Such increased Treasury control has been developing unobtrusively through mechanisms such as supposedly transparent 'objective-setting' and quantified 'performance targets' and indicators, across a range of activities of government. One consequence of such processes has been to generate new pressures within departments and devolved agencies for quantification in monetary terms of goods not previously understood as lending themselves to such approaches. In the environmental domain particularly, surrogate valuation methods of the kind discussed in this book have been taken up as ready tools for such processes.

My own recent experience within the Forestry Comission confirms the powerful pull of such dynamics. The 1995 conversion of Forest Enterprise (that part of the Forestry Commission which now operates and manages the Commission's 2.5 million acre forest estate for commercial returns) into a 'Next Steps Agency' has led to an escalating internal momentum in favour of the quantification of the so-called 'non-market' benefits of its woods and forests. Such benefits include environmental and nature conservation priorities, public recreational opportunities, and other similar public goods. Because of the corporate planning processes governing the new agency's

27

activities, commercial and non-commercial, there is now inexorable Treasury-driven pressure to convert such key activities into monetary units which can be considered and evaluated alongside the agency's more explicitly commercial timber production targets and activities. This is already beginning to lead to mounting reliance, for budgetary and PES (Public Expenditure Survey) purposes, on the outputs of contingent valuation and other surrogate valuation exercises.[14]

This is anything but a solitary new example. In November 1995, the Department of Transport announced that it too was intending to explore the potential of such methods for capturing the environmental 'values' associated with noise levels resulting from new roads. Here, as in the case of Forest Enterprise's corporate planning, such methods are seen by government as potentially environmentally *benign*, rather than the reverse.

This last fact points to a significant further dimension of the new dilemmas posed by surrogate valuation methods. Since Chris Patten's 1989 elevation of environmental economics, overt disputes surrounding surrogate valuation methods have been muted for the most part (there is one significant exception, to which I refer below). It is useful to consider why events have apparently proceeded so smoothly.

First, in the period since 1989, as envisaged by Patten, the methods have been advanced in order to *assist* environmental ends rather than to diminish them. This has meant that, in terms of *realpolitik*, there has been little incentive for environmental NGOs – historically, as we have seen, the principal explicit critics of such methods – to dramatise the methods' limitations, whatever their private reservations. Indeed, the reverse may even have been the case. Thus NGOs such as the Royal Society for the Protection of Birds and World Wide Fund for Nature, and statutory agencies such as the National Rivers Authority, the Countryside Commission and English Nature have all tended to explore the tactical possibilities of the use of surrogate valuation methods for advancing their aims.

An exception which tends to prove this general rule is the late-1995 controversy surrounding the socio-economic impacts of climate change exercise undertaken by Pearce, Faukhauser, Tol and others for Working Group III of the Inter-governmental Panel on Climate Change (IPCC). A range of assumptions embodied in this analysis – most strikingly concerning the differential valuations to be made of the lives of individuals in Third World as opposed to OECD countries – precipitated a stinging critique from the Global Commons Institute, a small but determined NGO run by Aubrey Meyer. The latter's criticisms (see Meyer and Cooper 1995), highlighting a range of inherent softnesses in the valuation processes, were taken up vigorously within the IPCC by developing world countries such as Malaysia. Sir Crispin Tickell, one of the British Government's leading advisers on environmental policy, added his weight to the controversy by observing that such supposed values of statistical life were 'economist's artefacts of doubtful value and subjective character, with almost unlimited capacity to mislead'.[15]

In the present context, the significance of this episode lies in its demonstration of the inherent brittleness of surrogate valuation methods, when subjected to intellectual challenge, not least by interests likely to be affected 'adversely' by decisions based on the methods' outputs. The interests in this case were Third World countries asked to bear (in their view, disproportionate) burdens in reducing anticipated future levels of CO_2 emission. In such circumstances, the political force of the challenge to the inherently fragile surrogate valuation outputs arose from the threat the latters' environmental 'demands' appeared to pose to particular national interests.

But there are also signs, closer to home within the UK's domestic institutions of government, that the relative lack of overt controversy surrounding these economic appraisal methods may reflect the inherent malleability of the valuation 'outputs' to back-stairs Whitehall negotiation (or, more crudely, arm-twisting). Current research[16] is tending to suggest that a new administrative *politics* of valuation may now be emerging in negotiations between the Treasury and other official bodies, around the actual *numbers* (i.e. values) claimed to be produced by surrogate valuation exercises. Thus it appears that the numbers emerging from such exercises are being shaped significantly, in some if not most cases, by tacitly understood Treasury expectations of what levels of value might be thought to be 'realistic', for example, in terms of their cumulative public expenditure implications. In other words, however intellectually 'pure' the formal exercises involved in surrogate valuation studies undertaken by individual economists, in the real world circumstances of internal government horse-trading, the final outputs of the processes are politically shaped. Whilst this may have contributed so far to an absence of public controversy (not least because of the publicly opaque character of Whitehall's negotiating frameworks), it highlights the fact that, *pace* the pretensions of well-intentioned economic theorists, surrogate valuation methods may now be acting to *obscure* important arguments about major public priorities, rather than to provide the more truly transparent and 'objective' bases for policy debate and judgement asserted by their key political and academic protagonists in 1989–90. If this is indeed the case, it is unlikely to remain uncontroversial for long.

3. THE WIDER CONTEXT

Overall, the observations in this chapter have been intended to convey that surrogate valuation methods have had a far more complex and problematic history than tends to be acknowledged by those in Whitehall and Westminster who have been pressing their cause. With the cumulative pressures now mounting for the wider official deployment of such approaches in a manner comfortable for the new 'hands-off' fashions in public adminis-tration, it would be prudent to expect the strains to begin to show increasingly vividly.

This being so, let us set these issues and tensions within a still wider social and political context. Industrialised countries like Britain are passing through a period of accelerating change, reflecting cultural processes under-stood by contemporary social and political theorists in terms of globalisa-tion, social de-traditionalisation, cultural fragmentation, and individuation (Bauman 1991, Giddens 1990, Lasch 1979). Increasingly, the environmental movement of the past twenty years is coming to be seen as having reflected *inter alia* one form of collective response to the cultural tensions triggered by such processes (Eyerman and Jamison 1991, Lash *et al.* 1996, Melucci 1989). I have also argued (Grove-White 1993) that the world-wide purchase of environmental concerns in this 'communications' age has reflected, in myriad disguises, the ways in which specific environmental issues have tended to become symbols of collective concern and anxiety about ever-ramifying technological change, in an era of social fragmentation and individualism.

Economistic views of human nature – particularly when imposed in fields where economic idioms have previously had no cultural authority – are classic instances of the dominant 'modernist' ontology now under challenge in this domain. The passions lurking just beneath the surface surrounding surrogate valuation methods in environmental economics reflect anxieties. Thus these apparently technical, benignly intended tools are profoundly political in their import. It will not be long before this reality becomes more widely appreciated. When such an awakening occurs, the arguments will intensify.

Such a prospect points to the need for urgent new thinking about how to secure environmental values at the heart of public policy. As several of the subsequent contributions to the present volume suggest, where *controversial* issues are concerned, appropriate fresh approaches seem more likely to lie in the direction of institutional reform aimed at enriching and refining open political debates about public values, than in the worthy but increasingly unrewarding search for 'objective' methodologies of the kind hitherto urged, with the most constructive of intentions, by economists of the neo-classical school.

NOTES

1 The author was Director of the Council for the Protection of Rural England in 1981–7, has acted as a specialist adviser to Parliamentary Select Committee inquiries, and is currently a Forestry Commissioner – over and above an ongoing research role at the Centre for the Study of Environmental Change.

2 E.g. Beck 1992, Douglas 1970, Hayer 1995, Melucci 1989, Wynne and Mayer 1993.

3 See the chapters by Wynne and Foster in this volume.

4 See e.g. Pearce *et al.* 1989 and Pearce 1993.

5 E.g. a speech to the Chatham House Conference, London 5 December 1989, and the 1990 Wilson Lecture, 'Ethics and the environment' at Godolphin and Latimer School, London, 12 March 1990.

6 The Centre for Social and Economic Research on the Global Environment (CSERGE) is a designated ESRC research centre, created in 1991, jointly at University College, London and the University of East Anglia.

7 See National Motorways Action Committee, 'A case against the M16 motorway' (London, 1976), and Levin 1979.

8 HMSO, London, 1994.

9 Two piquant features of COBA illustrate the point. First, because COBA values drivers' time savings particularly, its tendency is *de facto* to select those road schemes that do most to generate traffic. And second, because its tendency is to value the best-protected (i.e. undeveloped) land at close to zero for precisely the reason that it *is* well protected, COBA tends to select routes through undeveloped (and hence often environmentally valued) parts of the country.

10 A graphic illustration of such limited institutional memory within government was provided at a March 1994 conference, sponsored by the Department of the Environment (DOE). The Department's then chief economist went out of his way to praise the Department of Transport's (DTp) pioneering use and development of surrogate valuation methods in the motorways programme since the 1970s, in contrast to DOE's own negligence concerning such methods. He omitted to notice the connections between the DTp's historical reliance on the surrogate valuations within COBA, and the mounting crisis of an overwhelmingly car-based transport policy in the mid-1990s, now documented thoroughly by the Royal Commission on Environmental Pollution (Report on 'Transport and the environment', 1994).

11 There were of course significant exceptions to this – for example, Bowers in Turner 1988b, and subsequently Jacobs 1991.

12 For details of a more empirical study documenting more recent responses, see 'Pounds and pence view of Nature provokes uprising', *New Scientist*, 3 February 1996.

13 See also, R. Amman, 'A Sovietological view of modern Britain', lecture at Edinburgh University, 1 December 1995 (Unpublished; text obtainable from ESRC, Swindon).

14 A major study, 'Valuing management for biodiversity in British forests', was undertaken in 1995–6 for the Forestry Commission by the consultants Environmental Resources Management.

15 'Temperature rises in dispute over costing climate change', in *Nature* 378, 30 November 1995.

16 E.g. the 1994–5 ESRC-funded study into environmental valuation methods and negotiation frameworks at the Centre for the Study of Environmental Change.

2

VALUES AND PREFERENCES IN NEO-CLASSICAL ENVIRONMENTAL ECONOMICS

Russell Keat

1. ENVIRONMENTAL PROBLEMS AND MARKET FAILURES

For many environmental economists, working within the framework of neo-classical theory, environmental problems are best conceived as cases of 'market failure' – the failure of actual markets to display the efficiency of resource allocation which 'ideal' markets can be demonstrated to achieve. Hence the solution to such problems consists in removing such inefficiencies, especially those due to externalities: costs and benefits which have not been incorporated into actual market transactions. One favoured means for doing this has been the use of some form of cost–benefit analysis (CBA).

But what exactly should be included in such analyses; what are to be regarded as the relevant costs and benefits of economic decisions with environmental effects? In the early days of CBA, a relatively narrow view was taken of these, restricting them, roughly speaking, to those which in other contexts were already subject to market-pricing. But in response to claims that this procedure still failed to take into account significant aspects of the 'value' people attributed to the environment, CBA came to be developed in a more extended form: the concept of externalities was broadened to include the so-called 'intangible' values involved in people's aesthetic appreciation of nature, or their valuing of wilderness, of kinds of natural landscape, of the sheer existence of certain species ('existence-value'), and so on.

The example of river pollution may be used to illustrate this difference between narrow and broad conceptions of externalities. Suppose a firm discharges its waste into a river, but that further down the river another firm makes use of this water for its own productive purposes. The effect of the first firm's discharges is that the second firm has to purify the river water before using it. This is a straightforward case of market failure due to 'narrow' externalities: the first firm is imposing a cost on the second, but since this cost does not register in its own calculations, CBA may be used to modify the decision that would otherwise be made, and restore efficiency.

But there may also, or instead, be people who attribute other kinds of value to the unpolluted river water: for instance, to its aesthetic or symbolic properties, or to its ability to support various species of fish or plant-life. They may regard the pollution as a desecration of nature, or as having effects that are ethically wrong or impermissible, and so on. By broadening the concept of externalities, an extended form of CBA will regard these too as relevant costs. Attempts will thus be made to put a price on them by the use of methods such as 'contingent valuation' (CVM), in which people are asked how much they are willing to pay (WTP) to preserve the river in its unpolluted condition, or willing to accept (WTA) in compensation for its being polluted.

But this seemingly more environmentally friendly form of CBA has met with considerable criticism. In a trenchant and influential critique (Sagoff 1988b), Mark Sagoff has argued that, in the kind of example just noted, it is a serious error to regard these ethical or aesthetic objections to pollution as further kinds of external cost that can and should be entered into an extended form of CBA in the same way that straightforwardly definable economic costs are included in its previous, restricted form. For any use of CBA remains tied to the overall theoretical framework of neo-classical economics, and in particular to its concepts of efficiency and preference-satisfaction. Costs and benefits are thus characterised in terms of the extent to which individuals' preferences are satisfied, as indicated by their WTP/WTA; and in Sagoff's view, the extension of the concept of externalities to incorporate 'intangibles' illicitly transforms the logically distinct category of *values* into that of *preferences*.[1]

The radical error involved here, Sagoff suggests, manifests itself in the considerable difficulties experienced by practitioners of CVM when they try to elicit answers to WTP/WTA questions. Many people simply refuse to specify any finite sum, either objecting to the very questions asked, or assigning infinite monetary values. Whilst CB analysts tend to regard such responses as indicating the need to refine their techniques, or as showing that people are behaving irrationally or unfairly ('strategically'), Sagoff interprets them as indicating the logical absurdity of the questions: in assimilating values and preferences, these involve what he terms a 'category mistake'.

To arrive at environmental decisions in this way, he suggests, would be the equivalent of trying to decide whether a person on trial was guilty by discovering, before any evidence had been heard, what the preferences of the jury were in this regard, and then calculating the net benefits of the two possible verdicts; or deciding whether creationist science, instead of Darwinian theory, should be taught in certain schools by finding out whether there were enough pupils or parents whose preferences for this were sufficiently strong, as indicated by their WTP, to meet the costs of doing so; or determining the justifiability of the Vietnam war by finding out whether this policy produced more preference satisfaction than its alternatives, with people's moral judgements about the war being included alongside every other kind of 'preference'.

Extrapolating from these examples to the environmental case, what the use of extended CBA/CVM implies is that the judgements people make about the (intangible) value of the environment, or about what it would be right or justifiable to do to it, are to be seen simply as statements about their individual preferences; so that, to the extent that the environment is treated in ways that are odds with these judgements, this is regarded simply as giving rise to costs or disbenefits due to the non-satisfaction of those 'preferences'.

But why is a 'category mistake' involved here? As Sagoff notes, following Ryle, this is 'the kind of mistake you make when you predicate of one concept another that makes no sense in relation to it' (1988b: 94). In the kinds of case with which he is concerned, the mistake consists in predicating of someone's judgements or beliefs concepts that make sense only when applied to their preferences or desires – an error which is further compounded by then responding to those beliefs and judgements in ways that only make sense in relation to preferences or desires.

More specifically, Sagoff claims, whereas judgements and beliefs can be said to be true or false, well or badly supported by the relevant evidence, justified or unjustified etc., so that we can appropriately ask those who make or state them to provide their reasons for them, we cannot sensibly ask how much they would be willing to pay for them (or for their being accepted, put into practice etc.). This kind of question is, however, quite intelligible and appropriate in the case of people's preferences and desires; and likewise we can talk of these being stronger or weaker, more or less intense, and so on.

According to Sagoff, when people make the kinds of ethical (and other value-regarding) claims about the environment which practitioners of extended CBA regard as preferences, these should be seen to involve:

> not desires or wants but opinions or views. They state what a person believes is right or best for the community or group as a whole. These opinions may be true or false, and we may meaningfully ask that person for the reasons that he or she holds them. But an analyst who asks how much citizens would pay to satisfy opinions that they advocate through political association commits a category mistake. The analyst asks of beliefs about objective facts a question that is appropriate only to subjective interests and desires.
>
> (1988b: 94)

Furthermore, he suggests, this category mistake of treating judgements as if they were preferences – asking the WTP question instead of engaging with and evaluating people's reasons for their judgements – is tantamount to assessing the credibility or validity of these judgements by their proponents' willingness to pay for their being accepted or acted upon:

> The reasons people give for their views (outside the journals of economic analysis, where *argument* apparently is to be respected) are not to be counted; what counts is how much individuals will pay to satisfy their wants. Those willing to pay the most, for all intents and purposes, have the right views; theirs is the better judgement, the deeper insight, and the more informed opinion.
>
> (1988b: 41–2)

This is not only logically absurd, it is an error that prevents policy makers arriving at sensible decisions, since:

> Policy makers need to know which beliefs about facts are credible and which arguments about values are sound. The credibility of a belief (e.g. that the earth is round) depends on evidence and expert opinion, not the amount people are willing to bet that it is true. Nor does the soundness of an ethical argument depend on willingness to pay, although economic information, of course, may be relevant. Thus cost–benefit techniques, when they go beyond the confines of determining efficiency in the narrow sense, do not provide useful information. Rather, they confuse preference with ethical and factual judgement.
>
> (1988b: 37)

Now although I agree that there are logical and categorial errors of some such kind at work here, I shall argue that they are not quite of the character that Sagoff suggests. They do not straightforwardly consist in treating judgements (or beliefs) as if they were preferences (or desires), which is how Sagoff presents the matter, but rather in treating judgements about what is morally right as if they were judgements about what would contribute to the well-being of the person who makes these judgements. Thus the crucial contrast is not between judgements and preferences, but between different kinds of judgement – and also, since each kind of judgement may itself operate as the basis for a certain kind of preference, between different kinds of preference.

2. JUDGEMENTS, PREFERENCES AND THE MARKET

One can begin by noting that, at least in their ordinary uses, some of the conceptual contrasts which Sagoff draws between 'judgements' and 'preferences' seem not to be correctly specified. For instance, one may talk of the intensity or strength of people's judgements or beliefs: these concepts are not restricted to preferences or desires. More importantly, one may talk of the *reasons* for people's preferences or desires, not confining this

35

concept's application to judgements or beliefs. One can thus intelligibly and legitimately ask people to justify their preferences – for example, their preference for football over hockey, for philosophy over mathematics, and so on; and likewise to justify their desires for various things.

In doing so, one is asking people to articulate – and then, often, to justify further – the judgements or beliefs that support their preferences or desires: it is the fact that the latter are normally based upon the former that makes such questions appropriate or intelligible. People desire things, typically, because they judge or believe them to be desirable; hence one may ask them what (in their view) makes them desirable, and then perhaps go on to question or argue with the answers they give.[2]

All this is true not only of preferences 'in general', but also, and more importantly, of the specific kinds of preferences which Sagoff often has in mind (as have those economists whose views he is opposing), namely the preferences of consumers in a market economy. For although there is a tendency for neo-classical theorists to ignore or even deny this, consumers likewise typically have reasons for their preferences, and their preferences are likewise based on (in principle contestable) judgements.

For example, I might have a preference for a certain kind or make of car. This preference will typically be based on a judgement I have made about the respective merits of this car as compared with others – or at least, about these merits insofar as they are relevant given what I wish to achieve by having a car. And this judgement can be questioned, in at least two ways. First, am I justified in believing this car actually has (to a greater extent than others at the same price etc.) the characteristics which, given what I want to achieve, are the relevant ones? And second, am I justified in believing that possessing an item which has these characteristics will contribute to my own well-being – and hence, are these correctly regarded by me as the relevant ones?

However, although consumer preferences are normally thus based on judgements, and can be questioned in these ways, it is a highly significant feature of the market – i.e. of the specific context in which these preferences are articulated, acted upon, responded to etc. – that such questions have no role or function in how it operates (see Keat 1993). Market transactions take place without reference to the reasons for which consumers prefer what they 'happen' to prefer: the market is, as it were, indifferent to these, 'blind to reasons'. All that matters in the market is the fact that consumers have – and act upon – preferences, and what these preferences are for; no notice is taken of the judgements they are based upon, let alone of whether these are justifiable. In particular, consumers' access to their preferred or desired items does not depend on their being able to justify these preferences or desires to anyone – and certainly not to the producers who provide them. All that concerns the producers is the consumers' willingness (and of course ability) to pay for the items concerned.

So in the market, (consumer) preferences are, although actually based on judgements open to critical evaluation, treated or responded to as if they were not. In other words, they are treated in just the way that, according to Sagoff, judgements should not be treated: 'merely' as stronger or weaker, more or less intense and – to the extent that one may talk here of evaluation – 'evaluated' merely by their possessors' willingness to pay for their satisfaction. Given all this, one might be tempted to say that the market 'makes category mistakes all the time'; or rather, that those who support the market as a way of making economic decisions are guilty of such mistakes.

That is, if Sagoff is right to regard 'treating judgements as preferences' as a category mistake, and to regard the error of extended CBA as consisting in this, then the market should likewise appear objectionable since it (or its advocates) makes the same mistake. Conversely, if the market could be defended from this objection, it might then be wrong to claim that this is the error of extended CBA – so that, if extended CBA does involve a radical conceptual/categorial error, it would be of a somewhat different kind from that identified by Sagoff. It is this latter alternative that I shall now pursue: I shall try to show how the market might be rescued from Sagoff's version of the category mistake objection, in a way that will indicate how to redefine the specific nature of the error involved in the use of extended CBA.[3]

3. MARKETS AND INDIVIDUAL WELL-BEING

As noted at the outset, the rationale for the use of CBA (in either its narrow or extended forms) in dealing with environmental problems is that this will restore the efficiency of ideal markets. Thus for the proponent of CBA, efficiency is the key normative consideration; and it is the achievement of this by markets that is seen as their chief virtue.

But why should efficiency be regarded as a desirable feature of economic systems and decision-making procedures? Only, it may be argued, on the basis of a broadly utilitarian ethical theory, which evaluates actions (and institutional systems of action) in terms of their contribution to aggregate individual well-being.[4] Hence the relevant justification for the market here – i.e. in the context of justifications for the use of CBA – is that it manages to achieve (for a given set of resources etc.) a greater amount of individual well-being than any alternative economic system.[5]

Now in order to show that the (ideal) market has this virtue, a number of assumptions have to be made. Some of these concern how the institutional procedures of the market are supposed to work – for example, that consumer preferences operate as effective controls over the decisions made by producers, through competitive pressures etc. Others, of more significance in this context, concern the supposed motivations and competencies of consumers. In particular, two assumptions are crucial here: (a) that individual consumers are, generally speaking, the best judges of their own well-being, and of what may be expected to contribute to it; and (b) that in making decisions about possible purchases, consumers are primarily concerned with their own well-being.

Both of these assumptions may well be challenged, and often are by critics of the market (or rather, of this particular justification for it).[6] But I shall not consider such objections here, since my argument will be that even if these assumptions, and the justification for the market by which they are required, are accepted, it will still turn out that the use of extended CBA involves a radical error – and hence that it is only the narrow form of CBA that could be justified. In other words, even the best that could be said for the market (including its avoidance of the Sagoffian category mistake), and hence also for the use of CBA to deal with market failures, provides no justification for extended CBA; indeed, it is precisely this justification for the market that reveals what is erroneous about that form of CBA.

To see why this is so, one must first show why it is that, if (a) and (b) are accepted, the market can be defended against the charge of making (Sagoff's version of) the category mistake. There are two main points to be made here. First, if (a) is accepted, then the fact that the market 'fails to respond to consumer preferences by evaluating them' (or the judgements they are based upon) does not matter, since no such evaluation could be expected to improve upon the judgements which consumers themselves make – i.e. about the likely contributions to their own well-being. So, whereas in other decision-making contexts, as Sagoff rightly notes, policy makers may well need to evaluate judgements by the relevant criteria – e.g. when these judgements are about 'whether the earth is round', whether creationist science has any credibility etc. – this is not so for the judgements made by consumers in the market.

Second, if (b) is accepted, and consumers' judgements are primarily about the expected contribution of prospective purchases to their own well-being, it seems quite reasonable – albeit in a rough and ready way – to regard their WTP as a measure or indication of this expected contribution. This is a context in which 'putting your money where your mouth is' seems an appropriate dictum. If a consumer judges one item to be better than another in this respect, being prepared to pay more for it (and hence to forego other purchases etc.) seems a quite suitable test or measure of the expected benefit.

It would thus be misleading to say that a terrible conceptual error is being made here – that the credibility of the consumer's judgement is being assessed by seeing how much he or she is willing to pay for its realisation. Rather, the judgement has 'already' been deemed to be credible (via (a) above, affirming the competence of the consumer as judge); and WTP is simply being taken as an indication of how much benefit the consumer expects to derive from the purchase. This is not an illicit way of assessing the merits of the judgement; it is a measure of the benefit (to the consumer) that the judgement (and hence also the preference based upon this) is about.

4. INDIVIDUAL WELL-BEING *VERSUS* ETHICAL JUDGEMENTS

I have argued so far that, if a certain rationale for the market − along with its necessary assumptions − is accepted, there is no obvious category mistake involved in the market's 'treating judgements as preferences'. This rationale consists in claiming that the (ideal) market is efficient, in the sense of maximising (for given resources) aggregate individual well-being; and it is in terms of this rationale that the use of CBA to deal with actual market failures is itself justified by its proponents. What I shall now argue is that, given this justification for CBA − which is the best justification it *could* have, even if one regards it, and the related justification for the market, as quite weak − the use of the extended form of CBA cannot be justified; for this involves the conceptual/categorial error of treating ethical judgements as if they were judgements about the well-being of those who make them.

The practitioners of extended CBA try to include in their calculations (what they call) preferences based both on people's judgements concerning expected contributions to their own well-being, and on people's ethical judgements concerning what they regard as morally right, justifiable and so on. Two main kinds of the latter, ethical judgements may be identified: those that concern the expected contribution of the proposed course of action to the well-being of all or some of those affected by it; and those which do not, or at least not exclusively so. The most obvious cases of the latter kind are ethical judgements involving the ascription of rights. For convenience, I shall call these two kinds of ethical judgement 'utilitarian' and 'non-utilitarian'; but in doing so I do not wish to imply that they are necessarily − respectively − associated with, or at odds with, Utilitarianism as an ethical theory.

The inclusion of either kind of ethical judgement (or judgement-based preference) in CBA calculations is illegitimate; indeed, it is inconsistent with the only plausible rationale for the use of CBA. 'Utilitarian' judgements should be excluded because, in effect, they are attempts to do the very same work that CBA is intended to do: to arrive at calculations of aggregate individual well-being. If they do this correctly, they make CBA calculations redundant; if they are then included alongside non-ethical judgements of (affected) people's own expected well-being, there will be a 'double-counting' problem; and anyway, since the market-justifying rationale for CBA relies *inter alia* on the claim that each person is the best judge of his or her own well-being, such 'utilitarian' judgements are likely to provide an inferior basis for the decision.

But 'non-utilitarian' judgements should also be excluded, since the rationale for the use of CBA must deny their legitimacy. For if one takes these judgements seriously, they imply that CBA is not the ethically correct way of making these decisions about the environment. So the proponent of CBA must either stick to its rationale, and exclude these judgements; or accept them, and abandon the use of CBA. To try to include them 'as if' they were non-ethical own-well-being judgements makes no sense either way; it would only make sense if these judgements were misinterpeted – and this is the category mistake made by the proponents of extended CBA.

To elaborate this argument, one can consider the case of rights-based judgements. I do not claim that all the ethical judgements typically made by those questioned in (extended) CB analyses of environmental issues have this character. But it seems reasonable to think that many of them do; and the argument via rights-based judgements could, I believe, be reproduced for other 'non-utilitarian' judgements. For example, in a recent study of the significance of enhancing the survival prospects of various wild species in New England, 79 per cent of the respondents endorsed the claim that 'all species of wildlife have a right to live independent of any benefit or harm to people'; and a majority of these refused to give WTP answers to the usual hypothetical valuation questions (Stevens *et al.* 1991: 396).[7]

Now broadly speaking, the attribution of rights implies a refusal to countenance actions which, whilst they might be preferable to others in terms of net benefits, involve unacceptable damage to the interests or well-being of particular individuals or groups. To claim that people – or animals etc. – have certain rights is to claim that they should never be treated in certain ways, even if the calculation of aggregative individual well-being shows that the action which has these effects would be the most beneficial one. Hence typical examples of rights-attributions imply claims such as 'the (known-to-be) innocent should never be punished', 'slavery can never be permitted', and so on.

Thus attributing (and enforcing) rights places limits on what would otherwise be the implications of aggregative welfare calculations. This then implies that any benefits which would result from rights-incompatible actions must be seen as having no positive ethical value: they are not to be 'counted in favour' (even if they turn out to be 'outweighed' by various costs), but excluded from the action-decision altogether. Applying this to the wildlife example noted above, the point is this: if these respondents' rights-attributing ethical judgements are accepted, then even if an action which led to species extinction could be shown through CBA to generate greater aggregate well-being than others which did not, this action is impermissible. None of the benefits resulting from it count for anything.

Of course, the rights-based judgements may be rejected, and the action may then be judged acceptable. But one simply cannot avoid deciding whether to accept or to reject these judgements. In particular, one cannot avoid making this decision by instead trying to include them within CBA calculations. For, in terms of the rationale for the use of CBA, they do not belong here at all: they are not judgements about the well-being of the individuals who make them, and are hence irrelevant. And from their own standpoint, the kind of calculation of net benefits made through CBA is the wrong basis for deciding these issues, and is likely to include, as benefits, what these judgements imply should not be counted. So neither party can accept these judgements' inclusion in an extended form of CBA.[8]

Hence Sagoff is right to claim, in this context at least, that 'Policy makers need to know which beliefs . . . are credible and which arguments about values are sound' (see the passages quoted in section 1 above). An evaluation of these ethical judgements must be made for any rational decision to be taken: the only appropriate or intelligible response to such judgements is 'to assess their merits'. Further, this clearly cannot be done by asking those who make them to 'put a price' on them. Respondents correctly resist this request which is indeed, as Sagoff suggests, tantamount to determining the credibility of judgements by reference to their advocates' willingness (and indeed ability) to pay. The judgements cannot be priced because they do not concern the expected benefits to those who make them: they are not the kind of judgement (or preference) which is, I argued earlier, given certain assumptions, intelligibly 'assessed' by WTP.

Indeed, this feature of at least some of the ethical judgements which practitioners of extended CBA try to include is itself 'admitted' by many advocates of this procedure. Here I have in mind the concept of 'existence-value', the most favoured way of trying to include concerns for species survival etc. in an extended form of CBA. The concept has quite rightly seemed problematic to many commentators, since on the one hand its definition typically excludes the presence of any perceived benefit to individuals, yet on the other hand it is supposed to be included in a procedure whose only intelligible rationale requires individuals to concern themselves only *with* such benefits.[9]

So ethical judgements, such as those based on rights (and those concerning 'existence-value'), cannot intelligibly or consistently be included in CBA; or at least, they cannot thus be included if they are correctly understood or interpreted. The only way they 'can' be included is by *mis*interpreting them – i.e. by understanding them as judgements concerned with their makers' own well-being. This is the error made, as Sagoff notes (1988b: 89–91), in trying to put a price on ethical judgements by treating them, in effect, as statements about the benefits or costs that would accrue to those who make them through becoming aware of the implementation or failure to implement the principles they espouse.

So, for example, instead of regarding the claim that it is unjust to punish the innocent as an ethical judgement that must be responded to as such, extended CB analysts respond by trying to measure how pleased or upset those who make it would be were their principle to be acted upon or not. The most that could be said for such bizarre attempts is that they may dimly indicate some recognition that, unless such judgements were concerned with their makers' own well-being, they could not be included in the CBA. But actually they are not. To justify the decision being taken by means of CBA, these judgements have to be rejected. If they are accepted, some alternative (or additional) basis for the decision must be found.

The points I have made here can be further illustrated by considering the well-known distinction between 'efficiency' and 'equity'. As standard discussions of welfare economics typically emphasise, demonstrating that a particular use of resources is efficient is not enough to justify it, since there are other considerations that may also be relevant, especially those of distributive justice or 'equity'. It is then also noted that there may often be some 'conflict' between these two desiderata, and that one may therefore have to decide 'how much of one is to be sacrificed for how much of the other'.

Now although this formulation of the problem may not be entirely satisfactory, it is at least preferable to any attempt to incorporate equity into an extended CBA by 'putting a price' on the judgements made by those who believe in it: by asking them, that is, how much they are WTP to see their principle realised. For this would be to obliterate the distinctiveness of the principles of efficiency and equity themselves – transforming the judgements people make about the latter into elements to be included in determining the former. The resolution of conflicts between efficiency and equity cannot take place *within* the procedure of CBA, since they are essentially conflicts between the ethical considerations which provide that procedure with its rationale, and others which are potentially at odds with them.

The same applies to conflicts between the outcomes of properly conducted CB analyses of environmental issues – i.e. those which restrict themselves to individuals' judgements or preferences concerning their own well-being – and (at least many of) the ethical judgements which those and other individuals may make about the environment. The resolution of these conflicts must take place outside the procedure of CBA – as Sagoff suggests, in the political realm where people operate as 'citizens'. To include such judgements within an extended form of CBA is, at best, a case of killing them with kindness.

5. PREFERENCES, VALUE-JUDGEMENTS AND SUBJECTIVISM

Two objections might be made to the overall argument I have presented here. The first is that I have illicitly assumed throughout that neo-classical theory in general, and the use of CBA in particular, are committed to a conception of efficiency understood in terms of (aggregate) individual welfare or well-being, and hence also to a conception of preferences as concerning what people see as contributing to their own well-being. But this, it may be objected, is not the only way in which the concept of preferences – and hence of efficiency – either can be or actually is interpreted by neo-classical economists. Instead, a more 'abstract' meaning may be given to this concept: agents may be said to prefer something simply in the sense that they would choose it in preference to other things, without any specification of the grounds for this choice. Preferences may in fact be based on any number of different grounds, including not only the agents' expected well-being but also various ethical principles, values, 'commitments' and so on. But such differences are ignored at this abstract level of conceptualisation.[10]

My response to this objection is that whilst it points to a perfectly intelligible interpretation of the concept of preferences, its employment denudes the related concept of efficiency of any prima-facie ethical significance: it is no longer at all clear why the achievement of efficiency – in particular, through the use of CBA to address market failures – should be seen as being ethically desirable. Efficiency, defined by reference to this abstract conception of preferences, becomes a purely technical concept dissociated from its only remotely plausible ethical rationale, namely the promotion of aggregative individual well-being. The connection is lost because the preferences being satisfied are no longer restricted to those concerning the agents' own well-being: they may have any basis whatsoever.

To put this response in a somewhat different way: whilst the abstract conception of preferences may be useful for certain purposes within neo-classical analytical-explanatory theory, it is far from so in welfare extensions or applications of this theory, of which CBA is a central case, and where questions about the ethical significance or value of efficiency (and hence preference-satisfaction) are crucial. CBA is intended to improve efficiency: the only coherent (even if flawed) ethical rationale for this depends on the increased degree of preference satisfaction consisting in improved levels of individual well-being, and hence CBA cannot plausibly be conducted on the basis of this purely abstract conception of preferences.

The second objection will require more extensive treatment. It is that, like Sagoff, I have illicitly assumed throughout that it is possible to evaluate the ethical judgements that people make about environmental issues, and hence that what I have presented as the 'appropriate response' to them, i.e. to engage rationally with the justifications that may be offered for them (rather than to put a price on them etc.) is one that can be made. But suppose that this is not so – that there is no way of rationally evaluating such judgements, which are thoroughly subjective and do no more than express the preferences of those who make them. Wouldn't it then be quite appropriate, indeed necessary, to 'respond' to them as the proponents of extended CBA do, i.e. to treat them simply *as* preferences, just as the market does with consumer preferences?

As Sagoff notes, this subjectivist view of ethical judgements is not only a widespread feature of contemporary culture, but is also adopted by many neo-classical economists themselves (along with members of the Austrian School, such as Hayek; see Sagoff 1988b: 40–2; also Plant 1989 and Roy 1989). As meta-ethical sceptics, they deny the possibility of any rational justification for ethical judgements. This is not just a denial that such judgements can be conclusively proved or established beyond any reasonable doubt. Rather, it involves claiming that there is no way of supporting any one judgement as against another: all are 'equally valid' as it is sometimes put, though only because none have any such 'validity' at all. More specifically, as subjectivists, they claim that saying 'X is right' is the equivalent of saying 'I like or prefer X', and so on – and no rational justification can be given for these 'ethical preferences'.[11]

Now it might seem that a subjectivist account of values supports the assimilation of ethical judgements to personal preferences, which Sagoff criticises as a category mistake: indeed, that this assimilation can only legitimately be regarded as such if subjectivism itself is rejected. If this were so, then the defence of any alternative to extended CBA as the way to make environmental decisions would require the defence of a non-subjectivist, non-sceptical meta-ethics. But whilst I believe that there is little to be said for subjectivism, I shall argue that it anyway provides no support for extended CBA, and that the category mistake in the form that I have characterised it – mistakenly interpreting ethical judgements as judgements of individuals' own well-being – remains one even if subjectivism is accepted.

The subjectivist denies that any rationally defensible grounds can be given for ethical judgements. But it does not follow from this that no distinction can be made between someone's 'preferring' some state of affairs because they regard it as ethically superior (for example, the continued existence of a species or some of its members), and their preferring it because of its expected contribution to their own well-being. This differentiation continues to exist, whatever view is taken about the possibility of justifying the respective grounds for these preferences. So even if, as the subjectivist maintains, the ethically-based preference is a 'mere' preference in the sense that it cannot be justified, its nature *as* an ethically-based preference remains; and the same is true of own-well-being-based preferences.

That is, although for the subjectivist both judgements about what is ethically right and judgements about one's own well-being are equally unjustifiable or subjective (since they involve judgements of value), and hence are (mere) 'preferences' in this subjectivist sense, it does not follow that they are both 'preferences' in the different sense of indicating what the person concerned wishes to achieve for his or her own well-being. Consequently, also, the various further differences between these kinds of preferences noted in earlier sections are not removed or obliterated by the adoption of subjectivism: ethically-based preferences cannot be 'priced', cannot coherently be included alongside own-well-being preferences in an extended CBA calculus, and so on.

Hence the need in environmental policy-making to decide whether these ethical judgements are to be accepted – and hence what significance if any to attach to own-well-being judgements – still exists, whether one is a subjectivist or not. All that subjectivism tells us is that this decision cannot itself be made for any good reason. But this unpleasant fact – were it to be one, which I doubt – cannot be circumvented by trying to include ethical judgements in a procedure which, if it has any coherent theoretical rationale at all, requires their exclusion, and which, were those judgements to be accepted, must itself be rejected.

The point that is being made here can be brought out in another way by returning to the 'abstract' conception of preferences noted earlier in this section. The subjectivist may initially find this an attractive conception, since it determinedly ignores any differences between the grounds for various preferences: in particular, between those referring to expected contributions to the agents' own well-being, and those referring to ethical principles etc. But this attractiveness is illusory. For, as I argued earlier, whilst the abstraction may be justifiable for analytical-explanatory purposes, it is not so for ethical ones, where the differences of grounds may prove crucial; and this is so whether or not, as the subjectivist maintains, there is no way of rationally evaluating these grounds. Subjectivism does not justify the use of this abstract conception of preferences in welfare contexts: it simply denies that ethically-based preferences can be evaluated.

Nor should it be thought that the use of CBA is supported by subjectivism because it avoids one having to make the kind of judgement which, according to the subjectivist, cannot be rationally made: that CBA, since it is an objective, 'value-free' procedure, enables (environmental) decisions to be made in a thoroughly scientific way that avoids problematic ethical judgements. For although it may be possible to make the calculations required by CBA in a value-free manner, the adoption of this particular means for making decisions clearly itself depends on the espousal of some ethical principle – specifically, I have argued, concerning the maximisation of aggregative individual well-being. But this must itself, according to subjectivism, be rationally unjustifiable, no better or worse than any alternative such principle. Thus the decision whether to adopt CBA still has to be made, albeit irrationally; CBA fares no better, on subjectivist assumptions, than any other basis for decision-making. Subjectivism cannot help one avoid the unavoidable nor, in the case of extended CBA, help justify the unjustifiable.

NOTES

1 Sagoff links this distinction between values and preferences to further distinctions between citizens and consumers, public and private interests, and virtues and methods; for a critical discussion of these linkages, see Keat 1994.
2 For a useful discussion of the concept of preferences in both everyday and economic contexts, see Sheffrin 1978; on the claim that 'preferences answer to reasons', see O'Neill 1993, ch.5.
3 It is perhaps significant here that Sagoff himself does not criticise the market for making the category mistake he attributes to extended CBA.
4 Other possible justifications for the market – for example, in terms of its promotion of individual liberty or autonomy, or of individual property rights – are not relevant here, since they do not serve also to justify the use of CBA, whose rationale is tied to a justification for the market via aggregate individual well-being.
5 Efficiency is more usually now defined not as maximising aggregate well-being, but as Pareto-optimality, a much 'weaker' principle (see e.g. Buchanan 1985, ch. 1). But although (even ideal) markets can only be demonstrated to be efficient in the latter sense, it is more convenient to use the less rigorous, and stronger formulation; the error I shall attribute to extended CBA would not be avoided by assuming that markets/CBA are able to achieve efficiency only in the weaker sense of Pareto-optimality.
6 See e.g. O'Neill 1993, ch. 5, and Sagoff 1988b, ch 5. It must also be assumed that it makes sense to attach a monetary value to the various expected contributions to such well-being, so that they are 'commensurable' with one another. Many criticisms of CBA have rightly focused on the problematic nature of this assumption, but I shall put these aside; they are explored elsewhere in this volume.
7 Whilst some philosophers may dispute the legitimacy of attributing rights to non-human entities, clearly many people believe they should at least be treated 'as if' this were legitimate: i.e. they believe there are some things that shouldn't be permitted to be done to them, including bringing about their or their species' extinction. In any case, even the inclusion of rights-based judgements restricted to humans generate problems for extended CBA.
8 I am not implying here that utilitarianism, as an ethical theory, entails the use of CBA, or that what I am calling 'non-utilitarian ethical judgements' could not find a place in a suitably sophisticated version of that theory. But such a version – which in effect would be one that managed to justify the recognition of 'rights' – would not be one that supported the use of CBA as the best way of arriving at ethically correct decisions.
9 For a lucid 'positive' account of existence-value, see Pearce and Turner 1990, ch. 9; on the paradox here, see Aldred 1994. A related problem concerns the

identification of the relevant group of people whose judgements of existence-value are to be included in the CBA calculation. One cannot employ the usual criterion of 'all those whose well-being is affected', since the point about existence-value is that it is has nothing to do with such 'effects'. The only plausible group might seem to be 'every member of the human species', though the rationale even for this is problematic.

10 On the dangers of ignoring the distinction between self-interest and commitment through the use of this abstract conception of preferences, see Sen 1977; cf. Aldred 1994.

11 It is often assumed or argued by such economists that scepticism or subjectivism is required or entailed by the doctrine of value-freedom, to which they are strongly committed. But as I have argued elsewhere (see Keat 1981, ch. 2) this is quite mistaken: to claim that value-judgements should be excluded from science does not entail that the latter cannot be rationally justified; and it is the irrelevance of the former to descriptive and explanatory enquiry, not their irrationality, that justifies their exclusion. See also Norton 1994.

3

ECONOMICS, ENVIRONMENTAL POLICY AND THE TRANSCENDENCE OF UTILITARIANISM

Geoffrey Hodgson

1. INTRODUCTION

This essay contrasts two different types of theoretical basis upon which environmental policy can be built. The first is neo-classical economics, where the core assumption of the rational, utility-maximising individual with given preference functions engenders an approach to policy based on individual incentives and disincentives. The philosophical foundation of neo-classical economics is utilitarianism, the essentials of which are traceable back to Jeremy Bentham and others. Utilitarianism presumes that all means find their justification in the ends they serve, and – at least in this predominant and hedonistic version – this end is seen as individual satisfaction or 'utility'.[1] From Bentham onwards, the policy focus in this tradition is on the material or pecuniary sticks and carrots of punishment and reward. Institutional design is concerned with calculable incentives and disincentives, so that the behaviours of utility-maximising individuals are altered. Hence pollution taxes, road pricing, environmental property rights, and so on.

Yet ever since its emergence, there has been persistent criticism of the moral barrenness of utilitarianism, in its applications to both economics and politics. Furthermore, by the end of the nineteenth century a major challenge to the neo-classical utilitarian view had emerged in the shape of the 'institutional' economics of Thorstein Veblen. He and his followers regarded individual character as subject to a degree of possible change along with cultural, technological and institutional development.[2] While the 'old' institutional economists did not deny that people often respond to cash and other incentives and disincentives, it was also argued that the utilitarian focus of neo-classical economics is too narrow. Utilitarianism side-steps the question of human needs that are not necessarily expressed in individual utility functions, the preservation of a sustainable environment

48

for the future being a case in point. Furthermore, the utilitarian outlook downplays individual integrity and commitment, associated with moral values and rules that are typically acquired through the individual's immersion in a social culture. Accordingly, institutional design would usefully – and should perhaps necessarily – be supplemented by measures to promote cultural values such as social commitment and trust.

The policy divergence is thus traceable to quite different assumptions about human agents. Part 2 of this essay critically discusses the type of environmental policy promoted by neo-classical economists. Part 3 reviews the basis of an alternative perspective and Part 4 concludes the essay. I am fully aware of the sketchy and incomplete nature of what follows. Nevertheless, a start must be made, however incomplete it may be.

2. NEO-CLASSICAL ECONOMICS AS A FOUNDATION FOR ENVIRONMENTAL POLICY

We may loosely define neo-classical economics as the type of economic theory built on the idea of rational, optimising agents with exogenously determined preference functions, focusing on the equilibrium outcomes and limited types of information problem associated with such optimising behaviour.[3] Neo-classical economics is presently dominant amongst academic economists in the world today, even if game theory and other prominent developments have begun to undermine some of its core assumptions (Rizvi 1994a, 1994b).

Right from the start, the assumption of utility-maximising 'economic man' was recognised as unrealistic but nevertheless as an allegedly acceptable abstraction. Even before the marginal revolution of the 1870s, John Stuart Mill (1844: 139) writes of the tenet of maximising 'economic man' that no 'political economist was ever so absurd as to suppose that mankind are really thus constituted'. Yet he defends the assumption as a tolerable abstraction. Subsequently the 'fiction' of humans as utility-maximising machines is defended, not on the basis of strict empirical validity, but because it is a useful foundation for theories that would make 'valid and meaningful predictions' (Friedman 1953: 7) or that it was simply necessary 'for the theoretical system in which it is employed' (Machlup 1972: 114).

Furthermore, with the objective of mathematical formalisation uppermost in mind, it seems much easier to assume agents with exogenous preference functions rather than considering more complex theoretical economic systems where individual preferences were endogenously determined. Individualistic ideology has played a part too. More recently neo-classical economics has become a machismo pastime in which its advocates show off their self-avowed 'imperialistic' prowess in explaining all sorts of social, political, biological and economic phenomena on the basis of maximising agents with given preference functions (Becker 1976b, Buckley and

Casson 1993, Hirshleifer 1977). Indeed, the neo-classical approach has become so widespread and persuasive that it is now having an increasing impact within sociology, particularly in the United States.

Despite their common preconceptions, neo-classical economists are not united in their policy approach to the environment. Broadly, there are two types of neo-classical environmental policy. The first is based on 'market failures' and is identified with neo-classical economists such as Arthur Pigou. In this approach, ways in which the market system fails to take into account environmental costs and benefits are identified. Consider the social and environmental cost imposed by a car driver who pollutes the air and adds to road congestion. The car driver does not individually suffer most of that cost; it is imposed on others. The market does not impose a penalty on the driver that is commensurate with the social cost. This is an example of what is termed an 'externality' (Pigou 1920). The market failures approach aims to identify such externalities and to use measures such as road taxes, fuel taxes, and so on to alleviate the problem. The idea is to impose some of the social costs on the individual driver and thereby reduce car use. It is suggested that these ideas can be applied broadly, relying on the identification of such externalities and social costs. In general, this approach relies on the use of government legislation, the tax system, and informed experts to estimate the economic costs and benefits involved.

The second neo-classical approach is associated with the 'Chicago school' and the Nobel Laureate Ronald Coase. It takes an earlier inspiration from members of the Austrian School, particularly Ludwig von Mises (Coase 1960, Demsetz 1967, von Mises 1949: 657–8). Here the policy focus is on the creation and distribution of clearly defined 'property rights'. Proponents of the 'property rights' approach argue that pollution, congestion and resource depletion can be dealt with by creating property rights in such resources and in the environment itself, and allowing the market and if necessary the courts to deal with the problem.[4] Hence the Pigovian externality problem is seen as arising primarily because of the absence of clearly defined and enforceable property rights. It is remedied in practice 'by rescinding the institutional barriers preventing the full operation of private ownership' (von Mises 1949: 658). Over-grazing of common land and over-fishing of the sea, for example, are regarded as results of a lack of clear and meaningful ownership of such resources. If pollution occurs, then the owners of the rivers or open spaces that suffer would have recourse to the courts to obtain compensation.

We shall not dwell here on the disputes between the two approaches, and the various information and enforcement problems involved in each case. These are discussed widely in the conventional environmental economics literature (Baumol and Oates 1988, Helm and Pearce 1991, Pearce and Turner 1990) and are not the subject of this essay. What is of concern here is that which is fundamental and common to both types of neo-classical policy. This is the assumption of individuals with given and complete cardinal or ordinal preference functions and the exclusive focus on the way in which various costs and benefits affect these presumed utility-maximising individuals. In short, both neo-classical approaches rely on individual self-interest to solve the problems of environmental degradation and resource depletion. Consistent with the underlying utilitarian philosophy, moral values and virtues such as duty to others, care for the planet, respect for other species and so on are considered only insofar as they yield utility for that individual. Altruism and cooperation are possible and seen as enhancing welfare, but only insofar as an individual gains utility from such acts (Becker 1974, 1976a, Hirshleifer 1978).

A fundamental objection to this is that the kind of 'cooperation' or 'altruism' that emerges from the interactions of these individuals is still based on the maximisation of individual utility. If an individual increases his or own utility by helping or cooperating with others then he or she is still self-serving, rather than being genuinely altruistic in a wider and more adequate sense. Accordingly, neo-classical treatments attempt to reduce such transcendent and intersubjective phenomena as trust and culture to characteristics of utility-maximising, individual agents. 'Cooperation' and 'altruism' are still self-seeking in that sense and therefore do not capture fuller and more adequate meanings of those two words (Khalil 1993).

The primary issue of concern here is the way in which moral values such as these are subsumed and otherwise disregarded in all neo-classical and utilitarian approaches. Thus, for instance, Dieter Helm, claiming without much argument or evidence that values are generally 'fragile' and 'highly uncertain', immediately brushes them aside:

> environmental policy must largely take values as given, and focus instead on the context within which humans act. Within this framework, the economic process plays a leading role. By changing the constraints that individuals face – by including the environment within economic calculations – the market can become less at odds with the environment.
>
> (Helm 1991: ix)

Herein are prejudices common to many mainstream economists: particularly that moral values are ephemeral and personal and have little to do with the social context or the economic process. Yet even in his own terms the argument seems contradictory. If values were so fragile and potentially variable that would seem to provide an additional argument for making them the centre of analysis.

Helm goes on to argue that the inclusion of the environment within economic calculations requires that we assign a monetary value to it and 'treat it as if is a commodity'. This latter theme is taken up by Partha Dasgupta, a contributor to Helm's book. Concerning environmental

51

problems such as the depletion of the Amazonian rain forest, Dasgupta (1991: 31) writes: 'I cannot think that it will do to look solemn and utter pious sentiments concerning our moral duty.' Discussions of moral values are thus rather contemptuously removed from debates on environmental policy.

In work of this genre there is some discussion of norms, but only in a narrow sense, typically as discussed in modern game theory. As in Robert Axelrod's (1984) celebrated work on *The Evolution of Cooperation*, norms of cooperation arise from indefinitely repeated plays of a two-person game. In such circumstances, individuals can find it to be in their own *self*-interest to cooperate with others. Such norms are sustained as long as people rationally appraise their own self-interest. But again this is a shallow and devalued concept of a norm, arising simply on the basis of an individual's own utility. There is no recognition that a moral norm – such as honesty, love or duty – may involve self-sacrifice and even transcend individual self-interest.

Equivalent problems arise in reconciling with utilitarianism concepts such as respect for nature. Albert Weale (1992: 167) identifies this weakness in a subjectivist conception of value:

> On this subjectivist account, the value of natural resources or of pollution control is to be assessed from the perspective of human individuals living in society . . . the argument of many environmentalists that nature is to be respected as having intrinsic value is simply assumed to be false or implausible.

In sum, moral values and norms appear in the neo-classical approach, but either they are rendered commensurate with everything else via the utilitarian calculus of satisfaction-seeking individuals, or they are simply disregarded. For example, it is a well-known neo-classical technique in environmental policy to ask people what they would be willing to pay to maintain an environmental asset. This is typically an attempt to render a person's commitment to environmental protection commensurate with an amount of money. Theoretically this is consistent with the idea that all evaluations and (moral) commitments can be reduced to subjective utility. As the institutional economist K. William Kapp (1978: 293) puts it, 'Subjective value theory recognizes only the individual as capable of feeling "pain and pleasure" and hence able to establish preference scales with respect to different commodities and alternative courses of action.' Accordingly, an attempt is made to give everything a price, to measure everything in terms of money. The neo-classical economist is thus like the cynic in Oscar Wilde's play *Lady Windermere's Fan* – a person who 'knows the price of everything and the value of nothing'.

However, many values and commitments cannot be expressed or measured in such terms. Even a market economy depends on values and commitments which are not tradable (Hodgson 1988). Concerns about such issues of commensurability or pecuniary reduction stretch beyond institutional economists. As Kenneth Arrow (1974: 23) remarks on trust, 'If you have to buy it, you already have some doubts about what you've bought'. Further, W. O. Hagstrom (1965: 20) argues that commitments to values cannot be engendered by offers of incentives or rewards:

> In general, *whenever strong commitments to values are expected, the rational calculation of punishments and rewards is regarded as an improper basis for making decisions.* Citizens who refrain from treason merely because it is against the law are, by that fact, of questionable loyalty; parents who refrain from incest merely because of fear of community reaction are, by that fact, unfit for parenthood.

Accordingly, there are values or commitments held by individuals which are not reducible to matters of incentive or deterrence. Likewise, commitments cannot be ascertained via a 'willingness to pay': an amenability to forego monetary or other resources. Indeed, their reduction purely to matters of individual incentive or disincentive precisely betrays such values or commitments (O'Neill 1993).

At its inception in the eighteenth century, much of the impetus behind the new science of political economy was its attempt to reduce moral values to a cost calculus. In reaction against this, many critics complained of this degradation of worthy values such as duty, loyalty, chivalry and trust. Thus in 1790 Edmund Burke wrote of the claims made for rational calculation of human affairs in the era of the French Revolution: 'the age of chivalry is gone. – That of sophisters, oeconomists, and calculators, has succeeded' (1968: 170). Subsequently, and with similar sentiments, Thomas Carlyle describes political economy as the 'dismal science' which had professed a 'pig philosophy'. And the great romantic critic of utilitarianism William Wordsworth writes in King's College Chapel, Cambridge: 'high Heaven rejects the lore of nicely-calculated less or more'.

However, despite the calculative impetus behind the new 'science', classical economists such as Adam Smith, Thomas Robert Malthus and John Stuart Mill always find a place for 'moral sentiments' and higher human values. While Malthus, in particular, endorses the idea popularised by Smith of the alleged global benefits of the pursuit of self-interest, he systematically adds the reservation that an individual should so act only 'while he adheres to the rules of justice' (1820: 3, 518). Furthermore, Smith, Ricardo, Malthus and Marx adopt and sustain Aristotle's distinction between 'use value' and 'exchange value', seeing the former as the irreducible, objective qualities of goods and services in providing for human and social needs.[5] Despite clear utilitarian traits in all their works, these classical economists are reluctant to pursue the logic of subjectivism to its limit and to establish a single measure of worth based on subjective utility.

With the 'marginal revolution' and the intellectual victory of neo-classical economics in the 1870s, such qualms are increasingly marginalised in the pursuit of an 'economic science' with measurable variables and mathematical models. It is hoped that economics will rival sciences such as physics, which have purportedly delivered so much on the basis of hard-headed reasoning and ubiquitous quantification. The ancient distinction between 'use value' and 'exchange value' disappears. William Stanley Jevons claims to have solved the so-called 'paradox of value' by formalising a relationship between price and marginal utility. The victory of individualism and subjectivism in economics is proclaimed.

We need not dwell on the common observation that the reduction of values to utility paralleled growing commodification and monetary measurement in society at large, reflecting the reality of rising capitalism in the nineteenth century. Importantly, there is a conceptual as well as a contextual link between subjective utility and monetary valuation. For example, and most transparently, the assumption of a constant marginal utility of money provides a direct linear relation between marginal utility and price. The conceptual reduction of value to utility thus suggests that everything could be somehow evaluated in monetary terms.

3. ALTERNATIVE PERSPECTIVES

Opposition to the reduction of all human values to a single calculus of money or utility has persisted ever since the publication of *The Wealth of Nations*.[6] John Ruskin is a prominent and influential nineteenth-century critic. In his book *Unto This Last* (1866: 17) he attacks the idea, promoted by economists then and now, that the social affections 'are accidental and disturbing elements in human nature; but avarice and the desire of progress are constant elements'. For him, faith, generosity, honesty and self-sacrifice were just as real and potentially durable. Furthermore, economic policies that appealed simply to hedonistic motives are ultimately self-defeating.

Writers such as John Hobson, Mahatma Gandhi and Richard Tawney are influenced by Ruskin and see the importance of appeals to moral values in economic and social policy. This does not mean that people are always regarded as virtuous. Human beings are often selfish and all-too-frequently capable of morally outrageous acts. This is not simply, or evenly mainly, a dispute between an 'optimistic' and a 'pessimistic' view of human nature. Instead, the key issues are best put in different terms.

First, whatever their failings, humans are not *entirely* motivated by self-interest. Even criminals, Mafia gangsters and mass murderers generally live by a moral code, albeit one that is often defective. Second, the pursuit of policies based solely on an appeal to self-interest is ultimately self-defeating. Even a competitive, capitalist economy itself depends on moral norms, as many writers including Joseph Schumpeter (1976), Karl Polanyi (1944), Fred Hirsch (1977) and Amitai Etzioni (1988) have repeatedly emphasised.

For example, Schumpeter wrote: 'no social system can work which is based exclusively upon a network of free contracts between (legally) equal contracting parties and in which everyone is supposed to be guided by nothing except his own (short-run) utilitarian ends' (1976: 423–4).

In contrast, neo-classical economists have preached the doctrine that it is sufficient to assume that all people are motivated solely by self-interest and greed to millions of students around the world. Accordingly, generations of workers, business people, journalists and politicians have become disposed to belittle moral values and to favour policies based on such presumptions. By assuming the ubiquity of selfishness, such behaviour is legitimated, in turn encouraging more greed and adding to other forces of social, economic and environmental disintegration.[7]

As Paul Ormerod (1994: 211) puts it: 'The promotion of the concept that the untrammelled, self-sufficient, competitive individual will maximise human welfare damages deeply the possibility of ever creating a truly affluent, cohesive society in which everyone can participate.' It was for such reasons that John Maynard Keynes (1933: 445–6) candidly wrote:

> I do now regard that [Benthamite] tradition as the worm which has been gnawing the insides of civilisation and is responsible for the present moral decay. . . . We used to regard the Christians as the enemy, because they appeared as the representatives of tradition, convention and hocus pocus. In truth it was the Benthamite calculus based on an over-valuation of the economic criterion, which was destroying the quality of the popular ideal.

The early institutionalists expressed similar concerns. At the end of the nineteenth century a crucial philosophical inspiration for institutionalism was provided by the philosopher and founder of pragmatism, Charles Sanders Peirce. Peirce criticises the 'greed philosophy' of neo-classical economics. For him, the suggestion in the economics textbooks that 'the motives which animate men in the pursuit of wealth' are 'in the highest degree beneficial' is an atrocious villainy, the most degrading of blasphemies (Peirce 1893). Peirce was one of Veblen's teachers and Veblen satirises the hedonistic, 'rational' agent of neo-classical economics in a famous article first published in 1898: 'The hedonistic conception of man is that of a lightning calculator of pleasures and pains, who oscillates like a homogeneous globule of desire of happiness under the impulse of stimuli that shift him about the area, but leave him intact' (1919: 73). Veblen (p. 276) also endorsed the view of Gustav von Schmoller and others that whilst self-interest is prominent 'this self-seeking motive is hemmed in and guided at all points in the course of its development by considerations and conventions that are not of a primarily self-seeking kind.'

Two critical themes thus enter institutionalism at its inception. One is the rejection of the idea that individuals are wholly self-seeking or hedonistic.

The other is the rejection of the idea that the individual has given prefer-ences. The latter has been a prominent theme of institutional economics since its inception. Notably eloquent presentations are present in the postwar writings of John Kenneth Galbraith (1969, 1970). Here we find strong echoes of Veblen, but in an updated context. Galbraith explains that the abandonment of the assumption of individuals with given preference functions challenges still-cherished tenets of mainstream economics. Thus he criticises the idea of consumer sovereignty – where these elemental, utility-maximising individuals are supposed to drive the whole economic system and through their choices be sovereign over production – and argues that individuals are subject to manipulation by corporate power and other vested interests. Gone too is the idea that if the individual chooses more – in pursuit of greater individual utility – then more is good for society as well. Instead, Galbraith (1970: 280) urges us to consider 'how extensively our present preconceptions, most of all that with the production of goods, are compelled by tradition and by myth'.

The role of social norms and values is particularly emphasised by Hob-son. This great heterodox economist was familiar with the writings of Veblen and is the one of the few English economists close to the 'old' American institutionalists. In his discussions of motives and incentives in the workplace, Hobson (1914: 302–4) places emphasis on 'organic' moral values and on the limitations of atomistic self-interest. Hobson combines the basic 'old' institutionalist tenet of the malleability of human purposes and preferences – prominent from Veblen to Galbraith – with an assertion of the centrality of social norms and moral values to economic policy. At the same time, Hobson insists on the importance of material and pecuniary incentives to motivate individuals. To some degree economic policy has to appeal to self-interest, but at the same time it has to transcend it by considering the 'organic' interests of society as a whole.

One of the very first social scientists to pay extended attention to environ-mental problems is the institutional economist Kapp.[8] A number of relevant themes emerge in his writings. First, he criticised the neo-classical attempt to base both theory and policy on the assumption of utility-maximising in-dividuals. This critique, however, was much more than a rejection of utilitar-ianism. In works such as *The Social Costs of Business Enterprise*, Kapp argues that economic, social and environmental policy questions cannot be reduced solely to the level of the individual alone. Parallel to an opposition to methodological individualism and reductionism in economic theory, Kapp and other institu-tionalists oppose the *ethical reductionism* of moral and policy issues to the subjective satisfactions of individuals.

Kapp (1978: 288) thus defends a concept of social cost:

Indeed the really important problems of economics are questions of collective decision-making which cannot be dealt with in terms of a calculus deductively derived from a formal concept of individual rationality under hypothetically assumed and transparent conditions.

His argument is a defence of the notion of social cost against some extreme individualists. The assertion of the irreducibility of the social level counters the proposition that externality and social cost are illusory categories, emerging from the lack of clear individual property rights. Furthermore, Kapp's notion of social cost is different from that promoted by many neo-classical economists, being established through 'collective decision-making' rather than impacts on individual utilities.

Kapp's invocation of a level of theoretical and policy analysis above that of the individual counters the reductionist thrust of neo-classical economics. There are attempts to reduce macroeconomics to microeconomics alone, in a misconceived and ill-fated quest to place macroeconomics on 'sound microeconomic foundations'. Arguably, however, there have to be distinct multiple levels of analysis of socio-economic systems, from the individual, the family, the community, to the nation and the ecosystem.[9] Similarly, as Kapp, Hobson and other institutional economists suggest, there are also stratified levels of moral pertinence and policy relevance. Moral and policy discourse should explore all of these but not attempt to reduce one to another. Just as there familiar dangers of reducing the interests of individuals to those of the state, there are also severe pitfalls involved in reducing the interests of humanity to the interests of individuals, and the interests of the ecosystem to either of these.

However, while there are multiple, irreducible levels of both analysis and ethical discourse, each level should not be considered in isolation. Indeed, Kapp and others[10] emphasise the *openness* of socio-economic systems, rejecting the view that economic processes

> can be adequately understood and analysed as closed, *i.e.* self-contained and self-sustaining systems isolated from a social and physical 'environment' of which the economic system is a part and from which it receives important inputs and with which it is related through manifold reciprocal dependencies.

The economy thus interacts with, and is irretrievably part of, 'a more comprehensive social and political as well as physical system' from which it receives both organising and disorganising impulses (Kapp 1976: 212–3.)

This idea of a stratified plurality of ethical considerations ties in with another persistent theme in the writings of Kapp and other institutional environmental economists. This is the idea that environmental and other policy issues are not reducible to a single (pecuniary) calculus. As Peter Söderbaum (1994: 195) emphasises: 'A step towards a broader approach . . . is to emphasize multidimensional thinking rather than one-dimensional thinking. Non-monetary impacts are no less "economic" than monetary ones.' Indeed, the meaningfulness and practicality of attempting to assign monetary values to the whole range of relevant environmental attributes has been persistently attacked.[11]

For those who yearn for commensurable quantification this is somewhat disconcerting. Indeed, the underdeveloped and problematic nature of the alternative approach advanced here must be openly admitted. Nevertheless, some important strands can be identified. Against the subjective and utilitarian approach, the strongest alternative foundation for socio-economic and environmental policy is one based on a conception of human (and ecological) need. Expressed in various ways, this idea has been central to institutionalism since its inception. The famous 'Veblenian dichotomy' (Waller 1994) is much to do with a distinction between a preoccupation with 'material serviceability' and a preoccupation with 'exchange value'. Later American institutionalists, influenced in particular by the writings of John Dewey, attempt to develop a 'theory of instrumental value' and establish a dynamic 'social value principle' which 'provides for the continuity of human life and the non-invidious recreation of community through the instrumental use of knowledge' (Tool 1979: 291).

Needs are distinguished from wants, the latter term being reserved for desires which are not necessarily individually or socially beneficial. Needs can be usefully defined as that which 'persons must achieve if they are to avoid sustained and serious harm' (Doyal and Gough 1991: 50). Instead of subjective utility, such needs or 'instrumental values' are revealed via some instituted social process of technical or scientific enquiry. Thus Kapp (1978: 297) writes:

> For social choices are made not in terms of subjectively experienced deficiencies and wants but in terms of objective requirements or scientifically determined standards. The relative urgency of these requirements is not subjectively felt but objectively (i.e. often technically) established.

This is not to deny the problematic nature of this venture, or indeed of science itself. For this reason, writings in this tradition emphasise the ongoing, fallible and open-ended nature of enquiry, and address the problem of designing institutions that are appropriate for the democratic evaluation and revision of declared needs. Important theoretical and empirical work on needs has been produced by Len Doyal and Ian Gough (Doyal and Gough 1991, Gough 1993). Their approach takes into account a range of biological, psychological, social and ecological considerations. They erect a theoretical system spanning the basic human, societal and ecological dimensions of need. Within this framework, ecological considerations are unavoidable. Whilst some needs are more obvious, such as food and shelter, the character of others is to some degree open-ended and subject to continuing discussion and appraisal.

The key contrast, however, is that approaches based on need see the formulation of environmental policy as driven by ongoing scientific analysis and public debate, rather than simply by attempts to quantify the wishes of individuals. For example, the matter of global warming would be evaluated by discussion of the impact on sea levels, agriculture, and so on, rather than by attempts to measure or harness subjective desires or preferences. *Both* approaches are messy, complicated and potentially controversial. But one is based on attempted evaluations of the impact on humanity and on the ecosystem as a whole, rather than being driven by measures of individual self-interest.

As indicated above, the effect of neo-classical teaching on environmental and other policy matters is to relegate explicit questions of moral value in social discourse. A contrary view, found in writings from Malthus to Keynes, is that economics must be less a mere technical or mathematical exercise and more a science involving moral judgement and the development of policy. Despite this, the over-arching policy questions concerning morals and values are typically omitted from the neo-classical textbooks on economic policy.

The prolonged influence of classical liberalism in western culture is also a significant factor here. In his book *After Virtue* (1985) Alasdair MacIntyre charts this modern terrain in which moral values are rendered relative and subjective, the gratification of emotions is seen as paramount, and the notion of the good is deemed to be a purely private matter. Each person is declared free to judge the moral good for herself, and is deemed to be at liberty to pursue that private vision subject to the constraint that it does not impinge on those like freedoms for others. The abandonment of the search for a greater 'common good' has tragically been proclaimed as the era of freedom and human liberation. As Brian Crowley (1987: 18) argues, 'Having dispensed with any claim to be able to judge the goodness of the ends that men pursue, the moral interest of society in individual or collective action turns from the ends to be achieved to focus exclusively on the means chosen to achieve them.'

4.   CONCLUSION

Institutional economists reject the evaluation of human or ecological welfare on the basis of individual human satisfaction or utility. It is stressed that individuals are motivated by moral commitments as well as self-interest. Indeed, self-interest is itself a concept constituted and inculcated via a specific social culture. Furthermore, individual preferences are malleable and endogenous to the economic system. Generally, economic behaviour is partly determined by social institutions, culture and norms. Accordingly, attempts to commensurate all outcomes, through such ideas as 'willingness to pay', by reducing values to cash simply reflect the prevailing, socially-specific and pecuniary culture, and belittle the role of morality and ideas of the 'common good'. Institutionalists argue that public policy is not usefully based on individual utility-maximisation but should be built on ideas of common good and human need.[12]

A prominent policy conclusion is clear. Appeals to appropriate moral values and not merely perceived self-interest should become part of economic policy. As Fred Hirsch (1977: 12) argues, instead of reliance on 'the self-interest principle' economic policy should pay much more heed to 'the role played by the supporting ethos of social obligation both in the formation of the relevant public policies and in their efficient transmission to market opportunities'. The dangers of reliance on 'the self-interest principle' are especially obvious in the context of the present essay. Hirsch points to the futility of positional, keeping-up-with-the-Joneses competition in the context of increasing scarcity. He argues that to break the circle there has to be a moral appeal, and one based on cooperation rather than self-interest. Those that instead stress the ecological rather than the social limits to growth come to a very similar policy conclusion.[13]

What does such an appeal to moral values involve? It means that environmental policy must address the instruments and content of political and moral debate and not simply the technicalities of established policy analysis. A government committed to the protection of the natural environment must campaign on the basis of moral imperatives such as duty and compassion, involving concern for animals and succeeding generations of humans, and not simply a calculus of costs and benefits. In contrast, if environmental policy is considered purely as a technocratic and 'value-free' exercise then moral values become dangerously subsumed. It also means that environmental policy analysts have to address the political context of their evaluations, and address the difficult problem of designing institutions within which democratic impulses and scientific knowledge can fruitfully interact.

This does not mean that policies based on pecuniary and monetary incentives have no place. Indeed, such proposals can be reinforced by complementary appeals to moral values. Indeed, it could be argued that appeals simply to moral duty, on the one hand, or reliance on perceived self-interest, on the other, are likely to be of limited effect as they are employed alone. Carefully structured combinations working on both levels are likely to be more successful.

These injunctions are much more than a matter of 'looking solemn and uttering pious sentiments concerning our moral duty'. Indeed, there is evidence that appeals to values such as fairness and cooperation can either enhance or even eclipse a reliance on self-interest alone. For instance, Mark Sagoff (1988a: 62) reports survey evidence which indicates that 'respondents believe that environmental policy – for example the degree of pollution permitted in national parks – involves ethical, cultural, and aesthetic questions on the merits of which society must deliberate, and that this has nothing to do with pricing the satisfaction of preferences at the margin'.

Contrary to the suggestion that they are ephemeral, values are difficult both to build and dislodge. Observe, for example, the two centuries of tenacity of American individualism, the grounding of Japanese social and corporate solidarity upon the foundation of a feudal epoch and the stubbornly persistent British deference to class and status. Despite the globalisation of the capitalist system and strong pressures of convergence and conformity, unique customs, cultures and systems of values still remain in each nation, and these can be explained typically by reference to hundreds of years of history. An appeal to values is no easy policy fix. Yet once norms such as cooperation and fairness become reinforced their effects can span both current and future generations. Unlike the appeal to self-interest, the transmission of such reinforced values is a way of addressing the intergenerational problem which has so perplexed utilitarians in general and neo-classical environmental economists in particular.

Neither have prominent economists been immune to such arguments. Amartya Sen (1987), for instance, argues that too much weight has been given to the 'engineering' tradition in economics since the 1870s, and the moral tradition, going back to Adam Smith, has to be strengthened. But the extent of the radical reform required of economic doctrines should not be underestimated. As Kapp (1978: 300–1) put it,

> Only by abandoning the philosophical premises of the seventeenth and eighteenth centuries; by reformulating and enlarging the meaning of its basic concepts of wealth production; and by supplementing its study of market prices by a study of social value, will economic science finally achieve an impartial and critical comprehension of the economic process which will be relevant to any form of economic organization.

The challenge to the modern economist concerned about environmental despoliation and the related processes of urban and social disintegration is to make this start, broadly along the lines suggested by Hobson, Kapp and other institutionalists, and continue the process of building economics on non-utilitarian foundations.

Clearly, this is not a matter of merely supplementing existing techniques of environmental policy analysis with an overtly moral discourse. Institutional economics promotes a quite different view of the nature of the economy. It involves a distinctive kind of analysis, emphasising the cultural and institutional framing of decision and action. Instead of being regarded as mere contraints or ephemera, institutions, culture and values are regarded as the stuff of socio-economic life.

However, especially in terms of environmental policy the institutionalist approach is, alas, underdeveloped. Furthermore, constraints of space forbid a further elaboration of the character and achievements of institutionalism in the present essay. The lack of a sufficiently developed alternative is not, however, an excuse to return to neo-classical orthodoxy. Whilst neo-classical economics seems to provide an engrossing engine of evaluation and calculation, the practical problems of its implementation are notorious. It is not that all its techniques have to be discarded, but instead that morally charged, scientifically informed and democratically guided debate about environmental problems should replace exclusive appeals to individual self-interest at the centre of the stage.[14]

NOTES

1 There are other, less hedonistic forms of utilitarianism, such as the varieties of 'indirect utilitarianism' found in the writings of Herbert Spencer, Friedrich Hayek and John Rawls. For example, it may be proposed that states of affairs may be somehow evaluated by reference to the utility they contain, for instance in regard to their utility for an anonymous individual. This essay concentrates on the hedonistic version as manifest in the writings of neo-classical economists.

2 Hereafter the 'old' institutional economics will be simply referred to as 'institutional economics' or 'institutionalism'. Since the 1960s a 'new' institutional economics has emerged, associated with Ronald Coase, Douglass North, Mancur Olson, Richard Posner, Oliver Williamson and others, but much of it is built on neo-classical and utilitarian foundations and can be addressed in such terms (Hodgson 1993a).

3 Some, but not all, neo-classical economists assume that firms are profit rather than utility maximisers. Although this is an important conceptual distinction it does not undermine the essentials of the foregoing argument and for reasons of exposition exclusive reference will be made to utility maximisation.

4 Thus, for example, Block (1989) proposes the fencing of the atmosphere with laser beams to establish and enforce property rights, just as the American range was fenced by barbed wire in the nineteenth century.

5 However, even in the writings of Marx appeals to self-interest still prevailed. He castigated those socialists who relied on appeals to morality rather than the material interests of the working class to bring about the new order. This reliance on the material self-interest of the working class was one of the reasons for Parsons's (1937: 110) observation that Marx's historical materialism is 'fundamentally, a version of utilitarian individualism'. Like the utilitarians, Marx separated ends from means and focused on the means that satisfied given ends. Hence: 'the end is justified by the means'. The limitations of Marx's 'extreme consequentialism' are explored extensively by Lukes (1985). Doyal and Gough (1991) criticise those Marxists who try to abandon a concept of objective need, arguing that a reliance on such a category is unavoidable.

6 See Lutz and Lux (1979, 1988) on the history of opposition to utilitarianism and Etzioni's (1988) notable attempt to supplement neo-classical economics with moral considerations.

7 There is evidence which suggests that taking university courses in mainstream economics actually discourages cooperative behaviour and the consideration of fairness by agents. Frank et al. (1993: 170) 'found evidence consistent with the view that differences in cooperation [between economists and non-economists] are caused in part by training in economics'. As the authors of this article suggest, this raises questions of whether economists should be taught such a

narrow view of human motivation. An education in mainstream economics may not be in the interests of society or even in the interests of the students themselves, apart from other questions of its scientific or descriptive adequacy.

8 Along with John Hobson, Gunnar Myrdal and Karl Polanyi, K. William Kapp (1910–76) is one of the few major economists coming from Europe who can be closely identified with American institutionalism. In fact, Kapp (1976) wrote one of the best short introductions to institutional economics. On Kapp see Steppacher (1994).

9 For an incisive discussion of the limitations and ultimate failure of the micro-foundations project see Rizvi (1994a). On emergent properties and the stratification of (socio-economic) reality see, for instance, Bhaskar (1975, 1979) and Hodgson (1993b).

10 An equivalent concern with the reality and implications of open systems is found in the writings of Bhaskar (1975, 1979). The treatment of the economy as an open system is also central to the pioneering application of the 'entropy law' to economic and ecological problems by Georgescu-Roegen (1971). However, the use of the entropy law in this context is challenged by Khalil (1990).

11 See, for example, Bergström 1993; Bowers 1993; Christensen 1991; Jacobs 1991, 1994; Martinez Alier 1987, 1991; Norgaard 1990; O'Neill 1993; Page 1991; Sagoff 1988b; Söderbaum 1992.

12 See Jacobs (1994) for an application of institutional economics to environmental problems.

13 See, for instance, Daly and Cobb 1989, Meadows *et al.* 1992.

14 This paper benefited greatly from discussions held at the seminars organised by the Centre for the Study of Environmental Change at Lancaster University and from the helpful and extensive comments of John Foster, Chris Hope and Michael Jacobs.

Part II

ENVIRONMENTAL VALUE: LIMITS OF AN ECONOMIC MODEL

4

RATIONALITY AND SOCIAL NORMS

Mark Peacock

It is commonly asserted that the approaches and subject matters of the disciplines of economics and sociology intersect little, if at all, the former dedicating itself to the explanation of action that may be deemed *rational*, the latter clearing up the rest of the field in which action is supposedly somewhat less than rational and hence to be explained by other means, e.g., by appealing to norms or internalised values (see Samuelson, 1961: 90).[1] More recently, there has been a tendency for the 'economic approach' to encroach upon the sociological domain, something which can scarcely be described as an *entente cordiale* between the two disciplines.[2] In this paper I highlight some of the inadequacies of the economic model of rationality, particularly its narrow, instrumental focus which deflects attention away from the indispensable role in action for normatively sanctioned interpretative schemas and expectancies. Rather than conceiving normatively guided action as a second-best alternative, either inferior, or in opposition, to its instrumentally rational counterpart, I show how the former is essential to the latter and how the two go very much together.

Having made the role of norms in rational action clear, I describe the effects of the institution of the market on norms, and note the implications of my analysis for a contractual account of the market. I then explain reactions to market expansion in terms of the transgression of pre-existing norms, relating my explanation to the field of environmental valuation using the methods of cost–benefit analysis. I conclude with some comments on the distinction, made by Sagoff (1988b, ch.5), between values and preferences.

In order to demonstrate the importance for action of normatively sanctioned interpretative schemas and expectancies (henceforth referred to as 'norms'), I draw on Garfinkel's (1963) experiments with trust, an approach which, subsequently, became known as *ethnomethodology* (Garfinkel 1967). Garfinkel starts by examining the role of norms or 'basic rules' in games (p. 190).[3] There are three basic rules to a game:

1 a set of 'legal' moves that players may choose whilst playing,
2 an assumption that those rules by which one's opponent is bound are those which bind oneself, and
3 'the player expects that, as he expects the above of the other, the other person expects it of him'.

These rules define certain modes of play as normatively acceptable, and when adhered to by players the latter enter into a relation of *trust*. Players may then be said to share a common frame of meaning – they define the situation identically (for all practical purposes).

Garfinkel's strategy is 'to start with a system with stable features, i.e. one in which the basic rules are upheld, and ask what can be done to make for trouble' (p. 187). In 'making trouble' for his subjects (Ss), Garfinkel proposes a game of noughts-and-crosses in which the experimenter (E) disturbs the unstated, but reciprocally binding, normative consensus defined by the basic rules. This disturbance was caused by E, after S made her or his mark, erasing that mark and moving it to another cell whilst giving no indication that such a move was illicit. Garfinkel suggests three possible responses to this disturbance (pp. 201–2):

1 S abandons the normative order of the game, electing a new one through which E's move is interpreted and normalised.
2 S abandons the normative order of the game without electing a new one with which to make sense of E's move.
3 S retains the normative order of the game in which E's move appears as a blatant transgression.

The degree of disturbance manifested by S was lowest under response (1) and highest under (3). Generally, Ss can be seen as trying to 'normalise the discrepancy' as a legally sanctioned move, but those who retain the original normative order found that they were unable to do so and hence suffered the most severe disturbance (pp. 204–6).

Garfinkel, after careful consideration of possible qualifications to his thesis, proposes that the three basic rules of a game are analogous to the taken-for-granted background assumptions of everyday life (pp. 206–9). That is, there exist in everyday life, normative expectations which are held in common with others; 'seen without being noticed' conditions for interaction which agents supply and expect others to do likewise under the assumption that these expectations are commonly held (pp. 216–7). To test his supposition, Garfinkel uses much the same method as he did in his examples with games, namely to call into question the taken-for-granted context of interaction, problematising it by modifying the natural attitude of everyday life.

In one set of experiments Garfinkel disrupts 'the expectancy that a knowledge of a relationship of interaction is a commonly entertained scheme of communication' (p. 226) by getting his students, when at home with their families, to act as if they were lodgers, i.e. being polite, using formal address, avoiding being personal, speaking only when spoken to, etc. In a small number of cases the family took it as a joke or put it down to undisclosed motives of the student. The majority of families, however, remained within the traditional family frame of meaning, resulting in the following sorts of reactions:

> 'What's the matter?' 'What's gotten into you?' 'Did you get fired?' 'Are you sick?' 'What are you being so superior about?' 'Why are you mad?' 'Are you out of your mind or are you just stupid?' 'I don't want any more of *that* out of *you*. And if you can't treat your mother decently you'd better move out!'

> (p. 227)

The students' families experienced severe discomfort and manifested the deepest moral indignation as shown by their blunt demands for explanations toward which they acted as if they had a right. Garfinkel reports one student's sister showing indignation about being made the subject of an experiment when it was revealed that this is what had occurred: 'Please, no more of these experiments. We're not rats you know' (p. 227).

The results of a further set of experiments are equally startling. In these, the ambiguity inherent in the most common expressions is exploited, as the experimenters suspend their normal interpretational abilities. Two examples run as follows (pp. 221–2):

> The victim waved his hand cheerily.
> (S) 'How are you?'
> (E) 'How am I in regard to what? My health, my finance, my school work, my peace of mind, my . . . '
> (S) (Red in the face and suddenly out of control) 'Look! I was just trying to be polite. Frankly I don't give a damn how you are.'

> (S) 'I had a flat tyre.'
> (E) 'What do you mean, you had a flat tyre?'
> She appeared momentarily stunned. Then she answered in a hostile way: 'What do you mean? What do you mean? A flat tyre is a flat tyre. That is what I meant. Nothing special. What a crazy question.'

Garfinkel's experiments identify a tissue of shared, background understandings which are vital to social interaction. These understandings are normally invisible, supplied effortlessly across the course of a situation, and agents assume that those with whom they interact will supply similar understandings, that is, identical for all practical purposes. Only by providing and sustaining the appropriate background expectancies can agents

69

demonstrate their competence. Failure so to do renders action altogether bemusing and peculiar; the normative order breaks down and transgressors are usually called to account for their demonstrably deviant behaviour. Normal social interaction is suspended and, obviously, goal-attainment is hindered. This leads me to draw an analytical distinction between a procedural form of rationality (associated with acting appropriately) and an instrumental type (concerning the efficient choice of means to designated ends).

It may, of course, be argued that the aforementioned procedural rationality is, in some way or other, reducible to its instrumental counterpart. People adhere to the norms of the situations in which they find themselves, so the argument might run, *because* to do so enhances the chances that they will be successful in achieving their instrumental ends. In one sense this can be construed as an unobjectionable truism; humans are goal-orientated beings, and acting appropriately is essential to the attainment of their goals. Indeed, it is senseless to posit agents acting appropriately without simultaneously positing the goals to which their actions are directed. In another sense, however, the proposed reduction is implausible. Norms are fundamentally different from instrumental rationality in that people do not choose the normative framework of their lives in the way in which they choose which items of food to purchase (means) to satisfy their hunger (ends). Acting in a normatively appropriate manner is something that agents simply learn to *do*, and, to the extent that agents are socially competent, acting appropriately requires no deliberation. Agents supply the requisite contextual understandings and expectancies in their interactions with others quite automatically. To conceive norms instrumentally is to put too much of a voluntaristic slant upon them. It is rare for agents to have a real opportunity to treat norms as instruments at the mercy of their individual whims because, unlike preferences for, say, food, norms are socially sanctioned. It is not up to agents, individually, or, for that matter, collectively, to decide whether or not to abide by norms. Norms are a given, unreflective part of agents' form of life.

From the foregoing it is apparent that the market, or any other social institution, cannot be conceived purely as a realm of instrumental reason, having eroded previously existing non-instrumental norms, leaving it afloat (disembedded) from normative foundations. Rather than the destruction of the moral fabric *per se*, it makes more sense to talk of a moral shift in capitalist societies whereby it becomes normatively acceptable to subject things to the cash nexus which were formerly exempted therefrom (cf. Atiyah 1979: 84). To conceive markets in terms of the extension, and singularity, of instrumental reason engenders problems of regress which can only be remedied by invoking a non-contractual element of contract (Durkheim 1933: 211), something akin to the normative sphere about which I have written above. Consider the following:

70

1 If a central pillar of the market is the obligation to enforce and fulfil contractual undertakings, from where does this obligation come? Might it be based on a second-order contract whereby agents freely, i.e. out of self-interest, agree that contracts, once contracted, be obligatory? But, if so, on what is this second-order contract based? Somewhere along the line something beyond the contracts of instrumentally motivated agents must be invoked.[4]

2 A modern variant of social contract theory appears in some parts of the game theoretic literature. Here, such things as rules and institutions are modelled as the outcomes of repeated games played by rational players. But how, one may ask, are the rules of these repeated games determined? Either they are agreed upon by players prior to the repeated games which leads one to ask by what rules such an agreement took place and how it was enforced (which again succumbs to the threat of a contractual regress); or one might explain these prior rules in terms of pre-existing rules and institutions – the very thing which were supposed to be the outcome of the repeated games.[5]

Thus it seems that neither contractual relationships nor rules can provide a foundation to social practices and institutions without the threat of an explanatory regress. Something else must be ascribed a foundational status, that something being our habitual ways of acting – neither a rational, nor an irrational, but a non-rational foundation to social life.[6]

Expanding markets into hitherto uncharted areas poses a challenge to the pre-existing norms operative in those areas. An analogy can be drawn between market expansion and the breaching experiments which Garfinkel undertook. If, say, asking one's parents for the bill after they have provided one with a meal, or asking a friend who has just given one a Christmas present how much it cost, then proffering to them the £5 which they spent on you as a fair exchange, can be regarded as breaching experiments, then so, I think, one can consider less frivolous examples of market extension similarly.[7] That is, practices delimiting what should and should not be commodified constitute, in part, the shared normative schemas which ethnomethodology so graphically reveals. It is in this context that I interpret the 'protests' which occur when agents refuse to state monetary payments or compensations in attempting to value the environment. Cost–benefit analysts, who pose the questions, 'How much would you be willing to pay . . . ?' or 'How much would you accept in compensation for . . . ?', are treating as a commodity that which agents see as intrinsically uncommodifiable. And the responses they often get in answer to these questions – Sagoff (1988a: 88) puts the proportion between 20 and 50 per cent – manifesting the same sort of suspicion and moral disapproval as those of the subjects of Garfinkel's experiments, indicating that some norm has been breached in the very asking of the question, a fact which may help to account for Sagoff's conceptualising such questions as category mistakes.

I am not positing as a universal claim that the environment is, in itself, intrinsically uncommodifiable. Rather, it is part of agents' form of life that certain things should remain outside the cash nexus. This is not, therefore, to say that environmental goods, like many others before them, cannot or will not be drawn into the realm of commodities, or that it is inconceivable that environmental commodities could become an accepted feature of modernity. After all, most of those, today, who are able to sell their labour power do so without seeing this practice as remarkable or immoral, even though the commodification of labour power was, and still can be today, a site of protracted struggle and conflict. What gives rise to disputes around the market/non-market divide are the social and moral norms in which agents are embedded, which draw boundaries regarding that which should and that which should not be regarded as a commodity, and facilitate recognition of breaches of these norms. These norms and expectations are akin to what E. P. Thompson terms a 'moral economy'. In voicing his opposition to a prevalent view of crowd action or 'riot' as some kind of animal reaction to hunger, Thompson writes:

> It is of course true that riots were triggered off by soaring prices, by malpractices among dealers, or by hunger. But these grievances operated within a popular consensus as to what were legitimate and what were illegitimate practices in marketing, milling, baking, etc. This in its turn was grounded upon a consistent traditional view of social norms and obligations, of the proper economic functions of several parties within the community, which, taken together, can be said to constitute the moral economy of the poor.
>
> (Thompson 1971: 188)

It is norms of this kind, manifested in people's everyday behaviour, which provide a ground for the critique of cost–benefit analysis.

To end, I would like to clarify Sagoff's (1988b, ch. 5) values–preferences distinction in a way that ties in with the comments upon this distinction which Russell Keat has made in another chapter of this volume. I drew analogies, above, between the type of reaction to cost–benefit analysis which Sagoff reports and the reactions of Garfinkel's subjects to his experiments. That is, to suggest that the environment be valued using cost–benefit techniques constitutes, at least for some people, the transgression of a norm regarding the way people think about, and act toward, the environment. Sagoff uses this datum, *inter alia*, to establish his values–preferences distinction. To recap, preferences are private, given and not subject to justification, whereas values are public, amenable to change through discussion and capable of rational justification. It is this last characteristic of values which I wish to interrogate further.

72

Sagoff is quite adamant that people adhere to values for reasons, they have opinions regarding values which may be right or wrong and are subject to argumentation. However, it is not values themselves which are amenable to rational justification and debate; rather, values provide a framework of criteria concerning what is to count as a valid argument in regard to a particular issue, what is a reasonable stance to take regarding it. Hence, values provide criteria as to what is a relevant consideration in a debate; they have a direct bearing on the content of debate and it is in this sense that they should be distinguished from Sagoff's (1988b: 12) 'method-' or 'criterion-free' intellectual virtues (as Russell Keat refers to them) which Sagoff locates in open, clear and honest debate.

In fact, values themselves are peculiarly resistant to justification. If we stop to think why we should not place monetary values on environmental goods, or offer payment for the gifts we receive, or sell our loved ones into slavery, we find that, before long, reasons give out and we come up against our ungrounded ways of acting, beyond which no justification is forth-coming (Wittgenstein 1958: § 217; 1969: §§ 110, 166, 253, 411). These ways of acting define the parameters of our forms of life which we find difficult to imagine being otherwise, and it is they, as much as, if not more than, our preferences, which are *given*. For those who transgress such norms, without indicating that there is anything amiss in so doing, we simply have to say that they have not grasped the point of our form of life, they are not 'going on' appropriately. Transgressors are liable to appear to us as odd, even demented or mentally disturbed, their behaviour as not simply mistaken but senseless (Wittgenstein 1969: §§ 71, 155, 220, 647). Thus, *pace* Sagoff (1988b: 94), it is not of values that truth and falsity are predicated but rather it is values which admit judgements of truth and falsity *vis-à-vis* particular issues. What makes it so hard to enter into a meaningful debate with one who does not share one's values is the fact that values facilitate debate primarily amongst those who recognise them as values. Sagoff's intellectual virtues will be insufficient to mediate between those with different value systems.[9]

I have argued that norms are not to be seen as antithetical to rationality, but are actually a crucial component of it. Drawing upon the work of Garfinkel, I showed the somewhat calamitous consequences of norm transgression, an occurrence which disrupts the normal flow of everyday social interaction. I then went on to discuss the fact that, despite not being normatively barren, the institution of the market, and its ever-expanding proclivities, represents a shift in the normative underpinning to social action which disturbs that which was previously extant. This can give market expansion the appearance of one of Garfinkel's breaching experiments, to be met with outrage and protest. To finish, I discussed, and recast, the distinction between values and preferences, depicting values, in spite of their foundational status in everyday life, as ultimately impervious

73

to rational grounding or redemption. Yet it is precisely, and only, these values which hold out the hope of forging a rational environmental policy.

NOTES

1 Sociologists themselves, e.g. Parsons 1968, have colluded in this intellectual division of labour as much as economists.
2 The economic approach has been inspired by economists such as Becker and finds its most developed sociological statement in Coleman 1991.
3 References unaccompanied by the author's name and publication date refer to Garfinkel 1963.
4 See Poole 1985 for similar arguments.
5 See Geoff Hodgson (this volume) for relevant comments.
6 I am drawing on Wittgenstein (1969), here, and will return to the theme of this non-rational foundation to social life at the end of this chapter.
7 Sagoff's (1988b: 87, 112–13) examples of deciding the outcome of a trial or of a football game according to the aggregation of preferences of the jury and the spectators, respectively, are analogous.
8 'If the true is what is grounded, then the ground is not *true*, nor yet false' (Wittgenstein, 1969: § 205; cf. also §§ 70–5, 94, 156).
9 One could, of course, say, following Gadamer 1989, that it is precisely different values which are productive of dialogue and debate. I do not dispute Gadamer's thesis, but draw attention to the skill and sensitivity with which one must conduct a debate with one whose tradition is different from one's own if that debate is to yield fruit.

5

VALUE PLURALISM, INCOMMENSURABILITY AND INSTITUTIONS

John O'Neill

1. ENVIRONMENTAL VALUES: PLURALISM AND CONFLICT

The environment is a prime site of conflict between competing values and interests, and institutions and communities that articulate those values and interests. Part of the promise of cost–benefit analysis is that it offers a rational procedure for resolving those conflicts. In this chapter I show that this promise is illusory. To give focus to the discussion I want to start by considering a few typical examples of local environmental conflicts. My examples are drawn from conflicts that have arisen in North Wales.

The Countryside Council for Wales was formed in April 1991 from the regional carve-up of the old Nature Conservancy Council and its amalgamation in Wales with the Countryside Commission. The pros and cons of that reorganisation and the political motivations for it I leave aside. Of interest here is that it brought together participants in quite distinct practices with different evaluative vocabularies.

The old Nature Conservancy Council was primarily scientific in orientation and concerned practically with management of environmentally significant sites of special scientific interest. Already within that organisation conflicts could occur, for example, between ornithologists and botanists over drainage in wetland. Crudely speaking, from the ornithologists' perspective, the more water, the greater reed beds and open water, and hence more kinds and numbers of birds; such considerations might lead to a recommendation to cease current drainage patterns and allow an area to flood. However, from the botanist's perspective, some of the most interesting plant communities might sometimes be destroyed by that policy. This conflict is already a conflict of values, not of facts.[1] These local conflicts of value, take place, however, within the context of a shared evaluative vocabulary and criteria about what goes to make a valuable habitat or ecological system: species richness, integrity, rarity, fragility, history and so on.[2] Judgements are made within a common framework.

75

The transition from the Nature Conservancy Council to the Countryside Council for Wales brought with it a quite new responsibility, for landscape evaluation. It would I think be false to claim that aesthetic considerations played no part in the evaluations of the older Nature Conservancy Council. An aesthetic response animates interests in both birds and plant life, and Leopold is right to point to the way ecology can develop an aesthetic sensibility for objects which might appear dull to the uneducated eye, for example for the diversity in wetland (Leopold 1989: 173–7). However, it remains the case that the introduction of landscape concerns appeals to a quite distinct set of practices with a distinct institutional history in the pictorial arts and with their own distinct evaluative vocabulary and criteria. The practical conflict between the traditional concerns of nature conservation and the landscape values is evident in the different responses they indicate towards the spread of rhododendron, for example around Beddgelert. While the rhododendron is a superb landscape feature, from the nature conservation view it has little to be said for it. It is an alien Himalayan intruder which spreads quickly and under whose dense thicket little else grows, and which destroys local ecological systems. While problems of value conflict can arise within a practice, it is often more acute when different practices with quite distinct evaluative criteria are concerned with the same object under different descriptions.

Such conflicts occur within a policy-making community educated within particular practices, sciences and arts which have formal institutional support. These can in turn conflict with the evaluations of an outside community. Consider for example the disused slate quarries on the Llanberis side of Elidir Fawr. From both landscape and ecological perspectives there is very little to said for them. They form a huge industrial scar up a mountainside and at present contain very little of interest to the natural scientist.[3] Plans to landscape the quarries were partially implemented. Some of the local people, however, were very unhappy about this, on the grounds that landscaping literally covers up the past. The quarries embody a sense of place and past for a community. My sympathies here are entirely with the locals. A walk through the quarries, especially the huts higher up, gives a much stronger sense of past and place than would be gained from a visit to the heritage museums in the valley below.[4]

We have then a number of conflicting sets of values invoked for or against flooded wetland, for or against rhododendron, for or against the landscaping of quarries. An initial point to note regarding those conflicts is that the environmental states and sites which are the objects of conflict are evaluated under different descriptions. They are not simply good or bad as such, beautiful or ugly as such, but good or bad, beautiful or ugly under different descriptions. A site can be at the same time 'a good A' and 'a bad B', 'a beautiful C' and 'an ugly D'. The slate quarries have considerable worth as a place that embodies the work and history of a community, but

76

none as a habitat or landscape. A wetland may have little worth as a landscape, but considerable value as a habitat.[5] Relatedly there are evaluative adjectives that apply to a site only under particular descriptions. It makes sense to talk of an 'evocative place' or an 'evocative landscape'; one would be less likely to talk of 'an evocative habitat' or an 'evocative ecosystem'.

These evaluations of the site under different descriptions invoke quite different institutional practices and perspectives, and make appeal to quite different standards and criteria of appraisal. The values appealed to for the appraisal of a site under the description of habitat, such as species richness and integrity, are distinct from those appealed to for its appraisal as a landscape or place. None seems reducible to others, nor to some other common value. None straightforwardly takes precedence over others: there is no privileged canonical description for the purposes of an over-arching evaluation. The different appraisals of the sites call upon an irreducible pluralism of values. That this is the case is often taken to raise problems of value incommensurability. The claim that the values are incommensurable, and the consequences this has for cost–benefit analysis forms the object of the following section.

2. VON MISES'S WATERFALL, COST-BENEFIT ANALYSIS AND INCOMMENSURABILITY

Arguments between proponents of the application of cost–benefit analysis to environmental policy and its critics concern in part the nature of rational action and decision-making. Consider the following observation by Pearce *et al.* on the use of physical descriptions of environmental goods:

> Physical accounts *are* useful in answering ecological questions of interest and in linking environment to economy . . . However, physical accounts are limited because they lack a common unit of measurement and it is not possible to gauge their importance relative to each other and non-environmental goods and services.
>
> (Pearce *et al.* 1989: 115)

The Pearce report assumes that to make a rational non-arbitrary choice between options there must exist 'some common unit of measurement' through which the relative importance of goods can be ascertained. Money provides that unit of measurement and cost–benefit analysis the method of using that unit in decision-making: 'CBA is the only [approach] which explicitly makes the effort to compare like with like using a single measuring rod of benefits and costs, money' (1989: 57). The problem for environmentalists on this view is to extend the 'measuring rod' of monetary units to include those environmental goods which are at present unpriced. The argument offered by Pearce is dependent on the view that rational choice between alternatives requires value commensurability: the existence of 'a single measuring rod' of their benefits and costs, of their goods and bads. Monetary evaluation is important, not for any value of its own, but because it offers such a measuring rod.

The assumption that rational choice requires a common monetary unit, and the problem of incorporating 'non-economic goods' which lack a price into monetary calculations, have a long history in economics.[6] Both are developed not only within the neo-classical tradition in which Pearce works, but also, with particular thoroughness in the Austrian tradition of economics which is, on the whole, critical of politically implemented cost–benefit procedures. Moreover, the special problems raised by environmental goods have also a long and often unrecorded history. The assumption that rationality requires commensurability and its implications for environmental goods were anticipated with clarity by von Mises in his opening salvo in the socialist calculation debate.[7]

Von Mises assumes that choices between options require computation and that 'computation demands units' (von Mises 1981: 98).[8] The 'subjective use-value of commodities' provides no units for computation: 'judgements of value do not measure: they arrange, they grade' (p. 98). Hence such values cannot enter directly into comparisons between options. A common unit is required. Money provides that unit: 'calculations based upon exchange values enable us to reduce values to a common unit' (p. 99). Von Mises recognises however that this creates a problem of how to include 'non-economic goods', those 'which are not the subject of exchange value' (p. 99). Environmental goods provide the exemplar of these:

> If, for example, we are considering whether a hydraulic power-works would be profitable we cannot include in the computation the damage which will be done to the beauty of the waterfalls unless the fall in values due to a fall in tourist traffic is taken into account. Yet we must certainly take such considerations into account when deciding whether the undertaking shall be carried out.
>
> (von Mises 1981: 99)

Von Mises's response to that problem is one that has become standard in the later literature. We cannot avoid making hard choices between 'non-economic' goods and economic goods, and in doing so, whether we like it or not, we are implicitly making economic evaluations of the non-economic:

> If we know precisely how much we have to pay for beauty, health, honour, pride, and the like, nothing need hinder us from giving them due consideration. Sensitive people may be pained to have to choose between the ideal and the material. But that is not the fault of a money economy. It is in the nature of things.
>
> (1981: 100)

In making that claim von Mises is assuming that every choice is implicitly an exercise in economic evaluation. In such hard choices, whether or not we like to admit it to ourselves, we are implicit accountants, putting a price on unpriced goods. The agent in a choice of this kind knows not only the value of everything but also its price. While von Mises explicitly rejects the attempt to put a shadow price on goods in decision-making of the kind offered by cost–benefit analysis – with all Austrians he holds that prices have to emerge from the market itself – the central strategy for bringing the 'non-economic' into the realm of the economic he shares with more recent environmental economists. Rational decision-making requires monetary units, and whether we like it or not, in making choices we are making monetary comparisons. The economist is merely making this explicit. The proponent of cost–benefit analysis goes further and attempts actually to state what the price is in the absence of the market in the good.

The assumption that every choice involves an implicit act of monetary evaluation should be rejected. Part of the problem here is with the view of monetary prices that economists in both the neo-classical and Austrian traditions assume. Monetary transactions are not exercises in the use of a measuring rod. They are social acts which have a social meaning. The proper implications to be drawn from willingness to pay surveys are those that are drawn from one of the earliest and most famous surveys, that of King Darius:

> When Darius was king of the Persian empire, he summoned the Greeks who were at his court and asked them how much money it would take for them to eat the corpses of their fathers. They responded they would not do it for any price. Afterwards, Darius summoned some Indians called Kallatiai who do eat their parents and asked in the presence of the Greeks . . . for what price they would agree to cremate their dead fathers. They cried out loudly and told him to keep still.[9]

Darius does not here act like the modern neo-classical economist when faced with 'protest bids'. He does not dismiss the reactions and attempt to look for some other way of discovering the real price which the respondents would place on the respective good. Rather he uses protest responses to the demand for a price precisely to discover what the basic commitments of a society are. One exhibits commitment to some good, here one's dead kin, by refusing to place a price upon it. One betrays that commitment by accepting a price. Correspondingly, to ask persons how much they would be willing to pay to forgo a good to which they are committed is to attempt to corrupt. Darius does not in his survey attempt to corrupt, but to illustrate commitments. His modern counterpart who asks of Aborigines in the Kakadu Conservation Zone in Australia how much they would be willing to accept in compensation for the mineral exploitation of the sacred burial sites of their dead ancestors, does attempt to corrupt the relationships constitutive of a culture. There are certain commitments and relationships that are constituted by a refusal to accept money for their gain or loss; thus with friends: to put a price on them would be to betray them, to offer money to corrupt. Only an agent thoroughly corrupted by a lifetime in markets or an economics department could sit back, consider the Darius survey in a 'cool and rational' fashion and come up with the monetary value they would accept.

This argument does not yet, however, reveal any general incommensurability between values, of the kind which I asserted to exist at the end of the last section. It reveals a particular incommensurability between certain kinds of relationships and commitments on the one hand and the relationships involved in monetary transactions on the other. It is open to modify cost–benefit analysis to arrive at some other measure that does not have the particular incommensurability problems of willingness to' pay. One might invoke something like the quality-adjusted life years (qalys) of the health economist or some other measure of welfare.[10] That move is made for environmental goods by the authors of the Ramsey Centre report on environmental values who entertain supplementing or replacing monetary units (Attfield and Dell 1989: 34–5). In doing so they make a second significant shift from the position of Mises and more recent neo-classical theorists, who assume that rational choice requires commensurability in a strong form, a cardinal measure, and hence that the mere ordering of different objects and states of affair will not do for proper measurement of alternatives. The Ramsey Centre Report rejects that assumption. Rational decision-making does not require strong commensurability, the existence of a single cardinal unit of measurement. It requires only weak commensurability, an ordering of betterness between items: 'All that commensurability of values requires is that one is able to make judgements such as This is more valuable than that' (p. 29). Environmental values are commensurable in this sense: 'the values that enter environmental disputes are commensurable, in our view, because they can enter judgements of the form, "This is more valuable than that"'(p. 30). On the Ramsey Centre account either money or some other unit of welfare provides an ordinal measure: 'our measure of social welfare needs only to rank options (i.e. be "ordinal") and need not contain information about the gaps between items so ranked (i.e. be "cardinal")' (p. 35). What the units measure is welfare conceived of as the satisfaction of informed preferences: 'where money measures are inappropriate, we need to translate the argument into units of welfare, understood as a measure of preferences based on adequate information' (p. 35). It is such ordinal measures that enter the aggregation procedures of an extended cost–benefit analysis which is then able to 'form a basis for sound decision-making in environmental matters' (p. 35). The Ramsey Centre position is flawed. It depends upon an illicit shift in the use of the commensurability concept.[11] The report shifts between a claim about commensurability that concerns the possibility of certain *outcomes* of decision-making processes and a claim about commensurability that concerns the decision-making *procedures* through which outcomes are arrived at. To say that all that is required for value commensurability is that our values be such that they allow us to arrive at judgements of the form 'This is more valuable than that' is to make value commensurability a question of the possibility of arriving at a certain outcome: a betterness ordering of options. There are other versions of the betterness ordering that might be more plausibly invoked here, such as 'this is at least as good as that' (Broome 1991). I have my doubts as to whether we can order all options in this way, but these I do not want to pursue here (but see O'Neill 1993, ch.7). The point to note in the present context is that the possibility of arriving at such outcomes is quite independent of questions of how one arrived at them, whether it be through some algorithmic procedure applied to ordinal or cardinal measures, deliberative procedures in which the force of argument determines the outcome, the appeal to authority or whatever. However, the Ramsey Centre report assumes not only the possibility of outcomes that can be ordered in terms of a betterness relation, but also that ordinal measures appear in the decision-making procedures through which such outcomes are reached. They assume that we ought to arrive at judgements of betterness by employing ordinal measures of the informed preference rankings of affected agents and aggregating these. Hence the defence of cost–benefit analysis. But this involves a shift to a value commensurability claim which concerns decision-making procedures, not outcomes.

The report illustrates a more general failing in many discussions of value commensurability to distinguish three independent questions:

1 Can we compare options across different and possibly irreducibly plural values?
2 Can we rank all options in terms of an ordinal 'betterness' relation?
3 Can we rationally determine a decision by employing ordinal or cardinal measures and applying some algorithmic aggregation procedure to them?

A positive answer to either or both of the first two question is quite consistent with a negative answer to the third. Even if the Ramsey Centre is right in claiming that we should answer 'yes' to the second question, it gives no support to a positive answer to the third question and hence no support to the acceptability of cost–benefit analysis.

While the Ramsey Centre report claims that environmental values are commensurable in a weaker sense than that of Mises, the argument for commensurability depends on the same assumption as that of Mises, that every choice is an act of mensuration (except that where Mises insists upon cardinal measures, the Ramsey Centre report assumes only ordinal measures need be employed). That assumption should be simply rejected.

d the orthodox economist are right: hard choices do have to be
.esources are finite and there is a variety of social, cultural, envir-
tal and material goods that make a call upon them. However, the
's are not of the kind that can be made according to either cardinal or
    al scales of measurement employed to allow the application of the
potential Pareto optimality criterion. Our choices are not of that kind. They
are choices between objects and states of affairs that combine a plurality of
different values in different ways. We apply not mathematics, but practical
judgement to the particular choices before us. To do this we do need to
compare objects across different values. Nothing I have said entails the
radical incomparability of values such that choices are arbitrary. We can
compare without the possibility of a measure of value of the kind that cost–
benefit analysis assumes. One needs to rely on good practical judgement –
the faculty of discerning what is required in particular cases with the
specific mixes of values they involve – not on algorithms that require
measures.[12]

Not only can choices be made without a common measure, that is often
how they *are* made. It is instructive to consider again my local examples of
the first section. No one resolves the kinds of conflict I outlined by looking
for some common unit. They weigh not measures but reasons for and
against a proposal. They argue, debate and come to some agreement.
Attempts by the economist to force the measuring rod of money on to
them are contrived, and get in the way of the process of reasoned deliberation. One does not need a common unit to 'compare like with like'.
Rather, the opposite is the case. The monetary units entered into the
balance sheet can have the appearance of an alien attempt to fix on
some number, which is ultimately quite arbitrary. To say this is not to say
there is not a subsidiary place in the process of deliberation for algorithmic
procedures: techniques for computing species richness of the fauna of a
site or for scoring the significance of different conservation and landscape
components of a particular site may assist deliberation. So also might
welfare measures. However, any such measures and techniques need to
be understood as aids to deliberation and reasoned judgement, not substitutes for it.

3. INSTITUTIONS, VALUES AND CONFLICT

What should a rational procedure for resolving value disputes be like? What
kinds of institutions do environmental conflicts require for their resolution?
What institutional forms are required? Cost–benefit analysis offers an
answer to those questions, although its institutional dimension is often
disguised. It is a procedure that attempts to produce the 'optimal' outcomes
of 'ideal markets' by bureaucratic means.[13] In the last section I argued that
the procedures which cost–benefit analysis offers are inadequate, and

offered the beginnings of an alternative that stresses the role of deliberation and judgement. In this section I consider the institutional dimension of that alternative.

Consider again my earlier examples. The preferences that individuals have – for or against flooded wetland, for or against rhododendron, for or against the landscaping of quarries – cannot be taken as simple givens of individuals. They themselves have an institutional context. They emerge from a specific background of a set of social practices and historically rooted communities and they can only be properly understood or explained against the background of these.[14] The relationship between such valuations and their institutional context is not merely a contingent one. It is only against the background of certain practices that certain evaluations are possible. Take the case of ornithology. As Raz notes, it is only in the context of particular social forms that an interest in 'bird-watching' is possible:

> Activities which do not appear to acquire their character from social forms in fact do so. Bird watching seems to be what any sighted person in the vicinity of birds can do. And so he can, except that that would not make him into a bird watcher. He can be that only in a society where this, or at least some other animal tracking activities, are recognized as leisure activities, and which furthermore shares certain attitudes to natural life generally.
>
> (Raz 1986: 310–11)

The dependence of the activity on the existence of the social practice is a matter of evaluative standards: in activities like bird-watching, patterns of observation and behaviour must be potentially checkable against some socially embodied standard. Not any observation of something with feathers counts. Correspondingly, it is through engagement in a social practice that the capacity to distinguish between good and bad performances of the activity are learned.

This feature of the values points to another feature of the preferences expressed about the locations in Snowdonia: the preferences expressed are not simple preferences of mere taste. They invoke a set of judgements that call upon values, and these judgements are open to appraisal by argument that appeals to criteria independent of personal likes and dislikes.[15] That this is the case has implications for the kinds of institutional procedures that are appropriate for the resolution of conflicts where judgements from within different practices come into conflict.

Institutions for resolving conflict can be of two kinds: reason-sensitive, i.e. the soundness of reasons enters directly into the processes of adjudication, or reason-blind, i.e. the process involves no reference to questions concerning the soundness of reasons for different preferences. One reason for holding that cost–benefit analysis of itself is inappropriate is that it is reason-blind in this sense. The strength and weaknesses of the *intensity* of a preference count, but the strength and weakness of the *reasons* for a preference do not. Preferences grounded in aesthetic, scientific, and communitarian judgements about a site are treated as on a par with preferences for this or that flavour of ice-cream. Preferences are treated as expressions of mere taste to be priced and weighed one with the other. It offers conflict resolution and policy without rational assessment and debate. Politics becomes a surrogate market which completes by bureaucratic means what, within neo-classical theory, the ideal market is supposed to do: aggregate given preferences efficiently. This reason-blindness is not peculiar to cost–benefit analysis. It is shared by the market itself. For example, the Austrian and public choice critics of cost–benefit analysis do not reject the view that institutions be reason-blind. They hold a non-cognitivist account of values that denies any role for reason.[16] What they reject is the particular political form that the reason-blind institutions required for cost–benefit analysis assume.

Reason-blindness is also shared by another influential model of conflict resolution, that of social negotiation, where this is understood as purely a dialogical way of resolving conflicts of interests. The claim that value differences should be negotiated in this sense has appealing features. It clearly has one apparent virtue that cost–benefit analysis lacks, namely that it is relatively democratic: negotiation involves the participation of the disputants or their representatives, where in cost–benefit analysis a group of bureaucratic experts decides by employing suitable algorithms to aggregate the preferences of disputants. It also, unlike the market, allows parties to enter into dialogue with one another. Resolution of conflict occurs through voice, not exit. However, negotiation is reason-blind. Negotiation is appropriate where there exist conflicts of interests, not judgements. The aim of negotiation is not to converge on an agreed judgement, but to arrive at some *modus vivendi*, a compromise, that allows individuals with quite different interests to operate in a common world. It is for that reason I take it that it is popular amongst the relativistically inclined students of science. Truth drops out. Truths are not objects of negotiation. Negotiation entails bargaining, not reasoned discussion and in bargaining, as every good shop steward knows, appeals to reason are simply masks to forward the satisfaction of interests. To say this is not to dismiss negotiation. Negotiation has its place. Civil peace is of value, and given that agreement is not always possible, negotiation is often desirable. Moreover, one part of the institutional dimension to environmental conflict is about power and interest. Negotiation is sometimes appropriate in these contexts. In others, the value of civil peace needs to be subordinate to other goods. There are contexts in which negotiation may simply be a means through which those who lack social power concede to those who do not; in such contexts, for the powerless, dialogue might not be the appropriate response.

The model of negotiation needs, however, to be distinguished from another with which it is often confused, and which does appear appropriate to the cases of conflict which I have outlined – the model of reasoned dialogue. To claim that a conflict is open to reasoned adjudication is to call upon discursive institutions as the appropriate form for conflict resolution. The forum, not the market, becomes the model institutional form (Elster 1986). The model of the discursive institution as the ideal political form was and still is crucial to the enlightenment model of politics. It is formulated in Kant's essay 'An answer to the question: What is enlightenment?'. What enlightenment requires is the 'freedom to make public use of one's reason in all matters' (Kant 1991b: 55). It requires institutions that allow public reasoned dialogue. That Kantian model of the discursive institutions necessary for enlightenment remains quite deservedly influential. It is central, for example, to Habermas's conception of rational public life.[17] To engage in reasoned dialogue is to aim not at compromise but at convergence in judgements. To argue for a belief is to seek to convince; to be open to the arguments of others is allow oneself to convinced. The activity of argument presupposes an ideal of convergence of judgement founded on good reason. To say that rational dialogue aims at convergence is not to assert, as Habermas does, that in an ideal speech situation beliefs would necessarily converge. Choices are often, although not always, underdetermined by the values of rationality. In the best of all possible conditions reasonable interlocutors could find themselves at the close of argument tied to their respective opposed positions: dialogue may succeed in arriving not at agreement, but at each appreciating the reasonableness of the opposing view, while remaining committed to his or her own. Civil peace through argument is attained through mutual toleration.[18]

There are however difficulties for this enlightenment model of discursive institutions. First, a certain wariness needs to be exercised in writing as if an ideal speech situation already existed. Environmental conflicts are not only about values, they are also about power and interests.[19] The two are in tension, and appreciation of the possibility of resolution through dialogue needs to be tempered by recognition of the actual existence of interest conflict.

The second difficulty concerns the limits of dialogue itself in evaluative disputes between social practices. Kant's defence of the public use of reason is founded on the ideal of enlightenment that is famously characterised thus:

Enlightenment is man's emergence from his self-incurred immaturity. Immaturity is the inability to use one's own understanding without the guidance of another. This immaturity is *self-incurred* if its cause is not lack of understanding, but lack of resolution or courage to use it without the guidance of another.

(Kant 1991b: 54)

The difficulty with this claim is that for all persons in many, if not most of their affairs, there exists a necessary lack of maturity which is not self-incurred. Evaluations presuppose a specific set of social practices and education within a practice is a condition of having the capacities to engage in evaluation. For example, I do not have, and without extensive training am unlikely ever to have, the capacities to make judgements about the ecological importance of some sites. I take the judgements of others, for example scientifically educated friends and strangers, as authoritative. I am not in a position to recognise the variety of plants in a wetland, let alone assess its significance. What I want is not some unattainable 'maturity' but some criteria, 'immature' as I am in most matters, to know when it is rational to trust the authoritative judgements of others and when scepticism is appropriate. The practical problem in a democratic community is the reconciliation of necessary 'immaturity' with democratic procedures. I suspect that some of the attraction of the reason-blind view in environmental matters, as of such views of cultural concerns, is that it short-cuts that problem by treating all judgement as mere taste, and hence immediately denying the existence of privileged standpoints. That generalised scepticism about values needs, I suggest, to be resisted. What is rather required is an understanding of the conditions in which trust in the authoritative utterances of others is rational and of the tools of proper scepticism. That question has in turn institutional and political dimensions. What institutions deserve epistemological trust in what conditions? The different institutional dimensions of evaluation are again significant here. The association of evaluative practices with positions of social power and wealth induces quite proper scepticism about their reliability. What is required to answer these difficulties is not a series of decision rules but a political epistemology concerning conditions of trust, and a corresponding social and political theory about its institutional preconditions. That problem is taken up elsewhere in this volume.[20]

NOTES

1 One unfortunate feature of scientific assessments is that like their economic counterparts they assume rational decision-making involves quantification. Hence the tendency to disguise values amongst numbers. For a good illustration of this and the problems that result see Yearley 1991: 140ff.
2 The discussion in Ratcliffe 1977: 6–10 and *passim* is still deservedly influential. However, it would be a mistake to believe that the values can all be explicated on a tick list. An education in the life sciences, at its best, develops not just knowledge about its object and intellectual virtues, but also an evaluative interest in and concern for its object (O'Neill 1993: 141–6). Such evaluations involve capacities and habits of perception which are passed on by apprenticeship not by book.
3 They do have some interest to those concerned with ecological colonisation and development.

4 The conflicts outlined are conflicts between different environmental values: ecological, aesthetic and communal. These can themselves conflict with other values, for example, those associated with the immediate welfare of individuals who need to gain a livelihood from a particular place. A flaw in some versions of environmentalism is a failure to appreciate the call upon us made by other goods apart from a narrowly defined set of environmental goods. Specifically environmental goods need to take their place amongst others.

5 In the terms that Geach introduced, the adjectives here are attributive not predicative (Geach 1967). For a discussion of the issue in these terms see O'Neill 1993, ch.7.

6 Not all of that literature within the classics of standard economic thought shares Pearce's account. Both Marshall and Pigou use the notion of economic goods to limit the proper scope of economics rather than to extend it. See Marshall 1920, Book I ch.2 and Book II ch.2 and Pigou 1920, ch.1.

7 For details of the socialist calculation debate see Buchanan 1985, ch. 4; Lavoie 1985 and Steele 1992. The debates around environmental economics can be understood as a long footnote to the first stage of the socialist calculation debate; see O'Neill 1993, ch.7, O'Neill 1995 and O'Neill forthcoming.

8 The part of von Mises's text from which I quote here is a reproduction of his first essay in the socialist calculation debate, 'Economic calculation in the socialist commonwealth' of 1920. A translation of this essay by Adler appears in Hayek 1935.

9 Herodotus, *Histories* 3.38.

10 Other measures that have been suggested in the past are energy units and labour time. For useful discussions of these see Martinez-Alier 1987 and Steele 1992, ch.6.

11 In the background is a related illicit shift between the claims:

1 For any decision between options, there is a way of comparing values such that the options can be ordered in an 'at least as good as' relation, and
2 There is a way of comparing values such that, for any decision, the options can be ordered in an 'at least as good as' relation.

For discussion of this illicit shift in the scope of the quantifiers, see Wiggins 1980, sections VI–VIII.

12 See Aristotle's *Nicomachean Ethics*, Book VI chs 5–10 and Book X ch.10, and Kant 1991a, 'On the common saying: This may be true in theory but it does not apply in practice'.

13 The institutional dimensions of cost–benefit analysis are disguised in standard accounts. Cost–benefit analysis is not merely an algorithm for making decisions. It has particular institutional preconditions. That institutional background to cost–benefit analysis has rendered it open to criticism from standard market-based approaches to economics – from public choice perspectives within the neo-classical paradigm and from the Austrian tradition without. Whatever else they get wrong, these critics are quite right to criticise cost–benefit analysis for its disguising of its institutional presuppositions. I discuss these criticisms in detail in O'Neill forthcoming and 1994.

14 I develop the points here in more detail in O'Neill forthcoming.

15 See the contribution by Russell Keat to this volume for more on this.

16 For a more detailed discussion of this point see O'Neill forthcoming.

17 See Habermas 1984. For the use of Habermas in the environmental sphere see Dryzek 1990a and 1990b.

18 The virtue of tolerance is difficult to sustain because it can be exhibited only

towards that one holds to be not as it ought to be. A virtue of non-converging argument is that it can issue in tolerance. See Raz 1986, ch.15.

19 To that extent there is something to Sen's comment on Elster's version of Habermas: 'it is not really easy to see how antagonistic interests, including class interests, would all get submerged in "unanimous preferences" merely by "a rational discussion"' (Sen 1986: 234).

20 See the chapters by Jacobs and by Wynne, this volume. I discuss the issue in more detail in O'Neill 1993, ch.8.

6

PRICING THE COUNTRYSIDE

The example of Tir Cymen

Simon Bilsborough

1. INTRODUCTION

A review of the current economics literature reveals contradictory messages about the appropriate ways in which decisions about the environment 'should' be made. At one level, there is disagreement about exactly what is revealed by survey techniques that are designed to elicit willingness-to-pay for non-marketed goods. Thus it has been suggested that 'whatever it is that is measured by aggregating random consumer preferences, the numbers produced so far fail to convince as adequate surrogates for social choices and ethical judgements' (Lowe *et al.* 1993: 109). At another level, no clear view has emerged regarding the circumstances under which cost–benefit analysis can be legitimately used to set environmental objectives, targets or prices to generate environmental output. This paper aims to explore these issues in relation to the setting of objectives and prices for Tir Cymen, the Countryside Council for Wales's experimental farm land stewardship scheme.

2. TIR CYMEN

Tir Cymen (the English translation is 'well-crafted landscape') is a Welsh version of the English Countryside Stewardship scheme, and was launched by the Countryside Council for Wales (CCW) in 1992. It operates in three pilot areas in Wales: the districts of Meirionnydd in North Wales, Dinefwr[1] in mid-Wales and Swansea (which covers the Gower peninsula) in South Wales. The objectives of the scheme are to conserve and enhance important wildlife habitats and landscape features, and to provide additional opportunities for the public's enjoyment of the countryside. Tir Cymen has the following features:

1 It is a voluntary scheme, whereby entry is voluntary on the part of the farmer but discretionary on the part of CCW.[2] Resources are targeted towards those farms which offer the greatest potential for landscape and

wildlife conservation, and new access opportunities, and thereby provide the best value for money for Tir Cymen.

2 It is a whole-farm scheme. This means that the total area of the farm business is assessed for its wildlife, landscape and archaeological features, and for the potential to promote additional access opportunities. All important wildlife habitats and landscape features on the farm have to be managed following Tir Cymen management guidelines.

3 Farmers have to follow a whole-farm conservation code that ensures good environmental management (for instance, with regard to pollution control) across the whole farm. A sum of £20/per hectare is paid for following this code, with minimum and maximum payments.

4 Capital works (such as stone wall building) are funded through one-off capital payments, and annual management tasks receive annual per hectare payments.

A strong element of the philosophy that underlies Tir Cymen is the creation of a market in environmental goods, operated by CCW on behalf of the public who are the ultimate beneficiaries of Tir Cymen. Farmers can produce environmental goods to the required standard (set by Tir Cymen management prescriptions), 'sell' them in the market operated by CCW and receive rewards in the form of payments noted above. In this context the practical issues of establishing prices in a such a 'market', and the subsequent issue of targeting resources to achieve value for money, are explored.

3. SETTING PRICES: A DESCRIPTION OF THE PROCESS

Prices had to be seen to achieve value for money for the taxpayer. This was interpreted as meaning the least-cost achievement of Tir Cymen objectives: achieving the greatest environmental output at least cost to the taxpayer. Since there is no formal market in environmental goods, prices have to be set, and the market administered by CCW. The issue of how least-cost prices can be determined, artificially, is clearly of importance.

It was clear that pricing decisions had to be related to Tir Cymen targets. Targets are used to help measure the success of Tir Cymen, in that they provide a quantitative indicator of the amount of land under positive management. An assessment of the qualitative aspects of Tir Cymen management will be provided for by independent monitoring. This will monitor ecological change, change to important landscape features, and the quality of new access opportunities on a representative sample of farms. Results will be compared to change on a sample of similar 'control' farms outside Tir Cymen areas.

A target of achieving a rate of entry into Tir Cymen of about 10 per cent per year of the available farm land in the pilot areas for the first five years was considered appropriate. This would therefore aim to achieve a rate of uptake of 50 per cent after five years. A requirement for the setting of meaningful targets was accurate data sets concerning the extent of key habitats and landscape features in the three Tir Cymen pilot areas, although in some cases survey data were less comprehensive than ideal.

To help set minimum prices that would achieve these targets, market research was undertaken by independent consultants. This exercise in itself posed issues:

First, the sample to be chosen clearly had to be representative. Ideally, farms with environmental attributes that were representative of the spread of habitats and landscape features in each of the pilot areas would have been chosen. However, very little farm-level data exist that correlate farming type with its environmental resource. Representativeness with regard to the size and type of farms in each of the areas was therefore achieved, the assumption being that this sample would also be representative of habitats and landscape opportunities.

Second, time and resource constraints militated against using a sample size that would have produced statistically significant results. Results were therefore presented on the basis that they represented the view of an in-depth survey of representative farmers, rather than a statistically significant sample size that would have allowed degrees of confidence to be calculated.

Third, respondents were farmers in each of the three Tir Cymen pilot areas, and were given details about the philosophy of Tir Cymen, as well as the practical management details of the whole farm code and of management requirements for specific habitats or landscape features. Against the whole farm code, or individual habitats, respondents were asked for:

(a) the price at which they would definitely not enter the habitat or whole farm into Tir Cymen;
(b) the price at which they were very likely to enter;
(c) the price, between the two, at which they would give Tir Cymen very serious consideration.

The method of eliciting prices was to display a range of prices, from zero to an appropriate maximum, on a 'thermometer'.

This procedure of asking for three prices was undertaken to help minimise the obvious bias that might be introduced in a hypothetical situation; bias might arise from the following aspects:

● farmers, in anticipation of entering Tir Cymen at a later date, attempt to maximise personal returns by exaggerating required prices;
● farmers are asked at what price they would be willing to sell environmental goods, with no clear budget constraint on the response given;
● responses of farmers might be influenced by the range of prices suggested on the thermometer.

Later analysis, within CCW, showed that, as might be expected, the 'serious consideration price' was not mid-way between the 'definitely reject' and the 'very likely to accept' price, but was in fact skewed towards the latter. The mean responses were calculated and the mean 'very likely to enter' response was given an index of 100. This then revealed the following:

1 For a range of habitat management prescriptions, the mean 'definitely not' price measured 41, and the mean 'serious consideration' price measured 88.
2 For a range of typical capital works, the mean 'definitely not' price measured 45, and the mean 'serious consideration' price measured 86.
3 For additional access, the mean 'definitely not' price measured 88, and the 'serious consideration' price measured 110!

To engage a farmer's 'serious consideration' would require, if responses are to be believed, prices considerably higher than (and in some cases double) prices which would ensure rejection, and only slightly less than those which would secure definite participation.

It is clear that during the market-testing stage of the development of Tir Cymen, a much stronger antipathy towards the access provisions of the scheme was evident. This was focused on the provision for increased permissive access on farms. The management requirement to allow open access on to areas of moorland and upland unimproved grassland attracted no adverse comment, possibly because this requirement was one of a number of management requirements for these areas, others of which (such as limitations on stocking density) attracted more attention. Additionally, it may be that farmers are less averse to members of the public wandering freely across unenclosed moorland than to their walking, even on well delineated routes, across the main productive areas of the farm.

From the range of 'serious consideration' prices solicited for each management category, a price to attract enough farmers to secure Tir Cymen targets was required. A price that would attract 100 per cent of farmers, for a scheme with a target of securing 50 per cent of land into the scheme after 5 years, would clearly represent an inefficient use of resources. It was possible to construct a locus showing, for a particular management category, price from £0 to £x against the proportion of respondents who would give Tir Cymen 'serious consideration' at that price. It was thus possible to identify the 'serious consideration' price which (according to the responses), would mean that 50 per cent of the farmers would give serious consideration to entering Tir Cymen. This price gave the starting point for determining least cost prices.

Two problems with this procedure were apparent:

1 There was an upwards bias in responses, as noted earlier.
2 Farmers were responding to pricing questions for the whole farm code,

individual habitats, individual landscape features, and payments for introducing permissive access. In reality, a farmer would enter Tir Cymen on the basis of accepting these as a package, rather than being able to pick and choose which elements to accept and which to reject. The possibility existed that, by pricing each set of management prescriptions separately, each individual element was over-priced when compared with what was required when the scheme was entered into as a package of joint measures. There are therefore very real difficulties in pricing outputs that are, in effect, produced jointly.

These prices were then compared with existing information about incentive levels in existing Environmentally Sensitive Areas (ESAs) in Wales, with those available under the Countryside Stewardship scheme in England, and from CCW's internal data on SSSI management agreements. However, there are some reservations about the use of management agreement data for such an exercise. In particular:

1 Under section 28 of the 1981 Wildlife and Countryside Act, the use of compensation payments calculated according to the profits foregone by not carrying out an agricultural improvement to the SSSI (Site of Special Scientific Interest), means that resources are targeted according to threat, rather than targeted pro-actively to areas of greatest benefit. The use of resources in this way is likely to target a different range of habitats than would be targeted pro-actively.
2 Compensation payments, based on profits foregone, are highly specific according to the nature of the threat. In particular, the farmers' managerial ability, which may vary widely, will determine potential technical performance and thus strongly influence payment levels. SSSI management agreements expressed as payments per hectare, across a wide range of farming types situations, may not reveal accurately the minimum payments required to achieve whole-farm objectives, as opposed to the prevention of damage to a relatively small portion of a farm.

In view of these reservations, the procedure thus allowed some adjustment of the prices suggested through the market research exercise through comparisons with comparative incentives available elsewhere, and led to the current Tir Cymen prices. Subsequent monitoring of the uptake rate of Tir Cymen (assessed against targets), and of the number of farmers who initially show an interest in the scheme but who subsequently decide against participation, have tended to confirm that, overall, prices are those which will achieve Tir Cymen targets efficiently.

4. SETTING PRICES: DISCUSSION

This description of the process used by CCW to set prices illustrates some of the difficulties involved in price-setting for goods for which no market readily exists. CCW has a responsibility both to the taxpayer, to ensure that value for money is being achieved, and to the Welsh Office to ensure that prices are appropriate to ensure Tir Cymen targets are met. From the point of view of some economists, however, what is noticeable about the process is the lack of influence of formal economic welfare theory. Price is determined with regard to supply-side conditions, rather than demand-side considerations of social benefit. There might be several reasons for this:

1 the expected response of an agency which has inherited from a predecessor organisation (Nature Conservancy Council) a culture whereby conservation objectives on SSSI are agreed with farmers, as suppliers of environmental goods, rather than people as 'consumers' of environmental goods;
2 a strengthened emphasis upon 'partnership' with suppliers (farmers) to secure conservation objectives in the countryside;
3 a reluctance to see challenged the 'elitist' approach of scientists and landscape advisers to the setting of rural conservation objectives;
4 a desire on the part of CCW for success to be clearly demonstrated to its sponsors (the Welsh Office), leading to an approach that minimised risk of failure (an approach that invited comments or suggestions from 'consumers' of Tir Cymen might have challenged the perceived objectives or targets of the scheme, or the way in which it was proposed they would be achieved);
5 an urgent need to get Tir Cymen 'up and running' within a very tight time-scale and within a tight budget, that precluded the use of innovative or challenging methods of designing and planning Tir Cymen, especially if they were likely to be time-consuming or expensive.

So, for both practical reasons and reasons that concern the internal culture of a public organisation, Tir Cymen objectives and targets were determined internally, and prices to achieve these were determined with reference to supply-side conditions.

5. ALTERNATIVE WAYS OF SETTING OBJECTIVES, PRICES AND CHOICE CRITERIA TO SELECT FARMS

A central question concerns alternative models of securing the production of rural environmental goods, by seeking to establish and take account of people's preferences. The above approach is one which assumes that the objectives and targets for Tir Cymen are those that reflect accurately these preferences. How might an alternative approach seek to determine preferences for rural environmental conservation schemes, and what role (if any) might there be for the monetary valuation of environmental goods and for CBA-type models of decision-making?

It is clear that there exists potential to incorporate public preferences more systematically into the design of rural conservation schemes. If carried out rigorously, such exercises could help set a framework in which objectives, targets and more detailed management guidelines were refined to match public preferences.

For instance, it would be feasible to collect data concerning public preferences for nature and landscape conservation objectives, and on the relative strength of these preferences. Such an exercise could focus on, at a national level, broad objectives, with an increasing focus down to a regional then local level, aimed at ascertaining the strength of preferences for particular landscapes or wildlife habitats, or for the provision of additional access opportunities. The strength for various options could be ascertained through asking people to list, or weight, preferences. Thus, Garrod and Willis (1994) asked members of the Northumberland Wildlife Trust to allocate 100 points between ten different habitat types; mean scores ranged from 3.08 for conifer forest, to 22.2 for broadleaved woodland. In terms of making choices that reflected operational considerations, respondents could, for instance, choose conservation and access priorities from a realistic set of farm-level management options, within a hypothetical but typical farm. An extension would be to ask respondents to allocate sums from a given budget amongst the different management options.

The potential role for measuring the strength of preferences via monetary valuation is less clear. The rationale for carrying out such an exercise would need to be established. Three potential roles for contingent valuation could be imagined: to establish the strength of preferences; to set prices (equivalent to marginal social benefit); or to establish national or regional budgets for a countryside conservation scheme. Each of these possible uses of CV can be briefly examined.

1 *Strength of preferences.* Willingness-to-pay might be used as a mechanism simply to indicate differences in the intensity of preference for different habitats and landscape features. Such CV results might be used to influence scheme objectives and targets, with prices being those required to ensure farmer participation at a level that achieves these. However, compared with asking respondents to allocate points between preferences, there would seem little to recommend this use of CV. If pricing decisions are to be set according to supply-side conditions, willingness-to-pay information reflecting marginal increases in social welfare is not required.

2 *Setting prices.* Alternatively, results derived from willingness-to-pay studies might be used to set prices, the objective being to equate price with marginal social benefit, as measured by willingness-to-pay. For example, Maxwell (1994) estimates the present value of benefits associated with a proposed 'community forest' in Bedfordshire. Figures of £1,656 and £2,208 per hectare are calculated, for a 40 per cent and a 30 per cent coverage of land respectively.[3] It is argued that 'contingent valuation

95

methodology is able to provide valid assessments of the value of future environmental improvements' (Maxwell 1994: 398), and there is a clear policy conclusion: 'these sums [i.e £1,656 and £2,208 respectively] represent the amount a prudent government could afford to invest if it wished to match the public's valuation of the forest' (p. 393). The policy issue is thus interpreted by Maxwell as an investment decision, essentially about whether the predicted flow of annual benefits will justify the capital investment. The implication is that the 'market price' (in this case a one-off capital grant) for additional community forests should not exceed the quoted values.

An issue in this context is to what extent a menu of prices for rural environmental goods, reflecting social welfare as captured by CV, might ensure participation and deliver an increase in the quality profile of habitats and landscapes sufficient to satisfy both public demand and the requirements of wildlife. The comment that 'there is no guarantee that, even if all prices are assigned perfectly, the obtained result will be sustainable' (Castle *et al.* 1994: 382) is pertinent in this context. Within a countryside conservation scheme, there seems to be no reason to suppose that efficient resource allocation based on maximising net human welfare will create conditions under which wildlife thrives.

3 *Notional budgets.* A third option would be for mean *per capita* willingness-to-pay for improvements to Welsh habitats and landscapes to be aggregated up by an appropriate population into a notional budget. Defining the appropriate population in this context is crucial, and there is no agreed procedure for this.

Thus, in an American study concerning the Northern Spotted Owl, Rubin *et al.* (1991) assumed that mean annual willingness-to-pay decreased by 10 per cent for every 1,000 miles distance from the site where the owl is found in Washington State. By multiplying the mean figure by the total number of households, aggregate benefits increased from $102.7 million in Washington State to $1,481 million for the US as a whole. In a UK context, and with regard to willingness-to-pay for coastal protection works, Green and Tunstall (1993) found that whilst preferences for the preservation of coastal sites showed some decay with distance from the coast, they did not fall to zero even in the centre of the country. For a given level of preference, there was 'no direct effect of distance upon willingness-to-pay' (p. 11). It was concluded that 'the appropriate beneficial population is that of the whole country' (p. 11).

Since non-use values for wildlife are by definition unassociated with use, there can be no ready assumption that such values decrease exponentially with distance. However, the use of country-wide populations to aggregate mean willingness-to-pay sums will tend to produce 'junk numbers'. Thus, Cobbing and Slee (1992) suggest a value for the Mar Lodge estate in

Scotland of £108 million. This is derived from multiplying up, by the population of Scotland over 16 years of age, a mean willingness-to-pay of £26.64 derived from 279 respondents in Aberdeen, Dundee and Glasgow.

The point is not that the number of people that benefit from wildlife conservation is unimportant, but that these numbers should not be determined (hypothetically by a conservation agency) to make an argument in favour of a particular budget for a countryside conservation scheme.

Despite these problems with integrating preferences expressed in terms of willingness-to-pay in a form directly relevant to Tir Cymen, the view that the monetary valuation of environmental goods can in principle play an important role in issues of countryside conservation is widespread. For example, Garrod and Willis consider that:

> economic considerations of the benefits of local wildlife sites are . . .
> unlikely to be clouded by issues of irreversibility or safe minimum
> standards, and hence are amenable to conventional techniques of
> economic appraisal and the use of the efficiency criterion to prioritise
> decisions by capturing the trade-off between benefits and the resource
> costs necessary to achieve them.
>
> (Garrod and Willis 1994: 555)

Contingent valuation is the favoured tool. Pearce and Turner, in an optimistic assessment concerning the use of contingent valuation, argue that CV 'should, technically, be applicable to all circumstances and thus has two important features: (a) it will frequently be the *only* technique of benefit estimation; (b) it should be applicable to most contexts of environmental policy' (see Pearce and Turner 1990: 148). Results from CV studies are 'best interpreted as indicating respondent total economic valuation, i.e. a global assessment encompassing use, option and existence values' (p. 153).

There appears to be little doubt in this assessment that CV is a method that can capture all relevant benefits, and that a meaningful figure, amenable to policy decision-making, can be produced. The merits of adopting such an approach, however, are not clear-cut even at this level. Four issues are of concern.

First, there is no clear consistency in the results derived from CV surveys. To ensure a consistency of decision-making between farms and between different regions, CV surveys should generate results that are repeatable and checkable, and be capable of unambiguous interpretation. However, it is clear that even the way in which monetary values may be elicited profoundly affects results. Thus, Bateman and Bryan (1994) asked over 3,000 visitors to the Norfolk Broads whether or not they were prepared to pay for a flood alleviation scheme, using three different forms of question. An open-ended question yielded a mean per capita willingness-to-pay of £67.19; an iterative bidding approach produced a mean value of

£74.91; and a mean figure of £143.18 was recorded using dichotomous choice. Partial explanations for these differences, in terms of biased responses, are suggested by the authors. Nevertheless, the efficacy of a methodology that can produce such a range of values for a well-defined environmental issue must be open to doubt.

Second, it is questionable whether a process that aims to estimate the aggregated sum of private benefit accruing to individuals can fully capture the breadth and magnitude of all the benefits that arise from landscape and wildlife conservation. A key issue concerns the presentation and interpretation of information. Reconciling the need to present enough information, without leaving out important environmental data, to allow an informed decision to be made within the time constraints of a questionnaire process is a key challenge. It seems likely that the results derived from CV will always be highly sensitive to the degree of information, and the context in which it is presented. For example, following the completion of a CV questionnaire concerning the preservation of hump-back whales, Samples *et al.* (1986) showed one group of respondents a film about humpback whales, whilst a control group was shown an unrelated film. After the films, 32 per cent of the former and 20 per cent of the latter increased their willingness-to-pay, whilst 3 per cent of respondents in both groups reduced their bids. Mean bids increased by 33 per cent for the group shown the whale film, and by 20 per cent for the control group. It was suggested that this 'lends support to the view that preferences are learned during the interview process, even in the absence of new information' (p. 310). A less charitable observation might be that respondents were groping in the dark to consider a distinct environmental issue in a context that was that was highly unusual and not reflected in everyday experience. Answers to very specific questions concerning willingness-to-pay were therefore highly uncertain and consequently sensitive to alteration in response to stimuli. The sensitivity of response to information, and the lack of agreement as to the nature and context within which information is presented must generate concern regarding the consistency of decision-making that would result from more comprehensive use of CV within public sector decision-making.

Third, there are persistent difficulties with the problem of embedding. Thus, in a survey to estimate the value placed on preventing migratory waterfowl deaths in America, Boyle *et al.* (1994), surveying three different samples, found that estimated means for preventing 2,000, 20,000 and 200,000 bird deaths were $80, $78 and $88 respectively. In other words, 'the estimated contingent values do not increase significantly with the number of migratory waterfowl deaths prevented' (p. 78). The authors reflect on 'the extremely difficult task of valuing marginal changes in natural resources, when those changes represent small proportions of the total environmental assets in question' (p. 80).

Fourth, there is no clear consensus regarding the interpretation of CV results. From a survey of assessing willingness-to-pay for bald eagles and wild turkeys in New England, America, it was concluded that the contingent values derived:

> appear to reflect the aggregate value of a bundle of attributes associated with making a contribution for wildlife existence . . . a portion, but typically not all of an individual's payment might be motivated by consideration of fair share, or concern about environmental quality in general. Although payment of fair share might be interpreted as a lower bound of resource value, payment for a good cause, such as environmental quality in general, may prove little or no indication of the value of the resource itself. In fact, the 'cause' itself may not matter.
>
> (Stevens *et al.* 1994: 360)

6. PRIVATE BENEFIT AND PUBLIC GOODS

One of the issues concerning the use of contingent valuation is the degree to which a public agency, using public funds to promote the supply of public environmental goods, should rely on methodologies that treat public goods as private goods. The distinction between the 'citizen' and the 'consumer' (Sagoff 1988b) is well known. Tir Cymen aims to enhance the supply of public goods for the benefit of society as a whole, including future generations.

The key issue is whether decision criteria based only on aggregated private benefit should be used to make decisions about environmental goods whose production is for the public good. For instance, 'an ecological economics of sustainability implies an approach that privileges the requirements of the system above those of the individual' (Common and Perring 1992: 32). It is suggested that the idea of humankind's stewardship of wildlife and landscapes requires a decision-making framework that looks more broadly than aggregated private benefit. Toman (1994) considers that 'the stewardship perspective does not deny the relevance of human preferences, but it asserts the existence of larger societal concerns that members of society will feel (in varying degrees) beyond individual preferences' (p. 403). Similarly, Daly (1992) notes an obligation to trusteeship, which leads him to question the emphasis on personal benefit as a criterion for decision-making:

> we are related not only by a nexus of individual willingness-to-pay for different things, but also by relations of trusteeship for the poor, the future, and other species. The attempt to abstract from these concrete relations of trusteeship and reduce everything to a question on individual willingness-to-pay is a distortion of our concrete experience as

persons in community.

(Daly 1992: 191)

Common and Perring relate these issues back to the correct policy tools to use to make decisions about environmental resources:

> the tendency to seek an intertemporally efficient allocation of environ-
> mental resources through price corrections based on the contingent
> valuation of such resources in both surrogate and simulated markets
> . . . is further evidence of the dominance of the principle of consumer
> sovereignty over the relevance of the instruments.

(Common and Perring 1992: 30)

The common theme is that decisions regarding goods whose benefit is collective require decision-criteria with a wider focus than that provided by relying on the aggregation of private benefit across a sample of individuals.

The wider of use of CV in decision-making about rural environmental goods has implications for the operation of countryside agencies. In the context of Tir Cymen, for instance, the degree to which some degree of 'expert' input from CCW (regarding the wildlife, landscape, and access characteristics of a farm) would be required in the decision concerning the acceptance of the farm into the scheme is unclear. It may be possible that once prices are established through the use of CV, decisions about entry are made on an exclusively private basis by the farmer. Private decisions would reflect the product prices and environmental prices facing the farmer, along with the management requirements to produce both traditional output and environmental goods to the required standard. If he decides to enter the scheme, CCW would merely process the application form and offer a contract, although presumably some form of 'expert' assessment might be made to see if proposed contractual obligations could be met. Any use of discretion by CCW, however, might be limited to budgetary considerations, i.e. entry would be on a 'first come, first served' basis until an annual budget had been exhausted.

Using the market explicitly to allocate public funds to farmers on the basis of their marginal (private) costs of producing rural environmental goods might secure participation at least cost, but the degree to which this will correspond with a conservation strategy that reflects both scientific and aesthetic requirements is unclear. For instance, the 'development of local area conservation plans which could establish a context for both agencies and individual land holders within which particular conservation initiatives could be assessed' (Hodge et al. 1994: 210) has been argued for. Meeting locally-specific nature conservation, landscape and access targets is likely to require a more strategic approach to the allocation of public funds than that provided for by the market and the total reliance on farmers' perceptions of private conservation management costs.

100

7. CONCLUSIONS

There is undoubtedly scope for increased public participation in the design and delivery of countryside conservation schemes. In particular, public preferences can influence broad objectives and regional and local targets. In this context, the role for the economist is to design mechanisms that generate outputs consistent with these preferences in a cost-effective manner. This is consistent with the role of economists that is advocated by Goodstein (1994):

> the strength of normative economics is to make assumptions and clarify choices. By becoming uncritical advocates of an efficiency standard, economists have moved beyond that role. We are professionally better equipped to suggest how standards mandated by the political process can be achieved more cost-effectively. The suggestion in this paper is that the political process can be made more participatory.
>
> (Goodstein 1994: 190)

A key consideration is the setting of prices. Understanding the way in which the price mechanism can deliver rural environmental goods is of crucial importance if cost-effectiveness is to be achieved. This implies a much greater understanding of the motivations of farmers in their dual role as producers of food and fibre, and of environmental goods. It also requires greater understanding of the responsiveness of farmers to price and other signals regarding environmental output.

Securing farmer participation cost-effectively is only part of the picture. Price must also deliver environmental goods that, as well as reflecting public preferences, must ensure the conservation of the fragile and rare.

Securing public preferences for rural environmental goods therefore has to be seen in a broader context of policy formulation and delivery. In the case of policy formulation, the merits of collecting information on the strength of public preferences within a framework that reduces these down to monetary units are unclear. First, the sensitivity of the methodology, in particular to the 'payment vehicle' (the method of eliciting a response) and to the level of information (and context within which the information is presented) suggests that the correct response of policy makers to CV results is one of caution, at best, or, at worst, scepticism. Second, there is clear uncertainty in the interpretation of derived monetary values. Third, even if we assume an unambiguous interpretation of derived monetary values, the relationship between mean per capita values and price signals for rural environmental goods is unclear. The issue is whether CV, as a tool for influencing decision criteria in this way, is:

- sensitive to the multi-faceted ways in which wildlife and landscapes can benefit people;
- rigorous enough to estimate these benefits in an unambiguous manner;

101

- dependable enough to allow clear decisions to be made on a consistent basis.

There is a clear research agenda for the proponents of valuation methodologies. The wider agenda, however, concerns the relationship between people and their environments; the degree to which models of market behaviour can fully capture this relationship; and the extent to which the stewardship and trusteeship of environmental resources require a wider framework of decision-making than that based on private benefit. It is, for instance, argued that:

> what is important is the ability of the system to retain the resilience to cope with random shocks, and this is not served by operating as if the present structure of private preferences is the sole criterion against which to judge system performance.
>
> (Common and Perring 1992: 32)

The oft-quoted 'CBA is but a guide to decision-making' therefore needs refining in the case of rural environmental goods. Given the uncertainties regarding the derivation and interpretation of CV results, what is required is a clearer indication of the reliability of CV, and less ambiguous criteria regarding the relationship between CV and decision-making. The alternative is for public agencies to continue to derive cost-effective mechanisms for enhancing rural environmental quality in the absence of any role for CV whatsoever.[4]

NOTES

1 Excluding that part of Dinefwr that is within the Cambrian Mountains ESA.
2 From 1995, Tir Cymen will be included as part of the Government's Agri-Environment measures in Wales, and entry will no longer be discretionary. Minimum entry criteria, however, will be applicable.
3 Total annual willingness-to-pay is calculated by multiplying mean willingness-to-pay (derived from a CV survey) with the population over 15 years of age living within 6 km of the proposed forest. Over a 50-year period, this value is then assumed to show an annual real growth of 1 per cent. Discounting at 8 per cent derives present values.
4 The opinions expressed in this paper are those of the author and not of the Countryside Council for Wales.

7

THE RELATIONS BETWEE̲ PRESERVATION VALUE AN̲D EXISTENCE VALUE

Jeremy Roxbee Cox

1. INTRODUCTION: TWO DISTINCTIONS AMONGST EVALUATIONS

In this paper I am concerned with the value of the continued existence of environmental goods, which may be called 'preservation value': what economists have sought to capture as 'existence value'. To simplify the discussion, I will consider only the cases where the thing is to be preserved after the life of the valuer. I will argue that the idea of a *total* preservation value, which is the sum of the preservation values attached to a good by a number of individuals, is meaningless, and also that it is wrong to identify preservation value with existence value, as this is ordinarily interpreted in practice. From each of these conclusions it follows that the use of contingent valuation to elicit a total value for continued existence is a mistaken procedure. A more detailed statement of the aims of the paper can be given when two important distinctions have been mentioned.

One distinction is between two things that have been understood by 'intrinsic value'. The other is between those things valued because they are beneficial to the valuer, and those valued by a valuer for other reasons.

In this section I will elaborate the two distinctions. In the next section I will look at the implications of the distinctions for the question of when things of intrinsic value should be preserved, and in section 3 apply the conclusions of these sections to economic assessment of preservation value.

The first distinction is that between *object value* and *moral standing*: the distinction between intrinsic value understood as the *intrinsic value of an object*, and intrinsic value understood as *having moral standing*.[1] I am not claiming to have discovered the distinction. I do suggest, however, that it is often overlooked.

This distinction is best introduced through examples of ascriptions of value that are often made and whose character a reader will appreciate, whether or not the reader agrees with any particular example. Examples of _veryday attributions of intrinsic value of the object kind would be: 'the rose is beautiful', 'being able to play the violin is enjoyable', 'running is exhilarating', 'the Alps are awe-inspiring'.

Examples of everyday claims that certain things have intrinsic value of the moral standing kind would be: 'Human beings matter'; 'dolphins matter', in contexts where it is clear that they are not being judged to have instrumental value. We will understand these familiar assertions as meaning that the things mentioned are the sorts of thing whose good, interests, or welfare must, morally, be taken into account.

There is a fundamental connection between moral standing and object value. Suppose a thing has object value for you. And suppose I think that you have moral standing. Then I must, morally, take your good into account, and I will think that, other things being equal, the thing's having object value for you is a reason for you to enjoy that thing.

This is the basis of our judgements that things that matter for other beings with moral standing (like other people) matter *morally*. My concern with what is of object value for another being depends on my believing that the being has moral standing. This will also make me believe that enabling others with moral standing to get things of object value is a worthwhile activity, that is, has object value for me.[2]

I will be emphasising a second distinction, whose implications are important for the issue of preservation. This is the distinction between things valued because they are *beneficial to the valuer* and *things valued for other reasons*. Thus I value a supply of food for myself because of the benefits, in terms of need-satisfaction and enjoyment, that I get from it. I may on the other hand think it important to protect the environment for the future, where this is not because doing this will benefit me in any way. 'Beneficial' is used broadly here, to include enjoyment, and the kind of rewardingness that comes from achievement or doing something one thinks worth doing.

In the light of these distinctions, the theses of the paper can be stated. These are: that where the value of the preservation of a good is not a beneficial value, then summing the preservation valuations of individuals is incoherent; and that where the thing whose preservation is in question is a thing with moral standing, or a thing with object value for a thing with moral standing other than the valuer, then the preservation value will be non-beneficial, and therefore not summable. Further, existence value, in the practice of economists, is a beneficial value, and thus not the same as preservation value. The relevance of these claims to environmental matters lies in the fact that for very many environmental things, when it is claimed that they are of intrinsic value, what is meant is that they are in the class of things with moral standing. (Only in the special cases where the value of the thing's continued existence lies in the benefit to the valuer, or where a number of valuers are prepared to regard their benefits as part of a single pool of benefits, will the summation be appropriate. These cases will not be considered here, as they are excluded by the restriction to the preservation of goods after the valuer's death.)[3]

To establish these conclusions, we may go further into the implications of the two distinctions.

Object value and moral standing

We can see from the examples that these are very different kinds of valuation. Nevertheless, the blanket use of 'intrinsic value' to cover both kinds of value has led to the distinction being blurred. There are fortunately ways of referring unambiguously to these valuations which are familiar in everyday contexts.

Thus there are things that are worth having, worth doing, worth getting, worth undergoing for themselves, in themselves, for their own sake: these things have intrinsic value, and of course in the object sense. Again, things that are good for a person to have, enjoy or do, and are not just instrumentally good, will have intrinsic value of the object kind. According to how much they are worth doing, having, etc., they matter more or less, are more or less important, for the person who values them in this way. There will also be things of instrumental value for doing or getting, etc. the things held to be intrinsically valuable in the object sense, and here again the valuation will be of the object kind.

Other things matter, or are important, but are not the sorts of things that are worth having, worth doing, worth getting, worth undergoing, nor are they things that are good for a valuer.[4] We presumably believe this to be true of human beings: we each, who read this, think this of ourselves, and of any other human being. Many people will make the same claim about other animals, and some will make it about non-animal organisms, and some about ecosystems and rivers.[5]

Our belief that they matter in this way entails, as I said earlier, that we believe we must take account of what is good or bad for them, their good, or their interests (if they are the sort of thing that has interests), when considering actions that may affect them for good or ill. This is why the term 'moral standing' is appropriate.

The concepts of moral standing and of object value are clearly very different. I will give three main differences between them, which entail that the implications of such claims, and the ways in which the two kinds of value claims can be elaborated and supported, are importantly different.

1 First, the claim that some being is of intrinsic value in the sense of moral standing, involves a moral judgement: that human beings matter, that dolphins do or do not matter, in the relevant sense, are moral judgements. By contrast, the judgement that something has intrinsic value of the object

105

kind, that, for example it is beautiful, or enjoyable, is not a moral judgement.

2 An immediate consequence of this is that the kinds of reason that are needed in order to show that a thing should be preserved are different, according to whether we are claiming they have intrinsic value of the object kind or of the moral standing kind. That a thing is, for example, beautiful or enjoyable, and thus has value of the object kind, will not by itself show that, other things being equal, we ought to preserve it. Some further premise is clearly needed. This will be pursued further in section 2.

In the most familiar cases of the things that have moral standing, a concern with their good will no doubt include a concern with their continued life, and thus provide some reason for their preservation. In the cases of things such a landscapes and rivers, for which some have claimed moral standing, there will remain the question of what constitutes their good, and thus what it is that is required in the way of protection from harm or of preservation.

3 Third, whereas a thing that has intrinsic object value will be of value *in some specific way*, the same is not true of things with intrinsic value in the sense of moral standing. Thus, if someone says that a rose, or music, is 'of value', there is always a more specific claim that can be made: that it is beautiful, enjoyable, makes life more interesting, for example.

There is nothing analogous with things of intrinsic value in the sense of moral standing. If by a thing's importance, mattering or worth, we understand its having moral standing, there is not some *specific way* in which it is thus important, etc.

These differences should make us cautious when we consider the implications of a feature that the two kinds of intrinsic value share. In each case we can judge that one thing is more valuable than another: that one thing is more beautiful than another (object value) or a human being more important than a cat (moral standing). Given that things with moral standing and things with object value can both be more or less valuable in their respective ways, the question arises, in what ways we can compare a thing with moral standing and a thing with object value?

There is a class of cases where it is widely assumed that the object values of the things can be compared on a quantitative scale. In these cases, either the things are all good things or ills for a single human being, or although distributed among a number of human beings, are for the purposes of the valuer treated as if they were the good or ill of a single being. Thus we may say that this country is more prosperous, or is happier, today than one hundred years ago. Here the separate goods enjoyed by members of a group are totalled.

We must not assume that the simple quantitative character of the comparison in such cases will be found in the very different kinds of case where we put in order of importance a certain good or ill for one being with moral standing and a certain good or ill for another being with moral standing. An example would be where the severe suffering of a human is judged to be more important than the life of a dog, and the life of a dog to be more important than the passing discomfort of a human.

In such cases the valuer is putting in order of importance the states of affairs where the beings have their respective goods or ills. In more complex and difficult cases, we may have to decide between, for example, one human suffering a certain ill and ten dogs thereby gaining a certain good. Two points should be noticed about such cases. First, there is no reason to assume that the way we decide in such cases is analogous to the way we decide in the special case mentioned in the previous paragraph, where the goods with object value are, or are justifiably treated as being, goods enjoyed by a single being. That is, there is no reason to assume that a quantitative treatment is going to be available. Second, in the cases where the valuer is not one of the beings whose goods are being compared, and is not indirectly an interested party, the comparison will be essentially a moral judgement. These comparative judgements are about non-beneficial values.

Thus once the distinction between object value and moral standing is respected, there appears no reason to treat comparisons of the goods of things with moral standing, or comparisons of the object value of a thing with the good of a thing of moral standing, in a quantitative way.

Beneficial/non-beneficial

We may apply this distinction first to things that have moral standing. For beings other than the valuer, their having value in the sense of moral standing is clearly not a matter of their benefiting the valuer: they fall in the 'non-beneficial' class. In the special case where I judge that *I* matter in this way, we may ask whether this is because my good is of benefit to me, or because I think that I am the sort of thing whose good matters morally. The answer, surely, is the latter.

Turning to the application of the distinction to things valued as objects, an important difference between things with beneficial object value and things with non-beneficial object value can be illustrated with the following case of non-beneficial value. Suppose I think a certain painting beautiful. Suppose now that ninety-nine other people agree with me. What will these concurring judgements tell me? I may feel confirmed in my original judgement, but I will not conclude that the painting is one hundred times as beautiful as I at first thought. (If I had expressed my judgement by some such term as 'sublime', no one would be tempted in the slightest to 'add' my 'value' to those of the other valuers. If I have for some reason given it a quantitative form, the temptation is greater, but the summation is just as meaningless.)

On the other hand, if I believe that a hundred people have got the same pleasure from looking at the painting as I have, I can reasonably conclude that the painting has given more pleasure than if only one of us had looked at it. In certain contexts it may be reasonable to think in terms of the total pleasure got by the group, and to represent the pleasure in the one case as one hundred times the pleasure in the other.

Thus where the value of a thing is non-beneficial, the fact that many people agree in judging that it has that value does not entail that it has a larger value than if only one made that judgement. In the case of things whose value lies in their causing some enjoyment, need-satisfaction or other such good for the valuer, there will be a total value that is the sum of the value got by each individual valuer-beneficiary. We shall see that this point has been overlooked in the context of the contingent valuation procedure.

The value of objects for things of moral standing

Combining implications of the beneficial/non-beneficial distinction with what has been noticed about the relations between value of the object kind and value of the moral standing kind, we may notice a distinction that will be seen to be important for economic valuation.

When thinking about the relative importance of the good either (as in these last paragraphs) of different kinds of beings with moral standing, such as humans and dogs, or of different beings with moral standing of the same kind, there are two roles that a human valuer may occupy, and thus two kinds of valuation that he or she may make.

The valuer whose interests are not involved can make such judgements as 'This good for this being with moral standing is more important than that good for that being'. This judgement manifests the moral attitudes of the valuer to the different kinds of being with moral standing, as well as beliefs about how important or attractive to different kinds of thing with moral standing the various goods with object value are. In such a case, the value that the valuer arrives at will be non-beneficial. (Such a judgement may also be made when the valuer's interests are involved, but where the valuer succeeds in setting them aside at that time.)

The valuer may sometimes, of course, also be in a position where acting in accordance with such a judgement will involve some cost, and the decision about what to do in such a position will involve the valuer taking account of that cost. The price that I am prepared to pay to defend the interests of another being with moral standing, whether human or of another kind, while it will probably take into account this moral judgement, is affected also by considerations of self-interest. Thus if I am to pay, or if I imagine myself having to pay, to defend the interests of another being with moral standing, I will think of the price as a cost to weigh against other

108

goods that I could have had instead. The value that emerges from this course of thinking will be an object value: how much I think acting morally on this occasion is worth, in terms of the benefits and ills it brings. It is thus a beneficial object value. (This reminds us that goods with beneficial value need not be pleasant or enjoyable.)

We must bear in mind that there are these two kinds of valuation, when we come on to consider how far our judgements of the importance of the good of the preservation of things with moral standing can be manifested in the valuations made in contingent valuation enquiries.

2. WHY SHOULD THINGS OF INTRINSIC VALUE BE PRESERVED?

Why, or when, should a thing judged to have intrinsic value of either of these kinds be preserved (and thus, other things being equal, things with instrumental value related to them)? What is said will have obvious application also to the protection of things from changes that would be harmful to them. We may consider the question first for the case of beings with moral standing and then for things with object value.

For many beings to which moral standing may be ascribed there is at least one straightforward answer to the first question. If continued life is a good for the thing, then concern for its good will involve concern for its continued life. Some thinkers have extended the class of things with moral standing to include such natural phenomena as rivers. For such things without life the answer is not so clear. To answer the question about preservation, we have to discover what constitutes the good of such a thing, and whether continued existence is part of it.

However, for most candidates for the status of moral standing, it seems likely that continued existence is part of their good, and their destruction will count as seriously harmful to them.

For things with intrinsic value of object kind, we may consider three answers to the question about preservation. The first follows from what was said in section 1 about the implications of a thing having object value for a being with moral standing:

(1) A thing is of intrinsic value of the object kind if it is worth doing, worth having, good for its possessor, etc. If, then, a thing is worth having or good for other people, and we think they have moral standing so that what is good for them is relevant to our moral decisions, then we have a moral reason, other things being equal, not to deprive them of it.

This line of thought will show that, other things being equal, things of beauty ought to be preserved for so long as there will be beings of moral standing capable of benefiting from them. We can also see that it would

109

have been a good thing if they had existed at earlier times, in those cases where the beauty could have been appreciated earlier. Equally, there are implications for *where* the beautiful things should be preserved: where they can be appreciated. This line of thought does not provide any reason why beautiful things should be preserved in a world where they could not be appreciated.

It is worth emphasising how the distinction between things valued because they are beneficial to the valuer and things valued for other reasons applies here. If I am asked why things of beauty should be preserved, I can reply that for that large class of things of beauty that I myself will never have the opportunity to enjoy, my reason for thinking they ought to be preserved is that other people (beings with moral standing) will be able to enjoy them, and thus benefit from their existence. I, in this case the valuer, value these things for reasons other than their being beneficial to me, and out of a concern for other beings with moral standing. Thus both kinds of intrinsic value, object value and moral standing, feature in the account. The preservation of things with object value will be of benefit (object value) to other beings with moral standing. Thus the fundamental valuation reflects a concern with things of intrinsic value of the moral standing kind.

The question remains whether this is the only reason why things with value of the object kind should be preserved. Many people would say that the reason just given for preservation, although a relevant one, is distinct from what they have in mind when they say that things of beauty, or of intrinsic object value in other ways, should be preserved for their own sake. Are there then other reasons that do not have to do with the benefiting of beings with moral standing?

It is often argued that there is indeed another reason, independent of human or other beings' benefit:

(2) The existence of beautiful things, and other things of intrinsic value, is held to be good, and their preservation a duty, other things being equal, independently of whether anyone is or will be able to appreciate or enjoy their beauty.

It is held that things of beauty, or of environmental value, should be preserved, not merely because they will in the future benefit beings with moral standing, but 'for their own sakes'. It may be said, in a judgement reminiscent of a famous argument of G.E. Moore, that the existence of a world, or a place, with things of intrinsic value in it, is surely better than their not existing in that world or place, and that therefore one ought not to destroy such intrinsically valuable things (Moore 1903: 83).

Although this position is often asserted in environmental discussions, justification is seldom offered for it. Many writers seem to think it self-evident. However, this is to fail to distinguish the value that a thing may have, such as its beauty or exhilaratingness, and the value of the existence

110

of a thing that has some such property. We have seen that we can clearly distinguish between a thing being beautiful (and therein having value), for example, and the value, in enjoyment, that the existence of that thing may contribute. In this case what makes the existence of a thing valuable is quite different from what gives the thing its value. If it were true that the existence of a certain thing of value, such as a beautiful thing, was always itself of value, we might ask what kind of value it is that a valuable thing's existence would always have. (See point 3 in section 1.) (The *existence* of the beautiful thing would not be beautiful!) To show that a thing of value ought always to be preserved (other things being equal), it must be shown that there is *always* an answer to the question, what value the existence of the thing of value would have. Since it is not clear what sort of answer there could be, one may question the coherence of this position.

A third answer may be considered:

(3) The prospect of certain goods being preserved gives satisfaction to the valuer, and it is the gaining of this satisfaction that gives the object value to the preservation.

This view is sometimes stated in the explanation of existence value by economists, and it is often implied in the treatment of preservation value in contingent valuation. Thus an economist writes:

Even if the individual himself does not consume the services . . . he may still be concerned about the quality or existence of the asset. For example, he may derive satisfaction from the pure fact that the asset is available for other people – living now or in the future.

(Johannson 1990: 37–8)

Again, a natural interpretation of the following rather loosely worded passage from the report of a contingent valuation investigation is that the authors take the value we attach to preservation to be that of satisfaction. 'Existence value is the willingness to pay for the knowledge that a natural environment is protected by wilderness designation even though no recreation use is contemplated' (Walsh *et al.* 1984: 26).

This position is open to a simple objection. Taking the second example, suppose for the moment that someone does not attach any value at all to the future protection of a certain area of wilderness. Why then should they gain satisfaction from knowing that it will be protected? Clearly, no reason has been given. They will gain the satisfaction only if they think the protection of the wilderness important, that it has some value. The fundamental reason for preservation will thus not be the satisfaction but the value of whatever it is whose preservation gives them satisfaction (or of the consequences of the preservation of the thing).

Of the three answers to the question, why (or when) an environmental good should be preserved for the future, we may conclude that the first gives at least a partial answer to the question, and perhaps the only answer.[6] We will therefore go on to consider its implications. The second answer, that the existence of a thing of value has value in itself, suffers from incoherence. It is of interest to consider its implications, however, because it must be conceded that it is (I think) the answer that many environmentalists and many other people will give. The third answer I have rejected. It may well be true that it is what many environmental economists have in mind, and its implications therefore deserve comment. It will not be necessary to comment on it in detail here, however, beyond noticing that the reasons for denying the identity of preservation value and existence value, given in the next section, will not apply to an account of preservation value that treats it as satisfaction value.

We have seen that the two accounts that I propose we pursue both understand preservation value as a non-beneficial value. I shall argue that it is this that makes the summing of individuals' preservation values wrong, and that shows that preservation value is not the same as the economists' existence value. Only because preservation value is treated as if it was a beneficial value (perhaps through conscious or unconscious assumption of the satisfaction view) are these important points obscured.

3. PRESERVATION VALUE AND EXISTENCE VALUE

We may use the distinctions and conclusions of the preceding sections to examine the question, How far does the kind of valuation called 'existence value' represent the value that people attach to the continued existence of environmental and other things for their own sake, that is, for reasons other than any kind of benefit, direct or indirect, that the valuer expects to gain? We have called the value attached to continued existence 'preservation value'. The need for two terms in this discussion arises for the following reason. Although the technical notion of existence value has been introduced to cover what I am calling preservation value, it may reasonably be asked whether the procedure for eliciting existence value valuations does in fact yield preservation value.

I will argue that the conception of a total preservation value, which is the sum of the individual valuers' preservation values, is incoherent. This has implications for how the results of contingent valuation enquiries are used. Secondly, I will argue that the procedure for eliciting an individual's existence valuation does not in fact yield the person's preservation valuation. Thus the valuations relevant to the question whether various environmental things should be preserved are not, as environmental economists have argued or assumed, encapsulated in the existence valuation.

Summability: things with moral standing

We will consider separately the cases of the preservation value of a thing with moral standing, and of a thing with object value. What is said here covers both the continued existence of a thing with moral standing, where continued existence is a good for such a thing, and protection from changes that count as harmful for such a thing.

We saw in section 1 (point 3) that there was no reason to assume that judgements about the good of a thing with moral standing could be represented as a quantity amenable to arithmetical treatment alongside other such quantities. This shows that the procedure of adding the values that represent existence value to reach a total for the group is not applicable to the value of the preservation of a thing with moral standing. We also saw that a judgement of the object value of something for a thing with moral standing (other than the valuer) is a non-beneficial judgement. Thus the continued existence of a thing with moral standing other than the valuer, which is a good (of object value) for that thing, will have non-beneficial value for the valuer. And the non-beneficial valuations of something by a number of individuals cannot meaningfully be summed to reach a total. This was argued for in section 1 and illustrated with the example of the one person and the ninety-nine who give an aesthetic valuation of a painting.

Summability: things with object value

In seeing whether preservation valuations of things with object value can be summed, it is necessary to consider the different possible conceptions of preservation value, corresponding to the first two justifications distinguished in the previous section.

Consider first the view that the reason for preserving things of aesthetic or other object value is that their existence will be good for future beings of moral standing. If a valuer is assuming the future-beneficiaries account, then the valuer is reporting what they take to be the total benefits that they expect future people to reap from the thing's continued existence. Different people may put a different value on this. There may be grounds for trying to reach a compromise value, perhaps by averaging. But there is no reason to add their valuations, to reach a total value: the valuations do not correspond to benefits expected by each valuer, so the total would not be the sum of such benefits. As we have just recalled, the result of adding different valuers' valuations of things that have non-beneficial value (that is, are not valued for the benefit *to the valuer*) is meaningless. (It would in effect take the average valuation of the total benefits to be expected, and multiply this by the number of valuers. The resulting quantity would have no significance.)

We may consider the second view discussed in section 2: that the continued existence of things of aesthetic or other object value is of importance in itself, independently of any benefit that future people may gain from it. Despite the doubtful coherence of a view that cannot specify what it is about the existence of the thing that makes it (the existence of the thing) valuable, enough can be understood about the position to allow us to reach a conclusion about summability. For it is clear that this view of preservation value does not see it as involving a benefit to the valuer. It is, again, comparable to the example given in section 1 of ninety-nine people confirming my judgement of a painting. There is thus no reason to add the valuations (supposing they are in quantitative form) given by each individual valuer.

On each of these views of preservation value, then, no significance can be attached to the total that results from summing the quantitative valuations made by individuals.

I give two examples of valuations where this adding of individuals' valuations is involved. The first is from a well-known study. In the second, the significance of adding the individuals' existence values was, unusually, aired in public discussion.

A group of investigators report that residents of Colorado are prepared to pay a certain annual sum to protect wilderness in other states of the USA. The authors then extrapolate to suggest what sort of value would be set on the Colorado wilderness by residents of other states.

> Extrapolating this sample value to the general population of the United States results in a willingness-to-pay estimate of approximately $1.50 per household annually for protection of 10 million acres of wilderness in Colorado. Given the large number of households involved, even this low value would result in substantial aggregate nonresident values for Colorado wilderness.
>
> (Walsh *et al.* 1984: 26)

The values referred to are preservation values, which include option, bequest and existence value. Clearly part of the $1.50 corresponds to existence value. The aggregating thus adds up both values that can appropriately be added (the option values) and those that I have argued cannot, the existence values. (It is arguable that the bequest values should not be summed; but we need not go into this.) Since the option value is concerned with a benefit to the valuer, so that the valuers are each thinking of themselves as beneficiaries, totalling seems appropriate. But I have just argued that it is meaningless for existence value, where the valuer is not also a beneficiary. (We may note here that sometimes average values are calculated, as in the quoted passage. I am not denying that these values for existence value are significant. However, later in this section I argue that they do not signify average preservation value.)

Another case where what appear to be existence values are summed in

the way I have criticised occurred in the dispute over industrial develop-
ment between conservationists and the mining industry in Australia's
Kakadu National Park. According to a 1990 report, the Australian Resource
Assessment Commission carried out a survey.

> In the survey a random sample of 2,034 people were asked how much
> they would pay to stop mining in Kakadu. They volunteered figures
> between $52 and $128 each per year. This sort of money given by all
> Australians would dwarf earnings from the mine. Not surprisingly, the
> mining industry has called the survey results 'nonsensical' and unscien-
> tific.
>
> (Anderson 1990: 24)

The preceding discussion suggests that, if (as it would seem) these figures
represent existence value, then what is referred to as the sum of 'this sort of
money given by all Australians' is indeed a meaningless figure.This does not
of course imply that the bids do not support the conservation side in the
debate. (The foregoing argument has not called in question the meaningfulness of the figures of $52, etc. Again, however, the second point to
be made about contingent valuation raises a question about their interpretation.)

This case also illustrates an important corollary of the non-summability
point. A question that is often raised, in connection with user values and
existence values, but usually consigned to the periphery as a point of
technical detail, is, What is the relevant population for determining existence value?[7] We can now see that this must be divided into two questions:

What is the relevant population of *beneficiaries* in this case? and
What is the relevant population of *valuers* in this case?

Existence value and preservation value

The issue here is how far the monetary figure for existence value elicited in
a reliable contingent valuation procedure represents the aesthetic or other
valuation of the environmental good which is the reason for the preservation of the thing in question. We must consider separately the case of things
with moral standing and the case of things with object value.

For the goods of beings with moral standing, we saw there were two
kinds of valuation a valuer might make. One (such as 'The dog's life is
worth more than that man's inconvenience') is the result of a moral
judgement about the importance of a certain good for one being with
moral standing, compared to some good or ill of another being of moral
standing (of a different kind, or, in a special case, of the same kind).

The other kind of valuation takes account also of any cost there might be
to the valuer of acting in the light of the first judgement.

115

When we are concerned with the importance of preserving a thing of moral standing for the future, we may make a judgement based on the moral duty to take account of the good of the being in question, and the importance to that kind of being of its continued life. (A similar judgement may be made about preserving it unharmed. Here the importance of different kinds of alteration, and whether they amount to harm, slight or serious, will be judged.)

Only if the valuer is also expecting to pay for the preservation of the thing of moral standing will the second kind of valuation be relevant. Thus this valuation, which may be manifested as existence-value in a contingent valuation enquiry for a cost–benefit analysis, does not yield the value of the continued existence of the thing to be preserved.

Turning to the preservation value of things with object value, I will assume that, whatever the basis of the preservation valuation (the good of future beneficiaries or the value of existence of the thing in itself), the value attached to preservation will vary directly with the aesthetic or other value of the things whose preservation is in question. We may take aesthetic values as our example. The same line of argument will apply for any other kinds of object value that are thought to provide the basis for preservation.

We have a scale of aesthetic values that we use quite independently of (even prior to mastery of) a monetary scale. Thus we may agree with others about the quality of a number of landscapes, using various appropriate descriptions: beautiful, awe-inspiring, delightful, dull, etc.

When we are considering how important it is that things with aesthetic values should be preserved undamaged, it is this scale that is relevant. Other things being equal, the finest landscapes should be preserved rather than the less important. (Among things that might not be equal would be other, non-aesthetic, environmental features that also had value.)

How then does this relate to existence value? The restriction to the preservation of goods after the valuer's death means that we need not consider the case where there is also user value for the valuers. (In most actual cases where contingent valuation has elicited existence value, there have been user values also.)

We can accept that, for an individual valuer, the monetary sum given for existence value will reflect to some extent the aesthetic valuation, in that the order of the existence values for things with different aesthetic values will correspond to the ordering on aesthetic grounds. But the existence valuation will also take into account another important factor: how much, relative to other uses of their resources, people are prepared to pay to protect things they think aesthetically valuable but do not expect themselves to enjoy, which they think have preservation value for aesthetic reasons. The information on existence value elicited by contingent valuation is thus not only about preservation value.

There is a consequence of this that should be noticed. We saw that for a single valuer, the order of the aesthetic valuation will be preserved in the order of the existence valuation. It need not, however, be true that, in the case of two individuals, if A places a higher aesthetic value on X than does B, then A will place a higher existence value on X than does B. For it might still be true that one of them was inclined to devote more to the protection of things with aesthetic value than the other, even though their aesthetic valuations of the things in question were the same.

This is a consequence of the fact that the preservation values are not beneficial values. For a beneficial value, there is a strong case (not called in question here) for saying that the value, being the amount of benefit, is manifested in the monetary valuation. For a non-beneficial value we have seen that this is not so.

I conclude that existence value is not the same as, and does not correspond in any simple way to, preservation value, where preservation value is the importance of the continued existence of something for reasons other than any expected benefit for the valuer.

The relevance of this point, and the earlier conclusion about summability, to environmental matters is this. When we go beyond short-term considerations, we are considering the value of things that will exist after we, the valuers, have died. Any value will either be the value of things with moral standing, so that the value is non-beneficial (in the sense used here), so that each of our conclusions applies; or of goods that are of value to future things with moral standing, where, again, the value is non-beneficial and our conclusions apply.

NOTES

1 'Moral standing' is used in this sense by Andrew Brennan in the title of his paper of 1984, and by Robin Attfield (in Attfield 1987). They also use Goodpaster's term 'moral considerability' (Goodpaster 1978). Tom Regan uses 'inherent value' and Paul Taylor 'intrinsic worth' (as I understand these writers) for what I am calling moral standing (Regan 1984; Taylor 1986).

2 We can see at this point how the standard distinction between intrinsic and instrumental value fits in. Things may be useful for the achievement of things or states or activities that are of intrinsic value of the object kind, and thus be of instrumental value to the being for whom the things or states or activities are of intrinsic value of the object kind. Thus there are tools that are valuable, but not (let us suppose) intrinsically valuable, in either the object or moral standing sense. They enable people to create things of beauty. One reason they are valuable is, then, that they can be used to create things of intrinsic value of the object kind. The tools are being held to be of instrumental value; and their importance or value is due to their contributing to things of intrinsic value of the object kind for beings of moral standing. It will not be necessary to use the intrinsic/instrumental distinction in the present discussion.

3 If we did not restrict what is understood by preservation value, the main lines of the argument would still succeed; but exceptions have to be repeatedly mentioned, to allow for the cases where preservation value will be beneficial because

it is a user value. It should be noticed also that the conclusions of the paper will also apply to the case where the preservation valuation applies to the continued existence of the thing in the valuer's lifetime, and is based on considerations separate from those for use value and option value.

4 A more precise statement would allow for the fact that people, and other beings that we think important in the moral standing sense, may also have object value, and thus be worth employing as entertainers, porters, etc.

5 Tom Regan's attribution of inherent value to stretches of the Colorado River (Regan 1981) and Paul Taylor's attribution of inherent worth to many natural objects (Taylor 1986), may be so interpreted.

6 Estimating the total benefit for future beneficiaries would seldom be possible, as the number of future people who might benefit cannot be estimated. There may however be good reasons in many cases for saying that the total benefit will be very large, indeed large enough to outweigh the costs to the present generation of ensuring preservation.

7 Thus J.T. Winpenny, in a book aimed at practising economic valuers of the environment, commenting on an example of contingent valuation, writes:

> Grossing-up from the sample survey to the total relevant population is tricky in the case of non-user values such as option or existence-values. In the Grand Canyon example . . . the values from the sample were applied, successively, to all existing 'users' (visitors), to all residents of the Southwestern states, and to the whole of the United States. But why not to Canada, or to all potential international visitors? The correct definition of the appropriate population, to include existing non-users, the unborn, or all potential future users, is vital to the level of total values, and their credibility, but is inherently an open-ended problem.
>
> (Winpenny 1991: 60)

What is said in this passage appears to apply to option value. I argue in the text that the questions are not relevant to existence value.

8

SUBSTITUTABILITY

Or, why strong sustainability is weak and absurdly strong sustainability is not absurd[1]

Alan Holland

1. INTRODUCTION

'Weak' sustainability is here understood as the requirement to 'keep capital intact (over time)'; 'strong' sustainability is understood as the requirement to keep *natural* capital intact (over time) (El Serafy 1995). Interest in the issue of substitutability, which forms the focus of this chapter, arises from the fact that the distinction between weak and strong sustainability is supposed to turn on the question of whether human-made capital is 'in(de)finitely substitutable' for natural capital. After discussing some issues surrounding the concept of substitution, we shall reach the conclusion that no distinction of any substance can be drawn between weak and strong sustainability. It is further argued that what has been dubbed 'absurdly strong' sustainability (Daly 1995: 49), on the other hand, marks a genuinely distinct form of the doctrine of sustainability. A version of 'absurdly strong' sustainability is then articulated and defended.

2. PROBLEMS AND POSSIBILITIES

It has always been known that human economic activity affects the natural world. But until recently it has been the habit of economists to regard this as an 'external' phenomenon and not, strictly speaking, something with which economic theory should concern itself. The rise of environmental or 'ecological' economics, however, fuelled by increasing concern at both the degree and kind of human impact upon the natural world, signals the fact that many economists no longer regard this attitude as acceptable. Their response has been to look for ways of registering environmental impacts in economic terms. The most favoured way of introducing the natural world into economic thinking to date has involved the proposal to represent nature as capital, and the natural world as a set of marketable commodities. Adverse impacts can thereby be expressed in economic terms as diminutions of capital or decreases in commodities.

119

A consequence of this approach is that the adverse impacts of economic activity upon the natural environment will at least appear on the economic register, and can therefore no longer be overlooked. Paradoxically, however, such 'economistic' thinking about nature has created a deeply rooted unease among those very environmentalists who might have been expected to welcome such a development. One major source of unease is the assumptions about the relation between humans and the natural world which it seems to embody. These assumptions are seen, first, as colluding in a certain sort of betrayal and, secondly, as revealing a certain arrogance:

(1) The betrayal is of two kinds. One is a betrayal (mostly, a misrepresentation) of the human response to nature, and therefore a betrayal of human nature. The second is a betrayal (again, mostly, a misrepresentation) of nature itself. The two sorts of misrepresentation are connected. In the first case, human beings are construed as bundles of preferences seeking maximum satisfaction from the world around them; human nature is thus 'homogenised', not to say grossly simplified. In the second case and correspondingly, nature is construed as a bundle of commodities, affording greater or lesser degrees of satisfaction which constitute its economic value (Holland 1995: 24–33). The objective of policy, under this conception, is so to manage nature that it yields the maximum satisfaction in the long term; some versions of this policy objective go by the name of 'sustainability'.

(2) The arrogance is also of two kinds. The lesser arrogance is a failure to recognise the legitimate claims of non-humans, and a willingness to allow the minor interests of humans to override the major interests of non-humans. This is sometimes the result of the view that the interests of non-humans simply don't count; but it is sometimes also the result of what the Greeks knew as 'akrasia', or 'weakness of will': we know that our habits of consumption are often bad news for non-humans, but we are unable to kick the habit. The greater arrogance is the equating of the world with the human world – which the Greeks knew as 'hubris', and believed would be punished by 'nemesis'. Some critics of economistic thinking are apt to believe that nemesis also awaits us, and accordingly, like the prophetess Cassandra before them, are labelled 'doomsters' (North 1995: 8).

In defence against such charges, it might be protested that, even with the best of intentions – even if we set out not to misrepresent nature or human nature, and even if we aimed to coexist with, rather than exploit, the natural world – we should still need some system of accounting which would enable us to judge the degree and extent of the human impact upon the natural world. Assessing the economic (dis)value of different types of impact is one way of doing this – arguably, indeed, the only practicable way.

However, another major source of unease now emerges, which is the specific focus of this chapter. It stems from the fact that although, and even because, the adverse impacts of human economic activity upon the natural environment now receive their due economic 'weight', it also becomes possible at the same time to *offset* these adverse environmental impacts against 'beneficial' developments elsewhere. It is at this point that the issue of substitution begins to bite: the issue, namely, of the extent to which human-made capital can be supposed to substitute for, compensate or offset losses in natural capital. Here too, the alleged significance of the distinction between weak and strong sustainability begins to show. For whereas the advocates of weak sustainability will condone substitution wherever this yields an economic advantage, the advocates of strong sustainability hope to assuage the unease of the environmentalists by insisting that there are 'limits to substitution'.

3. THE ISSUE OF SUBSTITUTION

The debate over whether human-made capital is substitutable for natural capital is bedevilled by a lack of agreement over terms, and by not a little misrepresentation. Writers who are supposed to suggest that human-made capital might completely take the place of natural capital have attracted some scorn. In fact, they are probably being misinterpreted. To take one instance, both Herman Daly (1995: 55) and Vandana Shiva (1992: 192) attribute to Robert Solow the view that 'the world can, in effect, get along without natural resources'. This is indeed a direct quotation from Solow (1974: 11).[1] However, examination of the original text shows two things: first, that the comment occurs in a *hypothetical* context; second, that the author is using the term 'natural resources' to refer to *exhaustible*[2] resources only. What Solow in fact claims is that the world can get along without natural resources '*if* [my italics] it is very easy to substitute other factors for natural resources' – which is not, in the circumstances, a very surprising claim. His considered view is that the question of substitutability is an empirical one, but that what little evidence there is suggests that 'quite a lot' of substitutability is possible. The second point is, that the substitution of which he is speaking is that between 'exhaustible' and 'reproducible' resources, which is not necessarily the same as substitution between 'natural' and 'human-made' resources – for two reasons.

One is that 'reproducible' resources can be natural as well as human-made: reproduction is, after all, one of *nature*'s most brilliant 'ideas'. Furthermore, a reproducible resource can be both natural and human-made at the same time: for example, the original of a reproducible resource such as a variety of culinary vegetable might be natural, while its (humanly) reproduced form might be judged human-made. Whether it is or not turns on the second of the two reasons, which is that the crucial status of 'cultivated' capital – artificially selected plants and animals – has not yet been made clear: is this natural capital, or is it human-made? What follows from all this is that even if Solow were claiming that the world can get along without natural resources, he would be claiming not that it could get along

121

without natural capital but that it could get along without exhaustible resources. One might indeed think that, in a sense, this latter claim *had* to be true, unless there were an inexhaustible number of exhaustible resources; since, if a resource is exhaustible, it is either not used or, if used, will be used up.

But if we supposed that Solow was being interpreted correctly, and he had affirmed categorically that the world could 'get along without natural resources', it is worth asking whether he would necessarily be wrong. To even begin to address such a question, we need to be aware of the ambiguities it conceals. The first such ambiguity concerns the *purpose* which substitution is supposed to serve, the second concerns the *degree* of effectiveness which is required of the substitute and the third concerns the scope of the terms 'natural' and 'human-made' *capital*. But before discussing these ambiguities there is one important preliminary point to be made. Of course it is true that everything which is produced must be produced out of something, and ultimately, no doubt, something natural. So of course it is absurd to suppose that everything *could have been* human-made. However, that is not the issue under discussion, but rather, whether everything *could come to be* human-made – in other words, whether (human) life is sustainable in a purely artificial world; and it is far from obvious that it is not.

(1) *Purpose* We can illustrate the ambiguities which arise in connection with the concept of substitution by reference to linguistic contexts. For example, the terms 'the woman in red' and 'the person who delivered the letter' are in no way synonymous, and therefore cannot be substituted for one another in a sentence if we wish to keep its meaning intact. But if it is truth we are interested in preserving, then, if the two terms in question happen to refer to one and the same person, they can be substituted, as philosophers say, *salva veritate*. Whether two items can be substituted for each other partly depends, in other words, on the purpose of the substitution – in this case, on whether we are trying to preserve meaning, or truth. And in more common or garden contexts, the question of whether A is a substitute for B will also usually depend upon what we want B for. To take the simple case of food, if it is nutritional properties we are interested in, then one apple may be as good as another. But if we are concerned about flavour, then we may think that there is no substitute for a Cox's Orange Pippin. In the same way, in the dispute over whether human-made and natural capital are substitutable, the question must be asked: substitutable *salva* what?

In general, the answer which most discussions of sustainability seem to assume is that human-made capital is substitutable for natural capital if it preserves *the degree and kind of benefits which human beings derive from natural capital*. Moreover, this assumption seems to be common to both weak and strong forms of sustainability. However, as the previous example of the apples demonstrates, the question of whether any particular item of natural capital has a human-made substitute may depend entirely on *the degree of precision which is demanded in specifying the purpose.* Since it is hard to see how there could be a criterion for what constitutes the *right* degree of precision (do we demand that the substitute be fruit, or merely food?), it is correspondingly hard to see how there could be a determinate answer to the question.

(2) *Degree* A substitute is not usually supposed to have *all* the properties of the original. If it were, it is difficult to see how anything could be a substitute for something else. One item is usually regarded as a substitute for another if it is '*sufficient* for the purpose'. We sometimes speak of something as 'a poor substitute'; and we may mean by this that it will just do, or we may mean that it won't do at all. This introduces a further dimension of indeterminacy into the concept of substitution, in the light of which it is difficult to see how the issue of whether human-made capital can be substituted for natural is to be resolved. Even if we are agreed on the purpose, how good a substitute does something have to be to be 'sufficient for the purpose'? The answer will depend radically on circumstance, and degree of toleration. A cardboard box is no substitute for a centrally heated house as a means of shelter; but if the alternative is the gnawing cold, then it will suffice.

(3) *Cultivated capital* Yet another question is what is to count as a human-made substitute, and in particular whether cultivated capital is to count as human-made. Economists appear peculiarly coy about providing an answer to this question. We need to avoid two extreme answers which would tend to render the substitution question of little interest. The first would be to count as 'human-made' anything which has been affected by human activity. Since it is probable that most of the planet has been affected one way or another by human activity, it would follow not only that substitution is possible but that, to a large extent, it has already taken place. The second would be to count as 'natural' anything at all which is made of natural materials. Since virtually everything derives ultimately from natural materials, it would follow that substitution was virtually impossible because no purely human-made substitutes would be available.

There are few handrails here, but in attempting to provide our own answer to the question we might do worse than fall back upon the old Aristotelian distinction between 'form' and 'matter', which applies equally to living and to non-living things. A working suggestion might be to say that a human-made world would be one in which there was nothing which owed its form entirely to nature, but only its matter: it would be a world in which there was no 'natural expression'. According to Aristotle, everything can be analysed in terms of its *form*, or what it *is*, and its *matter*, or what it is made of: 'the underlying thing' (Charlton 1970: 17–18). In a human-made world, therefore, everything would *be* what humans had devised it to be, even if it was *made of* natural materials. Thus, sand – a natural material – is a constituent of glass; in Aristotelian terms sand is therefore (part of) the matter of a substance whose form is glass. In its pure state sand remains a natural substance, which is in turn *made of* fragments of shell, but the fact that glass is made from sand amongst other things is not enough to make glass itself a natural product; glass is a (human-made) artefact. The same applies to brick, concrete and the like.

Applying such a criterion to living things, the cultivated world as it stands would seem to fall betwixt and between the categories of 'natural' and 'human-made'. The domesticated cat retains enough of its natural form to be capable of surviving in a feral state; it might still be thought of, therefore, as a natural being. Some breeds of domestic turkey, on the other hand, require human assistance in order to reproduce – a fact we may take as indicating that it has lost its 'natural' form. Genetic engineering is likely to thrust the cultivated world ever more towards the human-made side of the fence. There is a glimpse of such a world in H. G. Wells's *Time Machine* where, the reader may recall, everything is a garden where gnats and nettles are no more.

On the basis of this working suggestion, and pending a rival account of how cultivated capital should be construed, one would have to conclude that so far as *living* natural capital is concerned, at any rate, there seems to be no reason in principle why natural capital should not come to be *entirely* replaced. For obvious reasons it is far less easy, though not logically impossible, to imagine a world devoid of *non-living* natural capital. But it is safe to assume that most environmentalists would regard a world in which only non-living natural capital remained as a godforsaken place. It is true that the absence of living natural capital would not be final: given the nature of living things its re-emergence would remain a permanent possibility – nicely illustrated by Antipho's remark, quoted by Aristotle, that a bed which is made of wood might yet sprout new growth, if buried (Charlton 1970: 24). However, such a possibility hardly vindicates the thesis of strong sustainability; rather, it would show that it was redundant, since it would reveal a sense in which natural capital was ineliminable, *whatever* we did.

We have seen that insofar as the question of substitution is empirical, its answer depends on the resolution of a number of ambiguities. At least one author, however – Herman Daly – appears to suggest that the question is amenable to determination a priori. Daly's basic claim is that natural and manmade capital are 'complements', not substitutes. He offers a number of arguments in support of this contention. At the common-sense level he makes the point rhetorically by asking, 'What good is a saw-mill without a forest; a fishing boat without populations of fish?' (1995: 51). However, he appears at once to undermine this rhetorical point by proceeding to draw attention, for purposes of illustration, to the complementary relation between cars and roads. The most obvious point about cars and roads is that *both* are human-made, which proves that human-made capital can sometimes substitute for natural capital (in this case, feet and earth) to perform a somewhat similar function. It would appear to follow that a given item can be both complement *and* substitute; and it is unlikely that those economists against whom Daly is arguing would assume that complementarity and substitutability are mutually exclusive. Moreover, even if the given item cannot (completely) substitute for the item which it complements, this does not preclude some other human-made item doing so. Thus, although Daly has provided some examples of complementary relationships between natural and human-made capital, this is far from showing that the natural capital in each case is ineliminable.

The first of his more formal arguments is ingenious. He points out that the substitution relation is symmetrical; so that if human-made capital can substitute for natural, then so can natural capital substitute for what is human-made. But if it can, the argument goes, there would have been no reason for our ancestors to develop human-made capital in the first place. Since they did just that, it follows that human-made and natural capital are not substitutes. However, there are several flaws in this argument:

1 Although the substitution relation is symmetrical *when it obtains*, it does not follow that there always *is* a substitute available. Our ancestors might have developed some forms of human-made capital because there was no natural equivalent – a prime example being the wheel. And from the fact that they made capital for which there was no natural equivalent it certainly cannot be inferred that they might not have been able to make human-made equivalents of the natural capital which was available *if* they had needed to.

2 Moreover, they might still have made equivalents even if they did not need to – out of curiosity, for example, or boredom.

3 And even if they had only done what they needed to, the argument only works on the assumption that the needs of people are given and unchangeable, and that it is in response to needs that goods are created. It would not work on the opposing assumption that goods themselves *create* needs.

4 Finally, the argument proves too much. The fact is that *some* human-made capital can substitute for *some* natural capital. But according to the argument, such human-made capital ought not to exist. Since it does, the argument must be wrong.

Daly's other arguments tend to be formalisations of the 'common-sense' argument rehearsed above, and to be open to a similar sort of response. He points out that human-made capital is always the product, and sometimes the agent, of a process of production, in which the raw materials must originally be natural resources yielded by the stock of natural capital. He further observes, let us suppose correctly, that none of these elements in the production process can substitute for the other. But from the fact that any production process requires material, agent and product as complementary elements, and therefore that *if* the raw material is natural then it cannot be replaced by the human-made agent or product of the process, it in no way follows that the material element must always be natural. The most that such an argument shows is that there must *have been* some natural resources in the ancestry of any given production process, not that there must always *continue to be*. Presumably, what supporters of the substitution thesis claim is that the human-made products of one process can increasingly provide the materials for another. There seems to be nothing in Daly's argument to answer this point.

4. WEAK AND STRONG SUSTAINABILITY

We have seen that the substitution question is not a simple one; it may not even have a determinate answer. At the same time it is held up as the key to the distinction between weak and strong sustainability. According to Michael Jacobs (1995c: 62) the advocates of weak sustainability affirm that natural capital and manmade capital are infinitely substitutable. Wilfred Beckerman, more cautiously, says simply that it 'allows for substitutability between different forms of natural capital and manmade capital, provided that, on balance, there is no decline in welfare' (1994: 195). In other words, proponents of weak sustainability hold that sustainability requires that we maintain the level of total capital assets, but that within this total any amount of substitution is allowed between the different kinds of capital. Proponents of strong sustainability, on the other hand, hold that because there are limits to which natural capital can be replaced or substituted by human-made capital, sustainability requires that we maintain the level of natural capital, or at any rate that we maintain natural capital at or above the level which is judged to be 'critical'.

The question now is: even if the issue of substitution were decidable, would it serve to differentiate weak from strong sustainability? The answer is that it would not. Weak sustainability allows for substitution *provided that* there is no decline in human welfare. Strong sustainability asserts that there are significant elements of natural capital for which no human-made substitutes can be found. As we have seen, the claim that no human-made substitutes can be found amounts to the claim that nothing human-made can provide humankind with the same degree or kind of benefits as those provided by the elements of natural capital in question. But if this is true, then the loss of such natural capital would inevitably mean a decline in human welfare and would not therefore be countenanced by weak sustainability. Since, therefore, nothing which is not countenanced by strong sustainability would be countenanced by weak sustainability, the two positions are indistinguishable. Thus, the idea that weak and strong sustainability differ in any important respect turns out to be a charade.[3]

In a separate attempt to affirm a non-collapsible version of strong sustainability, Michael Jacobs suggests we construe it as the proposal to ensure that environmental *capacities* (i.e. the ability of the environment to perform its various functions) are maintained over time (1991: 79–80). But the fact is, for as long as the maintaining of natural capital is understood as the maintaining of a *capacity* to deliver resource provision, waste assimilation, amenity and life support (for humans) (1991: 3–5), then the maintaining of natural capital will be compatible with any amount of diminution of the physical natural stock if the technology and socio-economic institutions are in place to realise the same degree of service to the human community. To take a simple example: if my eyesight is failing, then my capacity to read small print may be reduced. The simple device of spectacles, however, will restore my capacity; so that despite my failing eyesight, my capacity to read small print is maintained. Nor is this to be guilty of confusing the efficiency with which resources are used with human-made capital, and therefore illegitimately to regard the efficiency with which a resource is used as a substitute for the resource (Daly 1995: 52). What is being pointed out is that, given the understanding of natural capital as a certain kind of capacity, then if the level of capacity is maintained *because* of the efficient use of resources, then this will automatically count, not as substitution *for* natural capital but, *as the maintaining of the natural capital itself.*

It has been claimed that the quantity and quality of the natural environment 'or, to be more economic, the benefit streams humankind is obtaining from natural capital' are in decline, and that this is 'the reason why we are having a debate about sustainability at all' (Jacobs 1995a: 60). From the perspective being presented here, however, it is not at all clear that the benefit streams referred to *are* in decline, or that there is a specifically *economic* reason for having a debate about sustainability. For this reason it is in the long run unlikely that environmental economics will be able to contribute towards the solution of a problem which it is incapable of identifying as existing. The reason for this incapacity is that, insofar as there is a distinctively *environmental* crisis, it lies in the fact that the natural *world* is disappearing, not in the fact that natural *capital* – i.e. the natural world construed as a source of benefit streams – is disappearing. Of course there is not enough natural capital to go round, and of course we frequently waste what there is. But this is due partly to increasing human population coupled with absurd levels of consumption and gross inequalities of power; it certainly does nothing to show that there is not, or in the short-, medium- or long-term future will not be, as much natural capital as there has been. Indeed, we may well have to face up to the fact that if we wish to increase the level of natural *capital*, more of the natural *world* may need to disappear.[4]

Thus, the problem with letting sustainability, weak or strong, carry the flag for nature lies not in the issue over which weak and strong sustainability might be claimed to differ, namely in how they propose to measure the level or value of natural capital. The problem lies in what is common to both weak and strong sustainability, namely, the very conception of nature as capital, which provides little protection for the natural *world*. Indeed, so far as the environment as a factor in production is concerned, there is arguably a deep incoherence in the notion of 'natural capital'. Unlike the paradigm of monetary capital which yields interest while maintaining its own integrity, for so long as so-called 'natural capital' is functioning as capital (i.e. as yielding 'interest'), it can no longer remain natural, and while it remains natural, it cannot function as capital.[5]

5. ABSURDLY STRONG SUSTAINABILITY

But if natural capital is holding up, why should it matter if the natural world is disappearing? That it does matter, I take to be the defining claim of 'absurdly strong' sustainability. Because it does matter, an advocate of 'absurdly strong' sustainability will hold that nature ought not to be sub-stituted even where it can be substituted. 'Strong' sustainability, on the other hand, provides absolutely no obstacle to substitution *going through where it can*, i.e. where natural *capital* is thereby maintained.

Before attempting to defend absurdly strong sustainability, let us first empty it of some unnecessary absurdities. Herman Daly defines it as the view that 'no species could ever go extinct, nor any nonrenewable resource should ever be taken from the ground, no matter how many people are starving' (1995: 49). He is picking up a previous characterisation of Wilfred Beckerman's, who construes it as the requirement to 'preserve intact the environment as we find it today in all its forms' (1994: 194). But if we should always try to pick on the strongest possible version of any position we wish to attack, and we should, this is a far from satisfactory character-isation. For if we assume no more than this – that *any* form of strong sustainability carries a commitment to the natural environment – then it should be clear at once that both these characterisations are a travesty, due no doubt to an overly literal understanding of the notion of conservation. Since it is of the essence of natural processes that they are dynamic, no freeze-framing of any particular state of the natural world could possibly be construed as the conservation of nature: to pursue a freeze-framing pro-gramme would be to betray rather than serve the cause of conservation. On the other hand, as Daly's reference to starving people suggests, what absurdly strong sustainability does require is some defence of the natural world beyond the call of human interests. Why is this supposed to be absurd?

Beckerman himself argues that protection of the natural world when this is inimical to human interests is immoral. One response to this argument, as

Jacobs rightly observes (1995a: 63), is to point out that sustainability is unlikely to be our sole action-guiding principle, nor is it being proposed as such. While it is true that sustainability carries its own moral weight, it is not being claimed that it must therefore override all other considerations, especially other moral ones. After all, moral conflict is a real enough phenomenon.[6] It is important to note that this reply does not fudge the issue of what sustainability itself requires, as Beckerman appears to suggest (1995: 175). It does sometimes clearly enjoin that we forgo some human interest; it is just that we may sometimes choose not to follow it. Another response to the argument is that it appears to assume that human interests are given and immovable. It is perfectly possible, however, that in the light of moral reflection people may come to reassess where their interests lie; and they may, in the light of reflecting upon the claims of the natural world, be prepared to come to some sort of accommodation between those claims and their own interests. A final response is to point out that we do in fact endorse projects even when it is known they may lead to some harm for human beings which might otherwise be avoided. We persist in allowing private motorised systems even in the face of evidence that a system of wholly public transport would mean fewer fatalities, and do not appear to think this immoral. It would seem that the mere fact that a practice is judged inimical to human interests is not enough to make it immoral.

So far as environmental losses are concerned, a different kind of objection to absurdly strong sustainability might be based on the fact that it eschews economic valuation of the natural world. This is seen as 'impractical'. For economists, at least, are wont to suggest that we cannot get the measure of environmental losses until we can quantify them in some way, for example by comparing them with marketed commodities. Now there are two things we may wish to measure: (a) whether we have lost too much, and (b) how much we have lost. But it has to be questioned whether economics can help with either; for people's sense of loss hardly waited upon economists to come along and measure it. To take but one example, in his book *Our Vanishing Wildflowers* published in 1928, Henry Salt was able to cite a quip from no less a personage than Stanley Baldwin to the effect that 'There are three classes which need sanctuary more than others – birds, wildflowers, and Prime Ministers' (1928: 1). We suspected we were losing too much of the natural world, and causing too much damage, when figures started to come in about lifeless rivers and streams, increased desertification, loss of biodiversity and so forth. Indeed, it was not the measurable loss which concerned us so much as the immeasurable loss. Similarly, we suspect that the current generation of humans (some of them, at least) is appropriating an unfair amount of the earth's resources both in relation to future generations of humans and in relation to current and future generations of non-humans. These beliefs are simply 'abroad' in the community. It is far from clear that we need, or indeed that we can rely on, economic measuring to provide this information. Perhaps our suspicions are wrong? But we are unlikely to rely on economic measuring to put us right. Its precision would be suspect, not least because of the enormous number and kind of variables involved and the dependency of the results upon the values assigned to these variables on no very adequate grounds. Do we measure the loss of elephants only, or of African wildlife as a whole? And to whom do we attribute the loss? To the local population, or to the whole world? The problems are well known and scarcely require rehearsing here (Willis 1995). As a consequence, any discrepancy between our suspicions and the results of economic studies is as likely to feed our scepticism about the methods used in those studies as it is to make us question those suspicions.[7]

6. WHY NATURE – EVERY LAST DROP OF IT – IS GOOD

Absurdly strong sustainability, then, requires that we are sometimes called upon to defend the natural world, even when human interests seem not to be served by such action. In the previous section we have attempted to fend off some objections to such a stance; but why should we want to adopt the stance in the first place?

We shall treat this as the question whether the natural world, as such, presents any constraints upon how we should behave towards it. Along lines argued elsewhere in this volume (by Jeremy Roxbee Cox) we can identify two different kinds of constraint:

(1) The first arises from the fact that the natural world contains many items which, undeniably in the case of sentient animals, or arguably in the case of other animals and plants, have moral claims on us. This is a fact which the conception of nature as 'capital' conspires to hide from us.[8] In view of this fact, which far from making concern for the natural world immoral makes pure anthropocentrism itself morally reprehensible, it is clearly unjustified to conceive of nature *only* as capital. Although economists have taken to suggesting that these moral claims can be catered for by the device of existence value (Turner and Pearce 1993: 183), and thus construed as a kind of economic value, such a suggestion reveals a serious misconception about the *logical* nature of moral claims. Of course it may be debated whether the natural world does indeed make moral claims upon us, but that is a separate point. Once such moral claims are admitted, they have to be accorded the appropriate status. This means recognising their capacity to 'silence' other claims, their existence independently of their being recognised, and the fact that they cannot be the subject of a trade-off. Moral claims are the grounds for recognition, they are not constituted by their recognition – as they would be if subsumed under existence value; moral

claims are claims which *ought* to be recognised, not simply ones which *are* recognised.

(2) The second constraint arises from the idea that the natural world has a special significance and importance in our lives. Two major questions faced by the 'absurdly strong' position we have outlined are (a) whether there is any reason why we should value the natural world (for its naturalness) and (b) what this reason is. The task of supplying answers is no easy one. Apparently powerful reasons why we should not value nature for itself have been adduced in the classic essay 'Nature' by John Stuart Mill (1874), and his sentiments have been echoed by more recent writers. Mill draws attention to the basic indifference of natural processes, and the appalling sufferings to which they give rise; he thought they could only be admired by someone who was morally uncultivated (1874: 27); and Robert Elliot (1982) adduces sickness and disease as natural items which we would be better off without. The problem with such arguments, however, is that they fail to distinguish between what is good (unconditionally) and what is good for humans (Hurka 1987).[9] From the fact that some natural processes are not good for humans it cannot be inferred that they are not good unconditionally. And the fact that people sometimes sacrifice their lives for their ideals shows that we *can* value things even though they bring suffering or death. Nor is it permissible, as Mill shows, to pick and choose *which* natural items we value, if we are valuing them for their naturalness: 'If it is a sufficient reason for doing one thing, that nature does it, why not another thing? If not all things, why anything?' (1874: 31). However, to have shown (so far) that there is no reason for denying nature's goodness, is not to have given the slightest reason for affirming it. Perhaps nature's indifference suggests that it should be viewed as neither good nor bad but as value neutral.

We might begin the articulation of the view that it *is* appropriate to value the natural world for itself, over and above any moral constraints it may present, by observing that it must, in some sense at least, be 'beyond reproach' inasmuch as it constitutes the very conditions of life. This has to be true despite the fact that these conditions have evoked such deeply felt reproaches as, for example, Dylan Thomas's protest over the death of his father in the poem 'Do not go gentle into that good night'. This is not to say that we must value any event or process that is a necessary condition for our existence. This would not be appropriate, for example, if we were conceived as the result of a violent rape. But here we need to distinguish between events which are *contingently* (or as a matter of fact) necessary for our existence and those which are absolutely necessary. In the example given, we might have been conceived otherwise than as a result of the rape. But it is hard to imagine, on the other hand, how we might have existed if there had been no natural world. However, an initial weakness in this argument for the value of the natural world lies in the difficulty of seeing how to make the step from its value in bringing us to where we are now to the idea that we must therefore value its continuance.

A number of other promising lines of argument also reveal fault lines when put under pressure. Robert Elliot, for example, appealing persuasively to the analogy with works of art, has suggested that the distinctive value of natural objects lies in their origins (1982). There seems little doubt that, as with works of art, the natural origins of an object *do* matter to us and that in either case we are disappointed by 'fakes'. But we may still be left feeling that we want an answer to the question *why* they matter to us. Robert Goodin is therefore right to look further afield in his search for the appeal of the natural (1992: 32). According to Goodin, this appeal stems from the way in which the natural world serves to set our lives in a larger context, thereby providing them with some sense and pattern. Here, the objection might be put that if we need such a larger context we have the whole universe to go at, so to speak; so it is not clear why we should not feel at liberty to do what we like with the little bit of it which happens to lie close at hand.

For all their faults, these and other similar suggestions which connect our valuing of the natural world with the quest for meaning in our lives do rather put in the shade the glib dismissal of regard for nature, by writers such as Richard North, as some kind of romantic or nostalgic conceit (North 1995: ch.9). Talk of 'meaning', moreover, suggests we might do worse than revisit the idea we started with, which focused on the role of the natural world in providing the 'conditions of life', and as a modification to Goodin's suggestion, draw attention to the *significance* of the natural world in the human story, in both a global and a local sense, and at the species and individual level. We miss this if we focus too much on the life-support function of the natural world, and need instead to remind ourselves of the accuracy implicit in the notion of 'natural *history*'; for the natural world is indeed a unique historical phenomenon in which our own lives are embedded. What this means, for practical judgement, is neither the econ-omising of nature, nor (simply) the ecologising of economies, but the formation of policy under a governing principle such as 'diachronic integ-rity' (Holland and O'Neill 1996), which attempts to combine culture and nature into some meaningful historical sequence. The notion of 'significant history' can also help to explain our interest in the *continuation* of the natural world, which turns on a proper understanding of the nature of history. There is a temptation to think that history stops at the here and now. But nothing could be further from the truth. A history which was due to stop at the here and now would be dead, a matter of antiquarian interest only. For history to be alive and to matter, it is vital that we have some conception that it might continue, and how. Accordingly, as urged elsewhere (Rawles and Holland 1993: 19), conservation of the natural world has as much to do with conserving future nature as with conserving the past.

Nor, finally, is this approach incompatible with the suggestion by some writers that we find value in the 'otherness' of nature – in its very indifference. For an emphasis on the interrelation of human with natural history should not be misread as some kind of praise of cosiness (or indeed 'harmony'). The challenge, mystery and even terror (Mill 1874: 27; Williams 1992: 66–7) is itself part of the story whose continuation we seek.

7. CONCLUSION

There is some risk that environmentalism may become unnecessarily vulnerable to its critics if it permits a certain sort of split to develop. On the one hand there is the 'economic' wing, claiming that there is an environmental crisis in economic terms from which we need to rescue ourselves by more prudent economic accounting. This is vulnerable to the retort that in purely economic terms, there is nothing unprecedented afoot which cannot be solved by the fairer distribution of goods and power. On the other side there is the romantic/nostalgic wing perceived as clinging to some notion of nature which can be dismissed as a romantic luxury. This paper has attempted to reunite the environmentalist position into something a little less vulnerable, by emphasising on the one hand that the 'crisis' – the rate and extent of the loss of the natural world – is not (just) an economic crisis, and on the other hand that the loss of 'nature' is not (just) the loss of a romantic ideal, but the loss of our own history and that of the community of life to which we belong.[10]

NOTES

1 Twenty years on, a very similar claim is repeated by Edward Barbier who writes that 'in the long run even complete depletion of natural capital is economically "optimal"' (1993: 3). But exactly as with Solow, this is prefaced by a condition: complete depletion is optimal *if* the returns from alternative investments exceed the returns from holding on to natural capital.

2 I retain this somewhat unfortunate term from the original. It is unfortunate in appearing to imply the existence of resources which are *in*exhaustible, unlike the roughly equivalent term 'non-renewable'.

3 Indeed, Wilfred Beckerman has raised the question of whether the quest for sustainability adds anything of significance to the 'old-fashioned economist's' goal of optimising human welfare.

4 Contrary to what both Daly and Jacobs appear to suggest, it is not clear how the fact that there are fewer fish in the world, *of itself*, implies a lower level of natural capital. Consider a scenario in which all species of locusts have been eradicated. Would this constitute an increase, or a diminution in natural capital? The question is a meaningless one until some assumption is built in about the kind of service or disservice that locusts are expected to perform. It is not impossible

133

to imagine how the disappearance of the locusts might count as an increase in environmental 'capacity'.

5 For other grounds for concern about this concept, see for example O'Connor 1993 and Hinterberger *et al.* 1995.

6 The fact that Jacobs recognises the potential for moral conflict which strong sustainability brings with it, whereas Daly (1995) appears unwilling to concede this point, tends to confirm the claim being urged here, which is that strong sustainability is an inherently unstable position which either collapses into weak sustainability or must become 'absurdly strong'.

7 Nor should the fact that governments make use of such studies cut much philosophical ice. Governments may like to collude in the pretence that sensible economic estimates of environmental values can be produced, either because they can use such estimates to legitimate policies which they were in any case bent on pursuing, or to sustain the politically useful idea that their policies are the result of 'rational' procedures.

8 It can scarcely be regarded as the only source of moral 'invisibility', however, since humans themselves – presumably undeniable moral claimants – are also conceived of instrumentally, as 'labour', under the same set of economic concepts.

9 Although the point is contentious, the view taken here is that the notion of something's being good (or bad) unconditionally is unproblematic. For example, it is the notion involved when we say that a person's suffering is a bad thing: we do *not* just mean it is bad for him or for her.

10 This chapter attempts to develop ideas first sketched in 'Natural capital' (Holland 1994). I am particularly grateful to John Foster, Michael Jacobs, Kate Rawles and Jeremy Roxbee Cox for generous assistance.

9

METHODOLOGY AND INSTITUTIONS

Value as seen from the risk field

Brian Wynne

1. INTRODUCTION

One might expect that monetary valuation of environmental consequences could only seriously occur, if at all, following a definitive account of those environmental consequences. Yet such economic valuation has arisen in most of the mainstream domains of environmental policy, such as nature conservation, marine discharges, waste management, air pollution, and even climate change, despite the fact that the environmental causes and consequences themselves are still subject to enormous scientific disagreement and uncertainty.

Much valuation of the risks or environmental consequences of policies has been implicit. A typical approach has been to compare different activities according to their estimated risks normalised to a common unit such as deaths per year of exposure (Crouch and Wilson 1982). Thus one sees the argument (e.g. Fremlin 1985) that nuclear power is more acceptable than smoking because (in these terms) it is (to the average person) less risky. Such comparative risk-valuation ignores all other aspects of those activities which others may experience as highly important in a weighing of positive and negative attributes.

Here I will attempt to describe a sociological framework for understanding these valuation processes, methods, and the intellectual resources they draw upon. Decision methods have attempted to incorporate public values by introducing formal representations and values of public risk-perceptions. Surveys of people's expressed 'willingness to pay' to avoid a given increase of risk or environmental damage have been used, incorporating the resulting valuations of detriment into cost–benefit balancing (Hausman 1993; Jones-Lee 1989; Marin 1992). My main argument is that the incessant elaboration of methodologies for valuation of what are diverse forms of human experience in a single currency, is an inadequate and even self-defeating surrogate for more direct institutional means of addressing some

135

of the public concerns which are identified as constituting those environmental or risk issues. Thus I suggest that an obsession with methodology
obstructs responsible institutions from understanding their predicament –
which is not (the methodological) one of calculating and communicating
the right decision, but one broadly of public identification – and of the role
of those methods themselves in inadvertently corroding it.

Risk-perception research shows that people are valuing (positively and
negatively) important elements of the *social relations* of risk processes, indeed
that some of these negative dimensions themselves constitute authentic
risk experiences. Thus elaborating the *methods* of representing public values,
all the while enforcing the assumption that these are founded on the
objective physical risk, and that they are expressible in decontextualised,
inflexible and individualistic-utilitarian form (thus reproducing and extending those same problematic social relations), may be an obstacle to constructive *institutional changes*, that is, changes in the social relationships of the
relevant domain of decision-making.

I will describe how public risk perceptions have been framed as problems
for the economically efficient allocation of public resources. Originally
simply dismissed as scientifically unfounded, public perceptions are now
recognised as real politically (even if still not accepted as scientifically
based), and ways of interpreting and accommodating them within rational
decision methods have been advanced. I argue that work on public risk
perceptions, even when it recognises that dimensions such as trust are
central, systematically ignores evidence that public values and issue-defini-
tions, including the key one of investment of trust, are quintessentially
context-dependent and relational. Thus even multi-attribute utility analysis
(MAUA), which is advanced as a remedy to one-dimensional economistic
decision methods, nevertheless sustains central tenets of the decisionistic
neo-classical, rational choice paradigm of policy-making, including especially its inability to articulate institutional questions.

However, reflecting the discursive turn in much policy analysis (Dryzek
1990a), more enlightened proponents of MAUA (e.g. Stirling, this volume)
recognise that its claims lie as much in what it may do to change the social
relations of decision-making as in its result in any single case. This exposes
a final issue, that methodologies like monetary valuation, and MAUA,
should not – despite their typical self-representation – be treated literalis-
tically by their critics, as if they were *just* one-dimensional decision-truth
machines.

This would appear to invite a more charitable view of these methodologies and their incessant elaboration, because they can then avoid being
judged directly, for their immediate outcome, or truth-content, and more
on their indirect, performative contribution: do they support a decent
process? I will argue that on these grounds too there remain some unresolved
problems. These mainly relate to the unreflexive ways in which modern

136

expert institutions routinely translate challenges of contingency and indeterminacy in the very constitution of the knowledges upon which they
draw, into problems of deterministic uncertainty. They manage to objectify
and externalise the grounds of their own lack of public authority and trust,
thus also cutting themselves off from the broader cultural movements and
developments which can be understood as the source of the political
energy underpinning environmental experience and valuation at large.

2. RISK, SAFETY AND ECONOMIC FRAMEWORKS

Economic discipline has always cast a deep shadow over UK policies about
risk. UK regulatory principles have typically enshrined concepts such as 'as
low as reasonably achievable', and 'best available technology not entailing
excessive cost'. Even when these have not explicitly included a cost constraint, they have always legally accommodated informal expert judgements
about the social trade-offs of threatening industries with costly risk-
reduction measures. The key terms 'practicable', or 'reasonably achievable'
have been interpreted quite explicitly to mean that risk reduction has a cost
function, and that society will trade a reduction of risk for the extra costs
required to achieve it. The familiar risk–cost optimisation curves (Figure
9.1) have been widely promulgated as a scientific way of defining the
optimal level of regulation, say of investment in safety, or pollution control.

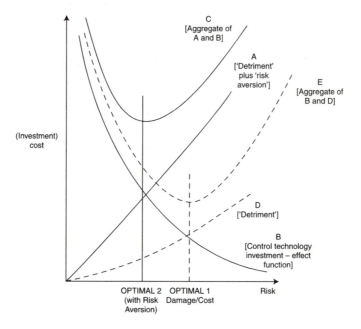

Figure 9.1 Optimisation with and without public concern ('risk aversion')

137

During the 1977 Windscale Inquiry into the nuclear fuels THOR plant (Wynne 1982), I cross-examined Ben Warner, then BNFL's Chief Engineer, about the rationale for not including in the plant design certain already-available technologies for reducing environmental emissions, such as flocculators for retaining alpha-emitters. He replied that cost–benefit calculations showed that this was not justified. Treated to the same answer about several different emissions, overnight I drew up a table for these different radioisotope discharges, with columns (all empty of values) for (a) the level of discharge avoided, (b) the estimated 'detriment' (i.e. human deaths) saved, and (c) the cost of the extra control technology needed to save that extra level of discharge. If Warner was right, then (c) ought to exceed (b) for each case, and the validity of their decisions could be openly scrutinised.

Next morning I confronted Warner with the table, requesting that the empty boxes be filled with the figures used in reaching their 'scientific' decisions. He then switched to emphasising how much expert judgement was needed for such complex and context-specific trade-offs, admitting that they had not actually based their decisions on anything so crude as actual magnitudes, but on the necessary judgement of qualified company and regulatory experts.

There was nothing especially surprising about this 'revelation' of the 'charismatic' nature of the decisions. The only surprise was the way it had originally been suggested that a more formal, transparent and 'scientific' method had been used.

In other situations however, where levels of protection from risks need to be decided and there is a reasonably clear function for the relationship between cost of controls and risk saved, if an accepted value of life is used on the risk–detriment side, then routine decisions are made in various situations, for example X-ray inspection of industrial welding. Values of life for such methods, like values for environmental goods, have been derived in several ways, such as revealed preferences from worker or consumer behaviour, expressed preference as in contingent valuation (willingness-to-pay) surveys, 'copying' other decision makers (the so-called 'literature review'), and wage differentials, 'loss of earnings' or loss of productivity estimates. A sample of such values actually used in different domains is given in Figure 9.2. Very similar problems surround these methods in this domain, as they do for valuing environmental goods and bads.

However, a wider set of issues arose for these kinds of quantification. This has resulted from two separate but convergent influences. One is implicit in the range shown in Figure 9.2, which could have been even wider, since BNFL have complained that if one works backwards from the levels of radioactive discharge actually set for the Sellafield site into the Irish Sea, from the risk estimates to the costs of the required control

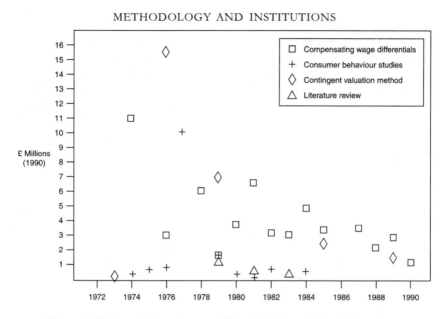

Figure 9.2 Value of life estimates 1973–90 (adjusted for real incomes)
(*Source*: Ives *et al.* 1991)

technologies, the implicit value of a life being used is about £25 million, which is way beyond even the highest figures shown in Figure 9.2. This kind of observation was very soon turned into the comparative argument, that it represented irrationally high levels of investment for little social benefit. It was associated with the kind of argument as to how many lives could be saved by building hospitals with the money that would be freed by relaxing the risk management demands on such nuclear plants.

Thus began a momentum towards prescriptive *comparative* analysis of the risk–cost balancing decisions taken in different policy domains by different government agencies. A recent inter-agency government working party report reflects the further progress of this movement (UKHMG 1995). An implication was that there was some super-agent which could actually make resources flow freely between these very different domains, say from nuclear power to hospitals, car-design or farming practices. A related implication was that this would be desirable – in other words that it would be of human benefit to reduce the multiple particular dimensions, relation-ships, interconnections and meanings of all these different domains of experience to one metric, that of (the estimated monetary costs of) physical risks of death.

A second strand contributing to this same comparative framing and the impetus towards standardisation, centralisation and reductionism was that introduced initially in the USA under Reagan, to curb the perceived regulatory zeal of the environmental agencies such as EPA and FDA

(Environmental Protection Agency and Food and Drug Administration). They were obliged by a Presidential Executive Order (recently reinforced by a Congressional Law) to perform cost–benefit assessments of any new regulation being proposed. (A similar cost–benefit constraint has been imposed on any regulations proposed by the new UK Environment Agency.) This provided yet more impetus towards monetarisation, and towards an assumed overall comparative framework of justification.

Thus both comparative analysis and cost–benefit requirements contributed towards a comprehensive, centralised framework for allocating resources to risk reduction across the whole sweep of government responsibility.

In 1993 an interdepartmental committee was set up within the British government, to examine the economics of safety regulation in the UK (UKHMG 1995). Its main concern was to eradicate inconsistency between different departments and agencies in the 'criteria used in determining safety regulations' (p.39). The committee's expressed objective was to 'provide a basis for a general initiative across government to promulgate consistent approaches to the valuation of safety benefits'.

Thus the different practices of different agencies faced with managing very different constellations of issues were perceived to be problematic because of fears about unduly stringent and costly – that is, 'inconsistent' – risk management decisions by some of them. The need for consistency was driven by an economic interest, and translated into the demand for valuation of safety benefits, of risk-cost avoided thanks to some level of safety investment. Thus, crucially:

- risk has been defined as something of universal meaning, which can be quantified into universal units;
- it has been defined as tradable against benefit, similarly defined;
- both have been defined as monetary values; and
- nothing more about the human experience of risky activities is recognised as having meaning, positive or negative. Risk has been translated and decontextualised.

Not surprisingly a monetary scale was assumed to unite these very different domains. Since these approaches have arisen at the same time as public perceptions and evaluations of risk have assumed growing political importance, it is now worth discussing how policy authorities have attempted to translate research on public perceptions of risks into decision-making. Since this has been well reviewed elsewhere (Royal Society 1992) it will be only outlined before discussing the issues of relevance here.

3. RISK PERCEPTIONS AND ATTRIBUTES

Expert knowledge of 'objective risks', institutionalised as a normative principle in policy, has frequently clashed with public perceptions, so frustrating rational expert decisions and plans. Nuclear power is the prime example, but many others have followed suit. Biotechnology is now thoroughly enmeshed in like concerns, with claims that the UK industry is over-regulated, owing to public overestimation of the risks.

When public divergence from expert risk knowledge over nuclear power began to rear its troublesome head in the early 1970s, it was assumed to be simply due to ignorance: public information would solve the problem. However when such programmes failed to rectify these conflicts and even made them worse, social research showed that the public was introducing considerations beyond just estimated magnitudes of risk of harm – which they could rank relatively well – into their *evaluation* of those risks or associated activities (Royal Society 1992).

Thus began a search for these unknown extra aspects of risks that appeared to be crucial to public evaluation. Psychometric research identified several factors which appeared to influence public judgements of risks in this way, for example the involuntary nature of many risks.

Several further such factors were found, such as: reversibility or irreversibility; the concentration of equal overall harm in single catastrophic events or dispersion in many smaller ones; whether harm was immediate or delayed; whether anonymous or known victims were involved; the familiarity of the risk or the processes involved; whether there was uncertainty and disagreement about the risks; and how equitable or not was the social distribution of the risks. These and other factors were defined as the different *attributes* of a risk, affecting public perceptions in ways which might be reasonable, but not connected with the 'objective' risks as estimated magnitudes (see e.g. Slovic 1992).

I proposed an additional factor (Wynne 1980), which is whether the public sees the *risk-controlling agents* (government regulators, or industry, or operators e.g. airline pilots) as trustworthy or not. I also argued that this factor, like others already identified, may not be just a 'perceptual' matter, but may influence the objective level of risk; and further, that the *scientific estimation of risks makes assumptions about these contingent factors too*. Proposal of this trust factor highlighted an aspect of the other risk attributes which their psychometric discoverers had overlooked. The attributes of 'risk' thus identified were in many cases attributes of the *social relationships* constituting the risky activity, not of some independently existent, context-free 'risk'. Thus the very nature and meaning of a risk was qualitatively different for a member of the public from what it was for an expert in a regulatory body because for the public it involved an objective element of risk through social dependency on such agents. These social relationships, though an important element of the risk itself for the public, exist *beyond* the risky activity, and cannot be reduced to it. Divergences over risks were often rooted in tacit differences of assumptions about such endogenous social

141

factors. Also, risk was seen to be historically rooted, in social relationships which had histories, and anticipated futures.

One implication, for example, was that it was meaningless to seek universal numerical values of 'acceptable risk' from whatever kind of risk, say one in a million annual risk of death, because this ignored so many contextual dimensions which people had been found to value. If this were not a precise form of valuation, it was no different in principle from the now-admitted informality of so-called formal methods. However this more cultural or sociological interpretation of risks and risk conflicts was not adopted by official policy and risk management agencies.[1] Despite the acceptance of these insights in some official studies (Royal Society 1992), continued use was made by government agencies and industry of context-free comparative numerical risk estimates for different activities, which reduced the social experiences of those activities only to the dimension of numerical risk of physical harm, from artificially isolated one-off cases. Sometimes these official approaches recognised the voluntariness dimension, but none of the others.[2]

In cost-effectiveness optimisation processes however the treatment of public risk perceptions did change markedly from the earlier assumptions about public ignorance and need to be informed of the facts of 'objective risks'. As the substantive realities behind the extra attributes were recognised, it was also tacitly recognised that where public perceptions appeared to be more severe than numerical estimates alone might portray, this should be reflected in levels of risk control and related investment. Already in the nuclear field, technical safety criteria and associated costs had been escalating in response to public concern. I suggested (Wynne 1986) that this was a self-made 'technological treadmill' for the industry, in that there was built into this escalation an extravagant dislocation between on one hand the (unarticulated) concerns of the public with a much more complex array of issues connected with the social relational issues and 'attributes' referred to above, and on the other the mistaken treatment of this by the authorities as a 'distorted' perception of physical risk alone, and as a demand for more safety.

At the same time the National Radiological Protection Board (NRPB) was integrating public perceptions into cost–benefit optimisation methods, by simply increasing the slope of the detriment curve (see Figure 9.1) by a notional amount deemed to represent public 'risk aversion'. Initially there was no pretence of quantification of this extra contribution to the detriment curve, though this was the natural place for contingent valuation methods and monetary values to be used. However the Health and Safety Executive (HSE) began in the mid-1980s to try out CV methods in order to use the results in this 'objective' way. Early in this exploration it was pointed out to the HSE that in addition to the usual methodological and ethical objections about CV techniques and monetarisation, people may effectively be forced to misrepresent concerns of a social relational kind, about risk-controlling institutions and decision-making processes, as if they were compensatable monetary costs. They would be asked in effect to confirm a questionable – and subsequently non-negotiable – model of themselves as human beings. It was suggested that extreme responses could thus be interpreted as tacit expressions of such unrecognised dimensions of concern, and should not be simply dropped as extreme outliers on the assumption of 'experimental error' or moral deviance.

These suggestions to take seriously and respond in kind to institutional, or social-relational bases of public 'risk' concern, were ignored[3] and replaced by methodological elaborations of a CV kind. The authorities' rigid and sanctimonious, if increasingly perplexed, approach to indirect attempts by respondents to express dissent from the very framing of the exercise was reflected in the exasperated comments of a senior HSE official at the time: 'there may be some to whom it is repugnant to ask such [WTP] questions – but what kind of people are these?'[4] The significance of the relational context was completely overlooked in the official defence: that since people are routinely in effect making such judgements in their lives, they should be happy to have these rendered 'more consistent' by these methods.

4. RISK METRICS AND DECISION ANALYSIS – DELETING INSTITUTIONS

Whereas CBA reduces all dimensions of (valued) damage into a single composite cost function (and implies the ability to do the same for the benefits), other approaches have attempted to address some of the criticisms of CBA by keeping separate dimensions separate. One such approach which has been advanced in the risk field is multi-attribute utility analysis (MAUA). Stirling (this volume) describes this technique and discusses some of its uses and implications. In this approach to its use from the risk field I hope to add some further considerations.

If valuation of risks occurs in several independent dimensions according to the factors noted above, this valuation process can be rendered more transparent and decisions about risks made more accountable and democratic by using frameworks which make the selection of attributes and relative weighting of them more transparent. Fischoff et al.. (1984) take the attributes of risk identified earlier, and propose that decision makers rather than experts can choose which attributes to give weights to, and thus choose explicitly and democratically how to construct a composite definition of risk which is socially recognised. The weighting distribution across the range of chosen attributes making up such a composite risk index is the utility function, since it expresses the negative utility for that decision maker of those aspects of harm represented by the chosen attributes. If, for example, injury to children is weighted more severely than a few years' life-shortening, these value-choices can be explicitly made and the effects on the overall best decision worked through. In theory, with accountability and consensus, this could be a societal choice. The implications of different value-choices of attributes and weightings can be openly explored.

In principle there is no reason why MAUA cannot include consideration of 'public concern', 'mistrust' or 'risk aversion'. Prospect theory in psychology has introduced to decision theory the relevance of anticipatory feelings of regret or fulfilment affecting weightings. Fischoff *et al.* (1984) were the first to propose that 'public concern' should be integrated in this way into formal risk–cost indices for decision-making.

As far as it goes, the MAUA elaboration of the usual risk decision methods is an admirable attempt not to ignore or patronise public perceptions, and to include them as a legitimate input to risk management decision-making. In principle MAUA avoids the limitations of reduction to a single (monetary or any other) metric. However, here I want to draw attention to four different problems which are not addressed by MAUA in its (legitimate) claim to offer improvements on the economistic CBA paradigm. I have argued that they are constitutive elements of the overall problem of risk and public evaluations. How far this applies in the somewhat newer domain of environmental valuation needs further exploration, but the indications are that very similar basic issues underlie both (overlapping) contexts. The four problems are:

1 the imposition of a unitary frame of meaning, of an assumed universal issue-object;
2 tacit institutional commitments shaping rational methods;
3 the *abrupt* (and irreversible) expropriation of meanings;
4 decisionism as a normative model of human society.

Imposing a unitary (risk-centred) frame

The first problem is that the MAUA framework takes for granted that the diverse actors and groups who may be involved in a decision process about risk activities are all focused on an identical problem-definition, one based on a risk and its attributes. They are all assumed to be bound in this same cultural space. The technology, system or institutional actor which gives rise to the defined risk is assumed to have the same basic meaning for all who experience it. All they are taken possibly to differ on are 'the' risk attributes and the relative weights they attach to them. This assumption therefore does not recognise people to be dealing with different problem-frames altogether, overlapping perhaps on this risk terrain but each embedded within different cross-cutting preoccupations, relationships, histories, commitments and constraints.

However definitions of technologies or risk systems and their boundaries are not objective and universal, but socially defined, not only as a matter of subjective perception but of objective social experience and relationships of the technology. Thus it is not only a question of allowing one-off participation in expressing what attributes to include with what weightings, from an assumed given decision issue, but of fostering widespread negotiation of what are the boundaries and shape of the risk-generating problem in the first place. What kinds of connection does it have with other possible issues and actions which may also present threats to actors in the process?

The issue of trust can best be used to illustrate the importance of this point. It is now routinely accepted that a central 'attribute' of risks is whether the public trusts the actors supposed to be controlling the risks. If they do not, they are more than likely to evaluate the physical risks more severely. Thus trust has been reified and objectified in this way as an attribute to be weighed alongside reversibility, voluntariness, etc. However if we take a proposal to operate a risky plant such as a nuclear reprocessing plant, the usual framing of the risk problem is around a single plant of given capacity. But if the public does not trust the authorities, it will logically feel that to accept such a 'separate' plant will inevitably lead to other risk-laden further developments, such as waste transport, plutonium exchange and diffusion into unknown hands, more nuclear reactors and further reprocessing; in other words a wholesale transformation of society as well as extra physical risks beyond those admitted in the rational frame.

To those who trust the authorities and their institutions, such possible developments can be bracketed out of the frame, as hypothetical possibilities whose risks can be impartially assessed at some appropriate future time. Nothing in the present discrete decision creates pressures that will influence future decision makers one way or the other. To those who experience such decision actors and processes as alien, on the other hand, this kind of bracketing and discrete framing of the risk issue is utterly unreal. Recognising the mistrust issue only then to reduce it to a weighted attribute within a MAUA framework, which assumes and imposes the limited prior framing of the overall issue, radically distorts those aspects of human interrelationship that generated the alienation and mistrust and the 'risk-concern' in the first place. And of course this institutional reduction via the methodology risks *exacerbating* that public sense of alienation and mistrust.

Thus, although it expressly allows for a certain range of value-choices, MAUA responds to public concerns by incorporating them within a decision method which still imposes a priori a single, discrete and context-free problem-definition.

Tacit institutional design

So one difficulty with MAUA as a means of valuation is that it imposes an arbitrary prior framing of risk problems, as well as a single and inflexible one, in the apparent guise of flexibility. Embedded within this framing, I argue, is the second difficulty: a tacit and problematic commitment to particular institutional forms, which need to be brought out from this taken-for-granted framing and subjected to debate. Elsewhere I have illustrated this point by reference to the tacit institutional commitment that the means of blocking horizontal nuclear weapons proliferation (the nuclear non-proliferation treaty and the International Atomic Energy Agency's safeguards programme) are adequate, which shapes the 'rational' exclusion of the 'irrational and merely symbolic' frequent public association of nuclear reactor risks with nuclear weapons risks (Wynne 1989). The assumption that there is a universal objective issue to be decided will always by default impose questionable tacit institutional commitments of some kind upon participants who may not share them.

Valuing as expropriation

Perhaps the most crucial element of institutional denial concerns the act of abrupt expropriation which is built into valuation methods, the third of the problems listed. It has been observed before that an inevitable problem with valuation methods as formal approaches to the question of value is that they forcefully attenuate the participation of public respondents in what they may have hoped or even expected to be a more open-ended process of continual (re)negotiation of values and identities. The formal methods for eliciting public values all take a fixed value such as willingness to pay, and assume it to represent a stable, intrinsic value of the respondent. Here we can see most clearly the reinforcement between the institutional relations of such methods, and the commitment of neo-classical paradigms to the idea of the sovereign individual self, with its own independent preferences and utilities, which can be unambiguously and decontextually expressed.

If the individual and her values are no longer seen in such essentialist terms, then it becomes manifestly indefensible to extract a 'final' value from respondents and treat it as fixed for all time – removed into an inaccessible expert world only to return eventually as a commitment said to represent the respondent. It may be this very abruptness, and the implicit essentialist model of human being and values which it imposes, which is the most damaging to the credibility of such deterministic methods in risk-valuation processes. Indeed the process decouples the human subject of the respondent from the value as if that is their intrinsic objective valuation, but then proceeds to manipulate that value as an object but in ways which utterly exclude its author from any further participation. Thus the malleability of such values is implicitly recognised, but is taken over and controlled by expert decision analysts rather than allowing their authors any further responsibility. Less essentialist models of the human would have to treat institutional relations of decisions as a part of the decision problem. Even MAUA, though it has been advanced as a form of process innovation, does not address this abrupt expropriation dilemma.

Decisionism

A final problem with MAUA is that like sister methods it is wedded to, and cultivates, a completely decisionistic model of society. As already argued there are systematic ways in which such methods delete the institutional and cultural dimensions of risk issues. This is tantamount to the further reinforcement of the sovereign individual, rational choice paradigm. I have elsewhere illustrated this problem of inadvertent undermining of institutional dimensions by taking a model decision analysis of risk problems, namely Raiffa's (1985) treatment of the coal-mine rescue dilemma. This attempts to incorporate the anticipation of regret, guilt, and satisfaction in a risk management decision about the rationality of conducting a rescue-bid for the trapped survivors in a coal-mine accident, but only by risking rescuers too.

The decision analysis cleverly navigates through the different odds to be weighed up and the various pathways of consequences to show the key role of perceptual factors in determining the rationally optimal calculated response to the rescue question. However as I earlier argued (Wynne 1987), apart from the obvious problem that the extra perceptual factors of regret, guilt, elation (and even the primary probabilities) are so slippery that a range of conflicting outcomes could be constructed as consistent with the rational decision model, the more serious point is that these factors – focused as they are on the individual utilities of the assumed sovereign decision maker – neglect a more basic human reality. This is that, in order for mining to exist at all as an institution, miners have to be able to trust that if ever they are trapped alive, a rescue will be attempted, virtually regardless of the odds. Thus managers are most likely to decide in favour of a rescue whatever a formal decision tree may indicate, because intuitively, as part of their culture, they are imbued morally with loyalty to fellow-miners which dictates a rescue-attempt. If in such a crisis managers were seen to be cold-bloodedly calculating the odds in the way suggested by the model, seriously contemplating triage, the very institution of mining would be in question because the necessary human mutual obligations, loyalties and common identities would be destroyed. This tacit *culturally embodied* institutional rationale is systematically deleted by the decisionistic MAUA method. In the latter, institutions are only seen instrumentally, as means to ends

147

(individual utilities), not as embodying value as such. Thus even big moral and political issues, and cultural questions such as equity, are reduced by this decisionistic worldview, to instrumental attributes which then allows them to be translated into mere utilities subject to decision weighting and trading in a preferences market-place.

A counter-argument to the above critique of decision-analytic reduction of the coal-mine rescue dilemma might be that it would be perfectly possible to defend the *institution* precisely by recognising it as an attribute and giving it a value within the decision-analytic frame. This may be especially persuasive when the decision-problem is clear-cut and may be assumed to be universally recognised, as when identified human lives are under threat. But even there when the responsibility for the decision is shared and different composite utility functions are put together, negotiation will commence about various uncertainties, assumptions, farther-reaching implications and connections, historically rooted loyalties and identities, and future hopes and expectations. In other words a familiar rather flexible, ill-defined and open-ended process of negotiative bargaining will most likely take place. The main difference from a more 'traditional' decision process not framed as a formal analytic method is that it is *represented* as something more analytically disciplined and superior. This representation seems to have the effect, whether deliberate or not (and I am inclined to think of it as innocent), of limiting the circle of participation in the negotiated decision. Perhaps this is a fortunate effect in that it may make decision *possible*; but it may not be, and anyway it is a misleadingly different rationale from those normally advanced.

The further problem with the comprehensively decisionist approach is that it leaves no room in principle for recognising that the assumed object of the decision may itself be a contingent human construct which excludes other legitimate concerns, values and experiences – even if these may not be easily articulable. Ultimately these lines of reasoning lead to an ethical problem with the MAUA framework, as to whether its clean formal separation of decision-issues, and of attributes and weightings as individually originating objects, offers a morally acceptable vision of human relations and interactions, regardless of the functional question about whether its results are good, bad or indifferent.

The model of society based on decisionism is consistent with the rational choice paradigm. It ignores the relational elements of social order and cohesion because it ignores the senses of historical experience and continuity across issues; issues are instead artificially insulated as discrete and decontextualised by expert decision-making institutions such as those of risk management. Thus judging the risks involved in dependency on existing institutions from past experience of their demeanour – something I have argued is a central and rational part of public risk perceptions and judgements – would be inconceivable within a decisionistic framework.

This is so because each decision is deemed to be entire unto itself, unrelated to anything but preferences that are assumed to be indigenous to the individual and focused on the object, not enculturated through past experience and influenced by collective cultural processes, emergent habits and continuing relationships which connect across issue-boundaries and time.

Decisionism is fundamentally anti-relational, and ahistorical. It negates human culture and institutions. It reinforces the idea of independent sovereign preferences rather than cultural shaping of individual identities and values. Based as it is originally in psychological experiment and related artificial situations, most of the risk literature falls into this decisionist fallacy. Thus even though it has been recognised that the challenges of sustainable development and preventive environmental policies will require cultural changes in modern society, dominant discourses and approaches still inadvertently undermine such change by inhibiting the kinds of public policy discourse which would facilitate it.

5. CONCLUSIONS: RISK AND IDENTITY, OR MAPPING OUT THE FOOTPRINTS

I have attempted to review approaches to measuring public risk perceptions and to valuing them alongside other factors in decision-making. I suggest that formalisation of such public 'perceptions' or evaluations is intrinsically problematic regardless of what precise metric is used, monetary or otherwise. All representations of 'public risk perceptions' used in decision methods are condemned fundamentally to distort them from the outset, by assuming them to be primarily defined by, and focused upon, an objectively existent and universally experienced risk problem. In official discourses of decision, people are normatively constructed in the very way 'the' issue is framed, since this already presumes to represent their worlds of meaning. I suggest this already engenders alienation between people and decision experts, because it ignores the autonomous and indigenous networks of relationships and issues in which people are differently engaged, and in which they find their own meanings, values and identities, including their own definitions of issues. It is not that these are entirely disconnected from expert discourses and definitions. Nor is it that they should be given sovereignty over expert frameworks. But if the mounting evidence of public alienation is to be addressed (Macnaghten *et al.* 1995) then they should be given forms of continuing representation and expression which allow interactive development and mutual learning. This implies institutional changes, rather than methodological elaborations which obscure the institutional questions.

Thus in the typical methodological representations of public perceptions and values, there is already a strong element of hidden, albeit inadvertent, coercion into an alien, externally controlled and standardised identity, even whilst such methods genuinely strive to represent people and their values more adequately than before. There are several aspects of this inadequate representation of the human dimension:

1 the imposed common issue-focus as mentioned above;
2 the assumption of complete separation between issues;
3 the assumption that social interaction is constituted solely by deliberate decision and choice (decisionism);
4 the assumption of sovereign individual values independent of social relations;
5 the assumption of a basic lack of ambiguity or indeterminacy in social values and preferences;
6 blindness to the importance of social *identity* as the basis of values, thus non-recognition of their shaping by social relations and institutional structures.

In the critical stance taken here towards these tenets, correspondences are evident with the 'old institutionalism' as discussed by Hodgson (1993a, and in this volume). These concepts of human value and relationships fundamentally contradict decisionistic approaches to public issues because the latter a priori assume the complete discreteness of issues, which is tantamount to assuming instrumental calculative reasoning and valuation on the part of social actors. Thus relationships are only treated as instrumental means to (preference-defined) individual ends; they are not recognised to have value in themselves (granted that this value can change).

Thus there is an intrinsic tension between any methods which attempt to formalise, represent and manage public values, and public processes of valuation in themselves. Those methods inevitably reify, decontextualise and objectify those values and processes, thereby reproducing alien models of people and social relationships. It is not surprising that social research should show deep public ambivalence about such methods and their institutional exponents, even when people may try to adapt to them, rather than overtly rejecting the whole framework. The intractable extreme values given in CV surveys which are usually dismissed as 'unreal' or 'distorted' should be seen not as real high valuations of whatever good is overtly in question, but an oblique way of expressing dissent from the underlying meaning and identity imposed by such methods and their associated institutional relationships.

The argument in defence of formal methods in this field is that, even if this formalisation does not fully capture the subtleties, its very transparency allows proper participation and recognition of all parties' valuations. Ultimately negotiation and compromise are required, but at least it will be between accountable positions. This parallels the observations about cost–benefit valuation, that not even exponents believe that such methods give true results (Craig *et al.* 1993). They are justified on other grounds, for example that the methods at least do force values and criteria out into the open, and that negotiation and interpretive flexibility can be conducted collectively by those who have joined the 'discursive community'. Without some such admittedly reductionist form of translation, and a corresponding rhetoric of objectivity, there would be no possible stabilisation of any collective decision-making.

It must be true that some form of reductionism in public decision methods is inevitable. Correspondingly, public rhetorics of decision processes will invariably emphasise their 'objectively-determined' character, concealing much of the actual contingency involved. Porter's (1995) argument that it is weak institutions which seek to objectify and quantify their self-rationales, seems to be borne out in this field too. Thus good practitioners would routinely treat accounts and 'methods' more poetically, never taking them as a literal version of how commitment is reached – just as BNFL's Chief Engineer did not cling to a literal reading of his quantitative cost-effectiveness language when pressed.

These points being accepted, any form of reductionism is not thereby justified. At least two problems remain, beyond a large problem of political effectiveness when one looks at the claims of valuation methods in the current domains of environmental policy or risk management. First, the justification that participation can be broadened because the valuations being used are more formalised and explicit *may* be fulfilled, but it is not automatic; and if the population of participants is formalistically broadened by including CV survey results for example, but the nature of that participation is limited and very inflexible (as described and criticised above for risk perceptions, for example), it is misleading to call this 'broadened participation'. Second, there is an implication that the discourse itself does not constrain the negotiations that may go on informally under its umbrella; but the very definition of the problems and the implicit models of the human on which the methods are based already pre-emptively shapes and limits the kinds of issue that can even be recognised and addressed. In this sense the case against existing methods of valuation echoes the philosophical stance that discourses have material-ordering implications. People are likely to be influenced by – and eventually likely to confirm – cultural models which unreflexively convey instrumental and individualist commitments, even if there is no intrinsic determinism involved.

However these responses could be seen still as failing to address the question of how ultimately the balance should be struck between the discursively reified and methodologised on one hand, and the endless relational negotiation of value on the other. There will never be *definite* evidence to show that the implicit assumptions embodied in such methods and their surrounding institutional commitments are wrong. Justification or refutation of these commitments will always be projected into the future; it will depend on what we make of them.

This sense of contingency, and the associated acknowledgement of limits to the impetus of control and instrumentality, seem to be precisely what most deeply alienates modern institutions from their publics, thus generating a further dimension to public senses of risk. It is not, as experts often patronisingly suggest, that ordinary people cannot cope with contingency, but that *those institutions and their typical scientistic culture cannot*, and they systematically convert contingency instead into deterministic forms of ('manageable') uncertainty, knowledge and value. Yet this contingency is the creative space for new and more ample human discourses, models, identities and values. In this sense we appear to be experiencing a growing dislocation between our institutions and our changing culture. Wheareas institutions tend normally to routinise, to reify and take for granted, culture poses the unsettling questions, such as, What kind of human situation are we in? Our self-consciously modern institutions appear unable to see that the spaces are being created, and filled out, by growing political and cultural constituencies in decreasing respect for the as-yet non-negotiable human assumptions and commitments which institutions and their methods increasingly tenuously express.

NOTES

1 This conclusion was eventually assimilated only to be retrieved in the concept of tolerable risk (HSE 1988), the idea of a more passive and perhaps reluctant acceptance, and with bands rather than precise magnitudes.
2 The Department of Environment (1995) *Guide*, for example, Annex 5, lists factors of familiarity, control, proximity and dread, but it is significant that it mistakenly refers to public evaluations influenced by these factors as *distorted estimates of magnitude*, rather than as evaluations which recognise more than bare magnitudes.
3 This account is based on my participation in a series of meetings in 1986 and 1987 with HSE and NRPB by a group of ESRC-funded researchers on risk perceptions and valuation methods, including amongst others, Jennifer Brown, Michael Jones-Lee, Richard Eiser, Tim O'Riordan, Alan Irwin, Jerry Ravetz, Sally MacGill, John Broome and Joyce Tait.
4 At one of the same meetings (see note 3).

Part III

VALUING NATURE: NEW DIRECTIONS

10

EXISTENCE VALUE, MORAL COMMITMENTS AND IN-KIND VALUATION

Jonathan Aldred

1. INTRODUCTION

Existence value has become an increasingly important concept as the use of cost–benefit analysis has spread from traditional applications to attempts to place monetary value on, for instance, a rare wetland habitat. It has been given various definitions, but a common element is *the value of an object in the natural world apart from any use of it by humans*. Existence value was introduced into environmental cost–benefit analysis to deal with a number of problems posed by recent, more ambitious applications of that method. The aim of this chapter is to investigate how far the concept succeeds in tackling these problems, or whether, as critics from outside economics allege, it is entirely flawed and should be abandoned altogether. A fundamental redefinition of existence value is proposed, which aims to address the concerns of these critics while remaining consistent with an essentially utilitarian approach to environmental decision-making. Two independent types of value are defended, existence value and well-being, implying the possibility of incommensurability between values. It is argued that this incommensurability can be overcome, although sometimes only after abandoning monetary measures of value. By distinguishing between commensurables, substitutes and replacements, it is shown when such 'in-kind valuation' might be necessary. The chapter concludes with a brief discussion of the implications of this theoretical analysis for operational problems such as protest bids.

Existence value does not fit easily into the methodology of neo-classical economics, where decision-making has become a 'black box'. A limited range of 'inputs' from the external environment of the agent are considered, most notably price, and related by theory directly to the 'outputs' of the decision, observed preferences. The intervening decision process *per se* is largely irrelevant because the objective is typically to predict behaviour. Theories which predict satisfactorily, *as if* the agent was a rational maximiser uninfluenced by social pressures and norms, are, according to the naïve positivist, satisfactory by definition. In contrast, with an environmental

155

existence value, understanding what has been observed, from what decision process the expressed value results, must be the first priority, since the concern is to satisfy preferences rather than determine how they change. As Madariaga and McConnell (1987) put it: 'When dealing with existence value, more than other sources of value, we need to concern ourselves with the question "What are we measuring?" rather than "What is the measurement?"' (p.936). Or again, 'Thus the central issues surrounding nonuse value would seem to revolve around what really is nonuse value' (Brookshire and Smith 1987: 932). Vatn and Bromley (1994) make a similar plea for environmental value more generally. The essential lesson is that since different questions are asked when analysing existence values rather than consumer preferences over market goods, a different analysis of the decision-making process is required.

Even within the narrow framework of the contingent valuation method (CVM), the objective is more comprehension than prediction. CVM seeks to elicit and interpret the monetary values individuals are 'willing to pay' for environmental preservation, whereas neo-classical economics is usually concerned with the ability to predict such variables. It is misleading when the willingness-to-pay measures from contingent valuation surveys are treated as predictions. For there simply does not exist a 'true' valuation or demand in the case of non-market environmental goods, against which the survey results can be compared. Thus the distinction between comprehension and prediction is not, here at least, an empty one.

2. PROBLEMS POSED BY THE DEFINITION OF EXISTENCE VALUE

Perhaps the only clear distinction to emerge from the literature is that between existence value and use value. The definition of existence value which has evolved is a residual definition, capturing all value which does *not* arise out of use of an environmental feature.[1] The channels through which the object under valuation benefits the agent remain obscure. Contingent valuation studies can never hope to elicit existence value directly, even supposing this were feasible, when researchers do not know which question has existence value as an answer. Questions such as 'What is the most you would be willing to pay simply to preserve the [environmental good] in its present state, even if you would never use it?' ask the respondent to perform the difficult conceptual exercise of determining a residual value, value in the absence of use, and there are obvious psychological reasons to doubt the validity of such responses. Such questions are unlikely to satisfy the doubts of theorists who suspect existence value is merely a chimera to the extent that it conflicts with self-interest and can be elicited by much more direct, motivationally explicit questions to the extent that it does not. The definition would be improved if 'use' was itself less arbitrarily defined.

156

For any given relation between object under valuation and subject valuer, environmental economics offers no procedure for determining whether this relation constitutes a use. Perhaps the boundary between use and non-use, use value and existence value, is of no great importance, but if not then neither is the recognition of the two distinct forms of value.

The merits of such a distinction will not be debated here but the need for one has been emphasised repeatedly in the literature. It is claimed below that the proposed definition, in drawing an important conceptual distinction, is self-justifying. Brookshire *et al.* (1986) are typical in rejecting several claimed motives for existence value because they do not permit this distinction: 'these values do not reflect a *different type* of economic value associated with the preservation of water resources that one would want to call "existence value"' (p. 1512). Unfortunately the distinctive feature of existence value lies in a paradox: value in the absence of value. This paradox has been often noted; Brookshire and Smith (1987: 932) in discussing Boyle and Bishop (1987) argue that they 'carefully avoid ethical considerations and the role of alternative motive structures. Thus they imply that a resource provides nonuse values only if someone has a use for it; this could be regarded as circular.' There is a paradox to the extent that so-called 'non-use' values imply the presence of a use.

Similarly, Mitchell and Carson (1989: 60) claim that the philosophical meaning of intrinsic value, that something has value in and of itself, is incompatible with 'the economic notion that something has value only if an economic agent is willing to give up scarce resources for it'. It is possible to reject the extreme ecocentric conclusion which the Routleys and others (see for instance Rolston 1988, Routley and Routley 1979) draw from their 'experience machine' examples, that a species would have value even if there were no humans on the planet to value it, while nevertheless denying the Mitchell and Carson argument. A truly intrinsic value consistent with the utilitarian foundations of economics is certainly conceivable. This middle position is reflected in the work of a number of environmental philosophers, including Callicott (1986), Norton's (1987) weak anthropocentrism, and Hare (1987), and will be assumed below. Briefly, an object O has intrinsic value if and only if the presence of O serves O's interests. A monkey has intrinsic value because it has an interest in its own continued existence. But unless trees have interests, they do not have intrinsic value. However a tree might have instrumental value to a monkey. For value to be meaningfully recognised in any of these categories, a human valuer is required. If his values are honestly held, the valuer will plausibly be willing to give up scarce resources to maintain them. Admittedly this last step is a contentious one, but even if some agents are unwilling in practice, this does not imply a logical incompatibility between economic and intrinsic value.[2]

This brief discussion has sought to illustrate the confusion in the literature over existence value, and raise some of the conceptual problems which must be addressed by any adequate formulation. The current treatment of existence value fully justifies Green *et al.*'s conclusion 'that no exhaustive and mutually exclusive set of motivations underlying individual preferences for environmental goods has yet been determined' (1990: 73). Critics from outside economics, on the other hand, typically claim that the very notion of existence value as understood in economics is flawed, and urge its abandonment altogether.[3] In the light of these observations, a redefinition of existence value will be proposed, rejecting the usual assumption of mainstream economics that welfare equals utility.[4] Brookshire and Smith (1987: 932) rightly suggest that 'To understand these [nonuse] values requires an inquiry into the psychological and ethical elements underlying preferences, as well as the physical meaning of consumption itself.'

3. UTILITY, WELFARE AND PSYCHOLOGICAL EGOISM

A first step is to overcome the considerable misunderstandings caused by terminology. In modern economic theory, the definition of utility as a cardinal representation of an agent's preferences has the advantage of being established, generally accepted and thoroughly clear (Broome 1991). This convention will be assumed in what follows: thus all chosen outcomes maximise utility by definition. Now of a pair of outcomes, is the agent necessarily better off with the preferred one, the one with greater utility, rather than its alternative? 'Better off' is here given its ordinary meaning. Mother tells us we would be better off not always doing what we want. We decide to do some act even though we know it will make us worse off. We may disagree with each other, or with Mother, over whether some outcome will *in fact* make us worse off, or merely be mistaken, but such claims as 'choosing to be worse off' are labelled as simply incoherent in mainstream economic theory. This can be true only tautologously, when defining welfare as what is preferred.

Mitchell and Carson's implied theory of welfare or the good, if it is a substantive theory at all, certainly equates utility with the good, in this case satisfaction. Thus the benefits of an environmental good are 'the paths through which the changes in the level of satisfaction indicated by an agent's utility function occur' (1989: 60). Only the implicit assumption of an identity between utility and welfare would require the assertion that 'existence values involve the notion that a person doesn't have to visit a recreational site to *gain utility* from its maintenance or improvement [emphasis added]' (p.63). More interesting still is their response to Brookshire *et al.* (1986):

[M]ost important, it is erroneous to assume that making choices on the basis of ethical beliefs necessarily involves self-sacrifice; in fact, those

> who make choices of this kind obtain utility from satisfying internalised social norms . . . Far from being counter-preferential, in properly conducted contingent valuation studies, choices based on these preferences are motivated by self-interested and egoistic considerations.
>
> (Mitchell and Carson 1989: 66)

Mitchell and Carson rightly assert that ethical influences on choice need not *necessarily* involve self-sacrifice but spuriously transform this into the claim that a *properly conducted* study involves *only* self-interested considerations.

An example of an ethical choice which does not necessitate self-sacrifice is that motivated by an ethic which attaches moral interests to non-human creatures.[5] According to Brookshire *et al.* (1986: 1515) 'this would necessarily involve a counterpreferential choice.' This is mistaken. For to maintain that such concern for animals is inconsistent with welfare-maximisation while a similar concern for other humans via altruism, bequest motives, or Sen-type sympathy is quite consistent, assumes the very asymmetry between the interests of humans and non-humans which the environmental ethic denies. Randall (1987: 84) certainly admits the possibility: 'Caring is extended [to nonhumans] because it gives the human satisfaction to do so.' So does the widely discussed idea of 'purchasing moral satisfaction' (Kahneman and Knetsch 1992). Brookshire's claim reduces to a criticism of an environmental ethic *per se*, rather than a fact about its implications. Either the concerns to preserve the environment for other humans, and for non-humans, can both be understood as welfare improving, or neither can be so understood. In both cases, it is plausible that the value placed on some environmental good may be attributed partly, but not exclusively, to welfare maximisation.

But this *possibility*, of support for the environment being essentially self-interested, improving the agent's welfare by giving them a 'warm glow' or preventing feelings of guilt, is not inevitable. The point is not that agents directly desire to reduce their own welfare, but that adherence to moral and other commitments will be an objective as well as welfare maximisation, and may conflict with it. The paradox underlying existence value can only be resolved by decoupling the two notions of value which are so commonly linked – welfare and utility; it is welfare gains, rather than nonuse values *per se*, which imply the presence of a use. Thus the defining characteristic of existence value becomes 'utility in the absence of welfare' or more strictly 'utility in the absence of well-being'. In short, Sen's (1977: 328) criticism that '[Commitment] drives a wedge between personal choice and personal welfare, and much of economic theory relies on the identity of the two' can certainly be applied to environmental value theory. 'One way to define commitment is in terms of a person choosing an act that he believes will yield a lower level of personal welfare to him than an alternative that is also available to him' (Sen 1977: 327). The welfare level is lower when compared to that obtained when the agent maximises welfare alone. The essential point is that choices driven by commitment will be utility-maximising but not welfare-maximising.

The claim that fully informed preference satisfaction implies welfare maximisation is an assumption labelled 'psychological egoism' by utilitarians, and precisely the identity which Sen disputes. Psychological egoism is the proposition that what an agent most wants, if he knows the facts and thinks clearly, is to do whatever would be best for him, or would best promote his long-term self-interest. Note that psychological egoism is sometimes defined crudely in terms of uninformed preferences ('an agent always acts in his own best interests') but, as Parfit (1984) has demonstrated, it becomes true by definition when so understood.[6] When defined in terms of informed preferences, psychological egoism has been almost entirely rejected by utilitarians. Parfit (1984: 129) concludes that it 'cannot survive a careful discussion'. Unfortunately this discussion inevitably requires a detailed examination of what is meant by an agent's well-being, or as Parfit puts it to avoid prejudicing the answer, 'what makes life go better'. A short answer therefore is not available; the discussion here will be limited to those conceptions of well-being which seem most likely to support the psychological egoism assumption. If psychological egoism cannot be defended in these circumstances, there is a good case for rejecting it altogether.

We should consider theories of well-being, or more precisely long-run self-interest (Parfit's theory S), which let the individual's well-being simply reflect his wants. The purest example of such a theory is the unrestricted desire fulfilment version of S. By this account of S, a person's self-interest is best served by what would most fulfil that person's desires throughout his life. Psychological egoism, on the other hand, claims that what would best fulfil my *present* desires, on due reflection (Parfit's 'deliberative present aim' theory: DP), is most in my self-interest, and this will imply different actions for many agents. If an agent follows unrestricted desire fulfilment, his present desire satisfaction is constrained by the requirement best to fulfil desires in the future too. Under DP, the agent's optimisation of present desires is not subject to such a constraint, leading to a different optimal path of acts whenever the agent's strongest desires vary over his lifetime. Parfit (1984: 127) further maintains that present desire fulfilment cannot subsume long-term self-interest, 'on any plausible theory of self-interest.' Simply defining S as equal to DP is unsatisfactory because, among other reasons, DP is not a 'plausible' theory of self-interest. Present desires need to be severely restricted, not just by future desires, but in more obvious senses if they are adequately to reflect individual self-interest or well-being.[7]

Parfit's 'success theory' version of S appears promising. It appeals 'only to our desires *about our own* lives' (emphasis added) (Parfit 1984: 494).

However, on this version, an agent's self-interest can be satisfied even after he is dead. Parfit gives an example where:

> all my children have wretched lives, because of the mistakes I made as their parent. Suppose that my children's lives go badly only after I am dead. My life turns out to have been a failure, in one of the ways I cared about most. A success theorist should claim that, here too, this makes it true that I had a worse life.
>
> (1984: 495)

Parfit is clearly right to argue that the desire to be a successful parent has not been fulfilled, regardless of whether the parent ever knew this, but it seems implausible to conclude that the parent had a worse life. There may be intelligible life after death for desires, but surely not well-being. The cause of the adverse effect on well-being does not prevail until after the agent's death, and it is unclear how the well-being of a dead individual can decrease. Parfit's claim that it can relates both to his distinctive conception of the nature of personhood and to the possibility of imperceptible harms and benefits, which cannot be discussed in the space available here.[8] However, the more conventional understanding of well-being does support a coherent notion of well-being improvement, readily distinguishable from desire fulfilment. It is this distinction that is so essential to the present discussion, made clear by requiring improvements in well-being to satisfy an introspection test. Preference-hedonism is the name given by Parfit to the success theory combined with the introspection requirement – that a feature of an outcome makes life go better or worse only if it is introspectively discernible. Consequences which prevail after an individual is dead are one category that is clearly not introspectively discernible.

In sum, the defeat of the psychological egoism assumption implies the logical possibility of non-self-interested, or altruistic, desires. The preference hedonism account offers a coherent distinction between self-interested and altruistic desires.[9] By that approach, the fulfilment of a self-interested desire must affect well-being in the sense of being introspectively discernible. Returning to terminological questions, since the definition of utility is so well established, it should be left undisturbed, and 'well-being' defined to be that which makes the agent better off, noting that an act which makes the agent better off is also by definition in the agent's self-interest.

For readers trained in philosophy, this section has undoubtedly laboured some simple points. However on a number of theories of well-being, these distinctions are quite subtle – and they appear to have been repeatedly overlooked by the dominant neo-classical model of decision-making in economics.

4. A DEFINITION OF EXISTENCE VALUE

In what sense, then, is existence value a unique and different economic value? The answer should by now be obvious, and therein lies a definition.

Existence value is problematic for environmental economics because it is assumed that all goods must bring a welfare gain to the agent – and it is only through a use that the welfare benefit can flow to the agent. Existence value seems to be a chimera if we are looking for welfare effects of the environmental good not related to use. For if an object has welfare benefits then the object has a use, since by definition the ability of an object to provide such benefits constitutes a use. Now because welfare benefits can only flow via a use, they are entirely captured by use value. Once the assumption that a good has value only insofar as it affects well-being has been abandoned, the role for existence value as non-welfare-improving value is clear.

The existence value of some environmental good is defined as the value assigned by the agent to the good in addition to any expected changes in the welfare of the agent contingent upon the good's continued existence. This formulation entails that welfare improvements are both a necessary and sufficient condition for positive use value.[10] More important, the welfare-improving independent variables found in a conventional utility function might be incommensurable with existence value since existence value is not measured in welfare units. This possible incommensurability is the essential rationale for continuing to treat existence value separately from welfare.

5. EXISTENCE VALUE AND SAGOFF

The approach taken here may appear to be simply a re-labelling of Sagoff's consumer/citizen dichotomy with other terminology:

> As a citizen, I am concerned with the public interest, rather than my own interest; with the good of the community rather than simply the well-being of my family . . . As a consumer . . . I concern myself with personal or self-regarding wants and interests . . . I look out for Number One.
>
> (Sagoff 1988b: 8)

Certainly my argument is consistent with that of Sagoff, and subsumes it by implying that agents can act as both citizens and consumers in valuing the environment, not just citizens as Sagoff alleges. Further, by tying the values of the agent as a citizen to existence value, precisely what aspects of any particular environmental good concern the individual as citizen is, I hope, made clearer. For plainly some aspects do not and Sagoff tends to ignore these. Crucially, Sagoff's justification for his dichotomy appears to rely on an appeal to intuition in a series of well-argued examples. However plausible, these do not demonstrate that the consumer/citizen, or altruistic/self-interested dichotomy is irreducible and cannot be compacted by, for instance, notions of enlightened self-interest.

The incorporation of the proposed measure of existence value in a utility

162

function does not imply such a reduction of the dichotomy to a conventional utility-maximising approach. To reiterate, utility is simply the cardinal representation of *ex post* (revealed) preferences. As has been emphasised above, in 'enlightened self-interest' explanations of altruism, the definition of utility will so often slide from the cardinal representation of preferences in one context, to a measure of individual welfare in another.

Margolis (1982), for example, posits two utilities for an agent, one from self-interested benefits, the other from public interest 'independent of any personal benefits arising'. So far this is consistent with my approach: utility equals cardinal preference representation and two independent preference orderings are implied. In Margolis, the two orderings are resolved to determine the agent's action by the familiar equalisation of marginal utilities. However, this only makes sense if the utilities are both cardinal and commensurable. Even then, although the maximisation exercise is now possible, it is not well motivated. At this stage, changing the definition of utility to mean individual welfare generates the requisite motivation for performing the maximisation. But the motive is strictly self-interested: thus Margolis ultimately fails to incorporate pure altruism (commitment) in the neo-classical model.

It may be better to describe the problem differently. Mainstream environmental economics may well accept the suggested form of the utility function but, crucially, assume that such a function exists *ex ante*. Incommensurabilities and other difficulties are resolved by the agent *ex ante*. Now with utility as the cardinal representation of preferences, utilities can of course be assigned and a function inferred *ex post*, but incommensurabilities may prevent it existing *ex ante*. In terms of the neo-classical choice model, the problem becomes one of establishing the axioms of completeness, transitivity, and continuity over an extended domain where variables representing the state of various environmental goods are elements in the vectors corresponding to the choice bundles.

6. VALUE PLURALISM, COMMENSURABLES AND SUBSTITUTES

The approach taken here, in acknowledging the presence of plural values, raises the possibility of ordinal incommensurability: it may be impossible to compare existence value and welfare against one another according to some common metric. If the alternative options facing the agent are incommensurable, then the agent will be unable to reach a rational decision, and any apparent decision will reflect, say, a desire to please the interviewer, rather than a meaningful ordering of the alternatives. Commensurability has been given diverse meanings and criticised on equally diverse grounds; it will be assumed to mean simply the possibility of ordinal comparison. Consider some good *X*. The following threefold categorisation will now be proposed:

1 *Y* is a *commensurable* for *X*, if and only if either *X* is more valuable than *Y* or *Y* is more valuable than *X* or they are of (roughly[11]) equal value.
2 *X'* is a *substitute* for *X*, if and only if *X'* evinces the same type of value as *X*, and to the same degree.
3 *X''* is a *replacement* for *X* if and only if *X''* is an identical token of value for all the values evinced by *X*. (Note that (3) implies (2): any replacement is necessarily a substitute.)

These distinctions are purposely vague in some respects. In particular, the source of the judgements of *X* over *Y* in (1), or 'to the same degree' in (2) is unspecified. Similarly for the 'relevant uses' of (3). Thus the categorisation is independent of how valuations are reached. In CVM – indeed in any environmental decision procedure grounded in individual choices – the source will be the valuer's preferences. The typology here may be contrasted with the notion of 'substitutes' in neo-classical economics, which appears to conflate all three categories above into one. This follows from value monism. Consider an example where *X* is ϵ, an environmental good, say an ancient woodland, which for simplicity is assumed not to improve the welfare of the valuer if preserved. It evinces existence value alone. Suppose an individual is asked to make a valuation of the woodland, and with some difficulty answers that he finds it is roughly as valuable as £*Y*. Such comparisons of an environmental good against money are unlikely to be easy, for they require two entirely different values, welfare and existence value, to be traded off against each other. Levi (1986) aptly calls them 'hard choices'.

Now clearly *Y* is a commensurable for ϵ here. However as conventionally understood in economics, it is also a substitute, because the agent is indifferent between ϵ and *Y*. Or in terms of (2), since there is only one value, welfare, both *Y* and ϵ must instantiate it and the willingness of the agent to exchange them is the sense in which they possess this value to the same degree. Moreover, since two goods matter to the agent only to the extent that they increase the agent's welfare, *Y* is identical to ϵ for 'all relevant uses' and is thus also a replacement for it.

The value duality defended here implies a different interpretation of the agent's valuation. Adopting the categorisation above, £*Y* is of course still commensurable with ϵ, but it is no longer a substitute. £*Y* yields welfare while ϵ evinces purely existence value. By (2), *Y* cannot be a substitute for ϵ.[12] From (3), it will not be a replacement either. This is made clearer by considering the forms of goods which *would* be substitutes or replacements for ϵ. If ϵ, an ancient woodland, is threatened, two substitutes are immediately obvious. One would be to regenerate (and subsequently preserve) another similarly old woodland which is currently in decline. Or ϵ' could be the preservation in perpetuity (through institutions such as trusts) of a similar old woodland which is currently unprotected and threatened with development. Both these options are potentially substitutes following (2) because they instantiate existence value, the same type of value as evinced by ϵ. Since ϵ has, by assumption, no use, definition (3) fails to define any replacements for ϵ. This is to be expected: the uniqueness of ϵ entails it is irreplaceable. Uniqueness here must not be misunderstood; trivially, a particular apple is unique but another apple of the same ripeness and variety will usually form a perfect replacement because it is an identical token of the sole value (value in consumption) of that apple. Considering the situation of a man whose (irreplaceable) wife has died, Griffin emphasises that the man could remarry, and 'It does not destroy grief that one can love again, or that the new love be as valuable as the old . . . The irreplaceability of individuals is not the incommensurability of values' (Griffin 1986: 338). Similarly the irreplaceability of an environmental good such as a unique ancient woodland does not entail the incommensurability of existence value against welfare, or indeed the absence of substitute goods evincing the same type of value as the woodland.

The proposed threefold distinction between commensurables, substitutes and replacements, although formally independent, only has substantive content when the irreducibility of existence value to welfare, and the uniqueness and indivisibility of environmental goods, is accepted. Given such status, it has significant implications. One puzzle illuminated is the often observed inequality between measures of willingness to pay and willingness to accept. The latter appears simply incoherent, since it implies the agent can receive money as proper 'compensation' for loss of existence value resulting from the destruction of some environmental good. A sum of money may be commensurable with the environmental good, but it cannot be a substitute for it, let alone a replacement as the language of 'compensation' implies. Money compensation is not merely inappropriate but unjustified. If the agent does not receive any welfare benefit from the preservation of the environmental good, there is, *ceteris paribus*, no welfare loss from its destruction for which he can be compensated. It is revealing to compare the meaning of a willingness-to-accept measure for an environmental good with that for some other project giving possibly no welfare benefit to the respondent, e.g. famine relief. For it is clearly meaningless in the latter case. If an agent is prepared to pay £100 in support of a famine relief project to save 100 people, this does not imply that £100, or even more, will compensate the individual for the absence of relief (Holland and Roxbee-Cox 1992). The individual does not need compensating; it is the famine victims whose welfare is affected by the absence of relief.

The famine example and the above discussion strongly suggests the appropriate form of compensation should be 'in kind': loss of existence value resulting from the destruction of an environmental good is properly balanced by attending to increases in existence value which might be had from sources elsewhere. Return to the agent who holds $£Y$ to be of roughly equal value to ϵ. Suppose the agent also agrees that ϵ' is a substitute for ϵ. The pertinent question becomes: will the agent be indifferent between ϵ' and Y? Surely ϵ' will be preferred to Y, even by the same agent. This is because the agent is much more certain that ϵ' is a substitute for ϵ than he is that Y is a commensurable – and knows he is.[13] Commensuration requires extremely difficult inter-value trade-offs, while the nature of the substitute must inevitably be well known to the agent, otherwise he would not know that it is a substitute. The statement that Y is of roughly equal value to ϵ expresses a relatively vague, generalised relationship between Y and ϵ – namely that neither is known to be preferable – while the statement that ϵ' is a substitute for ϵ appeals directly to a common property – the particular value which both goods instantiate – and is thus more confidently grounded. Uncertainty entails that judgements of commensuration should be regarded as conjectural judgements.[14]

Since the approach here claims ϵ' will be preferred to Y, ϵ' is rather more than just in-kind compensation, a non-monetary equivalent to Y, and represents what might be termed an in-kind valuation. The imputed value of ϵ entered into the CBA calculus for the purpose of informing a preservation decision becomes the cost of providing the substitute ϵ'. Space has allowed only the merest sketch of this radical approach to valuing, emphasising instead the necessity of a dual conception of value for any such departure.

7. IMPLICATIONS AND CONCLUSIONS

Existence value and hence total value does not measure how much better off the individual is made by the project or preservation under consideration, and certainly not the social welfare effects for society as a whole. Responses to CVM surveys must be understood for what they are: no more or less than subjective, conjectural, monetary valuations of the agent's current desires. As such they deserve much attention in the formation of policy, but alongside judgements concerning well-being and perhaps also non-utilitarian conceptions of value.

To want a species preserved on which one has placed existence value alone is to want what is not necessarily in one's self-interest. The welfare benefit to the agent from a species with existence value alone is zero, hence although by definition such a choice will be first in the agent's preference ordering, welfare maximisation is left undetermined. It may be unclear what theory of action drives existence value, if not self-interest. There are a number of possibilities consistent with the broadly utilitarian, or more strictly, consequentialist, approach underlying normative economics. One such theory is Parfit's (1984: 128) 'deliberative present aim theory' discussed earlier. This holds that the individual wants what would best fulfil her present desires if she 'had not been deceived and was thinking clearly' – or more realistically had undergone a process of 'cognitive psychotherapy' such as that proposed by Brandt (1979). Existence value then becomes a measure of the intensity of such desires, assuming the cardinality usually understood in WTP surveys. Norton (1986) defines 'weak anthropocentrism' as 'value influenced by both considered preferences and the consistency of such preferences with a rational world view'; this appears very close to the ideal preferences which would emerge from Brandt's cognitive psychotherapy. This possibility was raised merely to demonstrate that existence value does not demand a substantive 'objective' account of the goods in life in order to motivate action; further discussion of all possible theories is impossible here.[15]

An important advantage of the proposed approach to existence value is that it admits a structure of preferences which explains the refusal of many respondents to answer valuation questions which use WTA or WTP as a payment vehicle. Undoubtedly there exist moral commitments of the form which existence value as defined here seeks to capture. In a study of the importance of enhancing the survival possibilities for various wild species in New England, a majority of respondents (79 per cent) agreed with the statement that 'all species of wildlife have a right to live independent of any benefit or harm to people' (Stevens *et al.* 1991: 396). Equally certain is that these commitments will be associated with protest bids. Although 79 per cent of respondents in the Stevens study expressed an explicit commitment to preserving the species *per se*, the majority refused to pay when confronted with hypothetical valuation. Vadnjal and O'Connor (1994) provide further rich qualitative evidence in favour of this hypothesis. The close association of significant existence value, environmental moral commitments, and protest bids is empirically supported; this chapter has sought to explain the relationship.

A valuation process that allows for commitment can be sensitive to some of the valid philosophical objections to cost–benefit analysis made by Sagoff and others. As Sagoff (1988b) argues, the economist's conventional value neutrality is an illusion: it is neutral among preferences, but biased among theories of value, choosing welfare-maximisation as the ultimate good and preference satisfaction as the means of achieving it. The proposed understanding of existence value does not threaten value neutrality, and it strengthens preference neutrality because it does not reject certain preferences formed after due deliberation, such as those based on an environmental ethic, simply because they do not maximise an agent's welfare. It would be naïve to reject Turner's (1988a) conclusion that, 'On pragmatic grounds, arguments in favour of nonhuman individuals or collectivities, having interests and primary rights based on intrinsic value, are unlikely to make much headway in current policy-making circles.' However if this intrinsic value is recognised in the preferences of individuals, and hence in the existence value that they express, the practical problems are of the same kind as those involved in measuring most types of use value. Perhaps 'pragmatic' in Turner's statement ought best be interpreted to mean 'ideological'; in which case, those who wish policy to respond to some preferences but not others are at the very least obliged to defend such a distinction.[16]

NOTES

1 Throughout, 'use' will be assumed to include options to use. Economists have termed the value of having this opportunity 'option value'. Thus in what follows option value is always excluded from existence value.

2 While it is argued here that existence value may include intrinsic value, it is not claimed that they are equal. The set of entities possessing positive intrinsic value simply overlaps with the set possessing positive existence value. One reason for this has been pointed out by Brennan (1992: 19): 'To recognise [such] existence values we do not need to argue that rain forests have value in their own right. Rather, it may be that the existence of rain forests is instrumentally valuable, in that without them other things of value would be lost.' Here an instrumental value is included in existence value; the instrumental use of the rain forest is not captured by use value because its direct use is to *non-humans*. Use value reflects the preferences – and therefore uses – of humans alone. It is instructive to note that an object of instrumental value to non-humans would fall under class Γ in Hare's (1987) classification, providing non-humans have morally relevant interests. Hare invokes the 'Golden Rule' to suggest that all sentient creatures do; that approach is endorsed here.

3 Critics come from at least four different disciplines: Brennan 1992, Fischoff and Furby 1988, Rosenthal and Nelson 1992, Sagoff 1988a, 1988b.

4 But nowhere will any attempt be made to develop an approach devoid of utilitarian roots, such as a Rawlsian or rights-based analysis. This is simply because of the enormity of the challenge of relating a concept such as existence value, thoroughly grounded in (an arguably narrow) utilitarianism, to non-utilitarian ethics. The task attempted here is a much more limited one, working within a broadly consequentialist perspective. However no particular version of utilitarianism will be assumed.

5 Such an ethic is proposed in, among others, Attfield 1983, Callicott 1986, Hare 1987, Norton 1986, Regan 1981, Rolston 1988, and Singer 1979.

6 Psychological egoism defined over actual 'uninformed' preferences is the claim that, if some act would best fulfil someone's present desires, this act will inevitably maximise the agent's welfare, since present desire fulfilment is the definition of welfare maximisation. When psychological egoism is made true by definition, the independence of the concept 'self-interest' is sacrificed. It now means no more than uninformed present desire fulfilment. See next paragraph.

7 A full discussion would require several books. Edwards (1979), Gosling (1969), and Griffin (1986), have all influenced my approach.

8 Parfit (1984: 81) seems to argue for the possibility of imperceptible harms and benefits largely because of a wish to avoid a Sorites Paradox; this seems unsatisfactory but an inevitably technical discussion of that difficult paradox is far outside the scope of the present discussion.

9 I argue elsewhere (Aldred 1993) that altruistic motives are not merely a logical possibility but necessarily entailed by any account which seeks to reduce them to self-interest; relatedly preference hedonism has flaws which point to an Aristotelian 'objective list' approach. See O'Neill (1993).

10 This claim may appear to conflict with the idea that a good can have a use, in the strictly functional sense, without making the agent better off. Problems arise once the instrumental value of an object to sentient non-humans is morally considerable, as it is in Hare (1987), where it falls under class Γ. Such an object has a use (for instance the use of a wood to the animals living in it) but does not necessarily yield welfare benefits to humans. This leaves two possible conventions. Either these uses are held always to imply use value, corresponding to their instrumental value, or use value is held to cover only uses to humans. The latter convention, which reflects the understanding of use value in economics and permits a helpful distinction from instrumental value, is adopted here. Roxbee-Cox (this volume) adopts a radically different view and provides a much more detailed treatment of these questions.

11 X is roughly equal to Y if both X is not known to be worse than Y and Y is not known to be worse than X. Sen (1990) illustrates it using the problem of Buridan's Ass. It is applied to environmental valuing in Aldred (1994) but is a complication which can be ignored in what follows.

12 In this section money has been treated for simplicity as a source of welfare in exactly the same way that ϵ is a source of existence value. Of course the link is really more indirect with money, since it is not money itself which is the source of value but the goods which can be purchased with it. However this refinement does not recover a role for money as substitute for ϵ, because $£Y$ cannot buy substitutes for ϵ. True substitutes for ϵ (discussed below) are public goods and hence hardly ever available for purchase; when they are, their intrinsic indivisibility precludes their purchase by individuals. In short, if an agent receives $£y$ compensation, it will rarely be exchangeable for a substitute for ϵ, and only then in co-ordination with n other agents to pay $Y = f(n, y)$ to purchase the entire woodland. The essential point is that money can always 'buy' welfare but almost never buy existence value.

13 Assuming the agent prefers certainty. The irreversibility and enormity of environmental decisions provide grounding for this assumption, which is not that of risk-aversion (although it is consistent with it) because of the treatment of uncertainty; see next note 14.

14 Uncertainty refers to the Keynesian/Knightian distinction between risk and uncertainty, with probabilities being unknown or even unknowable. A somewhat weaker claim, but one which will suffice for the argument, is to invoke the ambiguity of probabilities in the sense used by Ellsberg in his famous paradox (Ellsberg 1961). Then the claim here is that the probability of a commensuration judgement being correct is ambiguous; a substitution judgement may be wrong, but its probability of correctness is assumed known. Thus substitution judgements are more certain than commensuration judgements not merely because they are more likely to be correct; the improvement is in the kind of certainty, not the degree.

15 See for instance Brandt (1979), Griffin (1986), Hardin (1988), or Parfit (1984).

16 In addition to members of the Environmental Economics group at Lancaster, I would like to acknowledge the helpful comments of Gay Meeks and Tim Swanson at Cambridge University.

11

ENVIRONMENTAL MANAGEMENT WITHOUT ENVIRONMENTAL VALUATION?

Clive Spash

1. INTRODUCTION: TWO MODELS OF ENVIRONMENTAL POLICY-MAKING

The concern underlying this paper is to identify principles for environmental policy and more specifically analyse the similarities and contrasts between environmental economics and a broader concept and discipline of environmental management. Advocates of environmental cost–benefit analysis (CBA) are often criticised as if they desired their approach to be used as a 'stand-alone' decision criterion, which would certainly be a blinkered way to proceed. Interestingly, however, the environmental economics literature generally focuses upon the selection of instruments that minimise the overall cost of achieving prescribed environmental objectives (Hahn 1989). This suggests an uneasiness within the economics profession over setting environmental objectives without regard to socio-political factors. Yet the rejection of a dominant role for environmental economics leaves unanswered the question of the extent to which the discipline should be allowed to operate within environmental decision-making, and whether the valuation methodology must be thrown out or merely constrained. In any case the likely alternatives require explicit attention.

The approach of mainstream or neo-classical economics to environmental policy formation can be compared with an alternative concept of environmental management derived from the natural sciences. The two approaches converge in the new field of ecological economics, but this fledgling discipline remains methodologically disunited. A conflict arises because economics is primarily concerned with trade-offs, while the natural science approach to environmental management has been concerned primarily with limits (e.g. sustainable fishing yields, carrying capacity, pollution thresholds). Although developments in environmental science are moving towards prediction of environmental change and scenario analysis, the core scientific approach referred to in this paper is still more common. A third approach to environmental management is the democratic political model,

170

where environmental targets are determined through public debate, i.e. targets set are social value judgements (see Jacobs 1991, Sagoff 1988b). Yet advocates of the political model often talk in terms such as 'natural capital' and 'carrying capacity' which implies targets are being scientifically derived. As Michael Jacobs discusses in this book, scientific sustainability and democratic choices can easily diverge. In this paper I largely ignore such issues and the political model (see instead Spash 1995).

Even for those who reject a role for environmental economics in the formation of environmental policy objectives there is still a requirement for cost effectiveness because resource wastage creates unnecessary pressure on other systems. This then raises the issue of how far there are substantive methodological differences between the alternative models of environmental policy-making. In the next section this issue is addressed with regard to the economic and scientific approaches, leading to concerns over the implications of cost effectiveness. Then, in order to provide a practical policy focus, two environmental problems are discussed: the enhanced greenhouse effect and land management for conservation and scientific ends. The argument put forward is that benefit estimation is unavoidable even in the standards-based, cost effective approach to environmental issues. Some suggestions for how environmental management might proceed are put forward although I hope this paper will act more as a basis for debate.

2. VALUE AND SCIENTISM IN ENVIRONMENTAL ECONOMICS

Many of the problems with environmental economics have arisen from an expectation that it can itself provide a scientific account of the 'true values' which environmental objects have for people. This expectation cannot in fact be met, nor can objective constraints on policy be established in this way.

Environmental economics has firm foundations in neo-classical economic theory. As a result the value as defined in economic studies and models is relative, i.e. an object is given value in relation to the scarcity of other objects. Value is described in terms of another object and becomes dependent upon the scarcity of natural resources; value is defined through a process of comparing objects via trade. The refined version of this theory leads through a market process to produce a market value of the traded item (the equilibrium price in supply and demand diagrams). An essential requirement of this explanation of value is the ability and willingness of parties involved in a trade to make comparisons and accept trade-offs, i.e. the loss of one thing or object in exchange for the gain of another. The theoretical outcome of free market trading is an optimal position in which all parties are better off and none worse off (Pareto optimality). This process of reasoning reflects the value of the environment by employing methods such as CBA, where trade-offs are explicitly considered in terms of the resource costs versus the benefits produced by changes in management.

Any wider concept of environmental management must share the concern of economics with providing incentives to achieve a given end, which in turn requires consideration of interactions between human social and economic systems in setting and achieving those ends. However, the foundations of what I refer to here as environmental management are in the natural sciences. Certain absolute values arise from adopting the core natural science methodology because this implies a search for 'the truth'. This may appear as a confusion of fact and value, but values are relevant for two reasons. First, the division between fact and value is blurred because a set of values determines the degree of belief in specific facts in an uncertain world. For example, an empirically testable hypothesis (at least theoretically) is the factual statement that 'the enhanced greenhouse effect will harm future generations', but the acceptance of the fact declines as attitudes move from environmental vanguard to technocentric optimists (Spash 1993). Idso (1984) has complained that scenario development with regard to the enhanced greenhouse effect has been influenced more by the psychological disposition of the protagonists than science, but given that humans are part of the process of scientific discovery the implied objectivity seems impossible. Some may prefer to regard allowing the psychology of the individual to influence 'facts' as unscientific, which still leaves open the methodology for the conduct of 'scientific' research. Second, the conception of facts as central to an issue can give a false sense of objectivity to decision-making where the 'facts' are taken to 'speak for themselves'. That is, amongst core natural scientists, there is a belief in an underlying objectivity which can be discovered and which should direct environmental management. Such a foundational truth may also imply social norms because if conditions are acknowledged, human behaviour can be changed to avoid passing thresholds. For example, Friends of the Earth Scotland (1995) has recently argued for the concept of 'environmental space' which calls for the definition of physical constraints required for the region to be sustainable (as measured by an input–output type of analysis) which then imply limits on individuals (e.g. per capita carbon dioxide emissions allowed).

Norgaard (1994: 66–7) critically explains such a core scientific approach as the acquisition of knowledge whereby individual minds investigate the parts and processes of nature, which he refers to as an atomistic-mechanistic view. This view is seen to be premissed upon unchanging parts and relations, allowing knowledge to be regarded as universal over space and time. Variations in natural and social systems are then regarded as due to differences in the proportions of parts and the strength of relations, rather than being an indication of fundamental differences. 'Thus, the idea of

172

underlying universal truths could be maintained across diverse environments and cultures' (Norgaard 1994: 67). This methodology leads in turn to the separation of facts from values and what is termed logical positivism (see Gordon 1991). While the logical positivist approach is flawed (e.g. in rejecting non-empirical knowledge) it still remains dominant in public beliefs and institutional structures. Thus the 'professional' natural scientist and neo-classical economist participate in public decision-making through this dominant belief pattern, which they then reinforce.

A powerful lobby amongst economists has for some time been eager to treat economics as methodologically scientific and has emphasised empiricism in order to confirm an objective reality, i.e. it has followed logical positivism (e.g. Hutchinson 1938). This view of economics as a science requires a belief in an objective truth and the ability of economists to reveal this truth. In the environmental economics literature this begins to appear in statements and approaches that suggest the 'correct' picture is being presented by the economic analysis. For example, the methodologically scientific idea that the values derived from preferences are universal, stable for an individual and therefore transferable has recently been expounded under the term 'benefit transfers'(see special issue of *Water Resources Research* 1992, volume 28 no. 3). Of course this also has the added advantage of reducing estimation cost (previous estimates of a similar environmental change can just be borrowed). The concept of truth can also be seen in the summing up of various categories of economic value (use, option, existence and bequest values) in the term 'total economic value' which implies that everything of importance is included in the concept (Pearce *et al.* 1989: 60). An application expressing the all-inclusive nature of economic value is presented by Boyce *et al.* (1992), who claim (as did Pearce *et al.*) that intrinsic value can be regarded as preference based and included in existence value. Boyce *et al.* undertake experimental research to validate empirically their hypothesis that intrinsic value can be measured in monetary units.

A danger arises in such extensions of objectivism to the idea of market values because those values begin to be regarded as absolute in the sense of the 'true value' of an object. For example, studies using the contingent valuation method may talk of trying to find the true value of an environmental commodity while the use of experimental economics tries to probe the 'true preferences' of individuals (e.g. Boyce *et al.* above). The true value here is regarded as the individual's preference-related willingness-to-pay or accept, and is seen to be 'untrue' when distorted by a lack of information, misinformation, free-riding, an unreal pseudo-market, disbelief in the trade-offs being required, property rights, perceived risks and so on. However, even accepting the existence of an underlying objective truth, the economist is handling a slippery fish.

An example of the difficulties faced by economists in searching for the underlying truth is the role of information. When providing information on a particular project in a contingent valuation study the formation of preferences as opposed to their being informed is unclear, especially when the object being valued is unfamiliar to the respondent, e.g. as in the case of biodiversity (Spash and Hanley 1995). The value given by a person's willingness to pay or willingness to accept compensation is highly contextual. Willis and Benson (1988) provide an example of testing for the role of information in a contingent valuation survey. They found the level of information (i.e. giving detail on ecological functioning) to be positively, but insignificantly, correlated to willingness to pay. They explain this result as follows (p. 258):

> Presumably an individual's bid will be affected by accurate information only if his perceptions concerning the site in relation to substitutes vary from reality. If, on the contrary, the individual's perceptions are correct, then no information bias will exist.

The terms 'reality' and 'correct' can be seen as indicative of belief in an objective truth and the extension of that objectivity to individual preferences and so by implication to the pseudo-market value.

Rejecting the ability of economics to discover the truth about environmental values from individual preferences can be compatible with maintaining a belief in the ability of natural sciences to find their own truth. Assuming some areas of study are 'hard' and factual, and that this applies to the natural sciences, will suffice. David Hume contended that demonstrating the truth of statements about moral or other value judgements is impossible. If this is correct, moral and other value judgements cannot be derived from empirical evidence. Thus scientists can be regarded as dealing solely with factual knowledge, so avoiding values; this is the appeal of the core natural science approach to environmental management. Of course an alternative would be to extend the criticism levelled at economics to all knowledge and reject any universal truths, but for present purposes I wish to focus upon the role of hard facts in the process of environmental management.

3. CONSTRAINTS ON POLICY: THE ROLE OF NATURAL SCIENCE

The extension or adoption of the scientific belief system by economics has led to the environment being treated atomistically and defined in terms of goods and services with an underlying value, which economists can discover. Rejecting this methodology for economics results in an appeal to constraints upon economic systems. For example, denying the ability of economists to value changes in the climatic controls of the earth suggests limiting the extent of human impact upon those controls. In this approach absolute constraints (e.g. thresholds) are found and imposed upon us by the operation of natural systems. This must deny the ability of humans to make trade-offs. Environmental management under the core scientific approach therefore regards the world as constituting systems which require analysis to find their operating conditions.

But the idea that these operating conditions are somehow 'naturally given' is a mistake. Allowing an area to be left to nature as a wilderness perhaps typifies the concern to ban human activity from spreading to every aspect of every ecosystem. This, however, raises the difficulty of defining a wilderness area. There can be few, if any, wilderness areas if this is defined in terms of an area being outside human influence. For example, the species roaming across the Scottish Highlands (e.g. red deer, sheep, goats) are the result of human actions, and the long-range transportation of air pollutants (e.g. acid deposition) has changed Scottish ecosystems in fundamental ways. Thus, to set up a wilderness area here requires human action to manage the environment towards some concept of an 'undisturbed' system, which seems counter-intuitive to the desired wilderness concept. In the United States large areas may be only distantly impacted by human action but decisions over the definition of wilderness still result in human action to try and influence the outcome, e.g. the controversy over the reintroduction of wolves in Yellowstone National Park. Thus the requirement for human action or inaction is a part of the process of even wilderness designation, and this implies a conception of objectives and environmental management. Correspondingly, socio-economic dimensions of the relevant constraints cannot be excluded.

As the range of intervention measures moves away from the wilderness area the role of management becomes less one of defining inaction and more one of deciding upon action. Protected areas and sites often require extensive management to avoid what is seen as undesirable change, e.g. invasion by non-native species. Recreation use of sites places the emphasis firmly on human management for human ends, but can be viewed in terms of multiple use management. The use of land for farming has also moved partially in the direction of multiple use and consideration of conservation (e.g., environmentally sensitive areas in the UK), although this conflicts with intensive chemical monoculture. At the opposite end of the spectrum from the wilderness area is the urban-industrial environment, where a human-designed and managed system is dominant. The role of human intervention and economics in the control of systems is readily accepted at this end of the spectrum. As we move from the wilderness concept to the built environment the objectives for management change from being natural-science-based to economic, from constraints to trade-offs.

The concern over the role of economics in environmental management can therefore be regarded as turning on the extent to which the systems are under human control. This might be viewed as the contrast between mankind as steward in command of nature versus mankind as a component of the environment with minimal control of the whole system. The implication is that 'mankind as a component' must have far greater concern for constraints which maintain the integrity of the system. The two issues here are (a) whether control can be achieved and (b) how control can be achieved? In the view of mankind as steward, and also in the economic model, the answer to the first question is assumed affirmative and attention is then focused entirely upon the second. Under the scientific environmental management approach the first question has no a priori answer.

Economics has conceptualised the control of systems as the achievement of a stable equilibrium, since Marshall's work became the dominant paradigm a hundred years ago. Uncertainty, ignorance, non-linearities and chaotic systems all argue away from this type of characterisation of the ability humans have to achieve systems control. Put simply, there may be aspects of the environment over which we have influence, but which we are unable to direct, or aspects that we are unaware we influence. The types of management and decision processes required under these circumstances are diametrically different from those under complete information and stable, resilient equilibrating systems.

The ability to control environmental systems will depend upon their characteristics. Following Lange (1970) the control of systems can be regarded as falling into seven aspects: speed, precision, reliability, stability, sensitivity, cost efficiency, and control range. Speed refers to how quickly disturbances can be eliminated so as to maintain equilibrium, although moving too fast can create stress. Precision is the ability of the manager to achieve a desired output pattern. Reliability describes the conditions under which management systems succeed or fail. Stability involves the conditions under which the manager will dampen or magnify a disturbance. Sensitivity is the response to a small deviation in control mechanisms. Cost efficiency is the ability to maintain control systems within a set cost boundary. Related to this is the range of disturbances – the control range – under which cost efficiency can be maintained.

There are two aspects to the consideration of cost efficiency here. 'Cost' refers to the cost of a particular control system, which is the concern when cost effectiveness is at issue. However, 'cost' also refers to the damages due to deviations from the target of control. Both these cost categories require valuation and therefore assessment of environmental impacts. In the former case there is a tendency to believe that the costs of a particular control system are easier to calculate, perhaps because they are regarded more as market-orientated values. Yet the definition of economic costs is wide and includes all externalities and opportunity costs (e.g. pollution associated with the systems). The range of damage costs is more obviously all-encompassing and therefore more clearly seen to raise the problematic issues surrounding the use of CBA in the assessment of non-market values.

In fact the problems commonly associated with benefit estimation pervade both cost categories, contradicting the view that the former are less controversial and more 'objective'.

In the next two sections these points are developed further and the extent to which environmental valuation pervades a wider concept of environmental management is explored. This is achieved by considering two case-studies to provide a policy focus for the problems environmental decision-making faces. One case-study is chosen at the global level: the enhanced greenhouse effect, and one at the regional or local level: land use planning for conservation.

4. GLOBAL ENVIRONMENTAL POLICY: THE ENHANCED GREENHOUSE EFFECT

In discussions of appropriate policy in the face of human ability to change climatic conditions all the most difficult issues of management arise: complexity, uncertainty, and disparate spatial and temporal impacts. The issue is complex, with numerous significant linkages across other systems, and is compounded by the global scale; thus the standard approach of simplifying assumptions such as *ceteris paribus* become unacceptable if our models are to be meaningful. A related problem is the uncertainty arising from human actions both in influencing climatic systems and in the results of changing climatic systems. Complexity and uncertainty are regarded as scientific while a somewhat neglected aspect of greenhouse gas control, but one which is central to the expression of concern, is the status given to future generations and geographically distant peoples in the policy decision. In order to tackle the policy question of what action to take, all these aspects of the problem must be considered; strict adherence to the environmental economic approach can be contrasted with environmental management.

Under environmental economics all pollution problems are in general simplified to the determination and achievement of the optimal level of pollution reduction. The appropriate question society must ask is, How much is society prepared and willing to pay for greenhouse gas reduction? The contentious issue becomes the size of the welfare benefits to humans from those reductions. In this approach to controlling greenhouse gases, environmental economics employs the techniques of CBA; some examples are Cline (1992), Fankhauser (1995) and Nordhaus (1991). An explicit recognition of the trade-offs required when making pollution control decisions is central to the methodology. The costs of control in the case of the enhanced greenhouse effect will relate to control of the source emissions (e.g. chloroflurocarbon production) and the expansion of sinks for greenhouse gases, such as forests, to absorb carbon dioxide. On the other side the benefits of control are the avoided damages which, at least in theory, are to be measured in marginal units, i.e. the effect of an increment in a gas in terms of the damages caused. Thus, in principle, the analyst would need to know, for example, the extent to which the release of one more tonne of carbon dioxide might lead to increased sea level rise and so flooding in Bangladesh resulting in the cost of relocating people, and simultaneously drought and starvation elsewhere. Even this is a gross simplification of the problem because there are many gases contributing to climate change, raising issues of synergism, and there are globally diverse impacts occurring simultaneously. Yet, this consequentialist approach requires that scenarios are made explicit.

An obvious difficulty with the consequentialist approach combined with marginal analysis is in establishing such refined cause–effect relationships; this is compounded by the time and scale of impacts. In addition, the treatment of potential loss of life and species raises contentious aspects of monetary valuation. The uncertainty surrounding future events might be reduced to the estimation of risk but this neglects the wider nature of our missing knowledge about future states of the world and about the dangers of the enhanced greenhouse effect. There is also the question of whether future damages should count in the utilitarian calculus as much as present damages. These are just some of the issues confounding the assessment of the benefits of greenhouse gas control (for others see Ayres and Walters 1991, Daily *et al.* 1991, Spash 1994a, 1994b).

An alternative approach is to try and avoid the explicit detailed analysis of the benefits and instead concentrate upon the costs. Thus, an environmental management approach would determine the capacity of systems to assimilate greenhouse gases by looking at the relationship between sources and sinks. This information would be used to estimate the thresholds beyond which systems become stressed and how that stress might materialise. As in environmental economics, this approach is fundamentally consequentialist, but here marginal analysis is avoided and, at least in theory, value judgements are excluded. The contentious issue then becomes the cost incurred in controlling to those thresholds.

Environmental management is therefore characterised here as being in favour of cost effectiveness, i.e. cost-effective control of source and sink functions. This preference reflects the belief that estimation of monetary benefits is susceptible to manipulation and makes unacceptable ethical assumptions, but scientists can present decision makers with 'facts' leaving control debates to the political process (see, for example, Sagoff 1988b). Greenhouse gas control will then be decided by negotiations between power groups within society. However, the extent to which this political decision-making process can free itself from the problems which confronted the environmental cost–benefit approach is unclear.

Let us assume some percentage reduction in carbon dioxide is scientifically or politically agreed upon, say of 30 per cent. The next step would be to employ environmental economics to determine the cost-effective control method, i.e. how control should be achieved. One option is to control source emissions, but this will affect the value of products associated with greenhouse gases. The emissions prior to control are a by-product of processes with outputs of importance to humans. For example, carbon dioxide is emitted during fossil fuel combustion, which occurs in the production of plastics and transportation services. The control of carbon dioxide relates to these uses. The cost of the control process requires assessment of the welfare impacts associated with these products, and that means monetary valuation of products to see how control affects social costs. A 30 per cent reduction in carbon dioxide might require large taxes on petrol to reduce car use, which is associated with many negative externalities such as tropospheric ozone; the reduction of these externalities must be accounted for as a reduction in control costs, i.e. a benefit of the control decision. In this way the benefits associated with tropospheric ozone control become part of the cost effective calculus. Alternatively, control might require the reduction of methane, one of the sources of which is wetlands. If wetlands are 'managed' to reduce methane emissions this carries with it impacts upon related goods and services; the 'products' of interest to humans in this case include recreation, wildlife conservation and biodiversity. These 'products' are of the same type as the class of environmental benefits which cost effectiveness is apparently supposed to avoid putting into monetary terms, because management here requires a political decision based upon scientific 'fact'.

Similarly, if control is to involve the expansion of sinks their valuation will become part of the cost effectiveness procedure. The value of sinks, in the utilitarian framework, again relates to the impact upon human use. For example, increasing the area of forest plantations to help carbon dioxide absorption will be associated with choices affecting tree species, which can conflict with or benefit recreation, timber production, and biodiversity. The costs of control relate to the value of these uses. The creation of beneficial side-effects lowers control costs but requires exactly the same benefit estimation as was necessary under the cost–benefit approach.

Thus, cost-effective greenhouse gas control requires estimating the extent to which sources or sinks are to be managed. So, for the 30 per cent reduction in carbon dioxide to be achieved efficiently, society needs to know how far to increase forestry versus reducing fossil fuel use. Part of the information requirement will be for the value of forest recreation to be compared with the value of fossil fuel use in transportation. Similarly, when considering cost-efficient responses to sea-level rise the options include migration and sea defences. Costs of the options include cultural, aesthetic and environmental values of the sort environmentalists are loath to see portrayed as purely monetary. The cost of reducing carbon dioxide by one tonne will be measured in part by the welfare losses and gains in related activities. There is then no distinction between cost effectiveness analysis and CBA in terms of the methodological criticisms of monetary benefit estimation. In fact, cost effectiveness is properly regarded as a restricted or constrained CBA.

5. LOCAL ENVIRONMENTAL POLICY: LAND USE

At the opposite extreme to proposals addressing the enhanced greenhouse effect is the set of decisions made by national and regional government agencies about the economic development of land. The recognition that development must be restrained if conservation of ecosystems and species is to be achieved has led to various approaches in different countries. In this section the experience of Great Britain is briefly discussed with respect to the class of land designated as Sites of Special Scientific Interest (SSSIs); in 1991 there were 5,671 such sites, covering 1,778,474 hectares. Threats to sites of high conservation value in Great Britain arise from urban and industrial development where planning legislation is relevant (except for statutory undertakers such as the military), and from rural development that bypasses planning requirements. Concern has arisen over such development because of the cost of preventing a class of actions by landowners which are officially designated as potentially damaging operations (Spash and Simpson 1993, 1994).

Potentially damaging operations are allowed in the majority of cases with only slight modification. This might be regarded as a violation of the designation of land as protected for environmental reasons but the need to cooperate with the landowners is seen as essential. More seriously damaging actions can be delayed in order to try and negotiate a management agreement, with side-payments for potential loss of development benefits; or the conservation agency concerned could make a compulsory purchase, but rarely has done (two cases in ten years). The management agreement requires the definition of objectives for conservation, and the imposition of restrictions.

SSSIs are selected and designated on scientific grounds as a representative stock, which is to be protected absolutely. This reflects the more general criteria of ecological designation for protected areas on the basis of rarity and representativeness (Smith and Theberge 1986). In theory the agency has no choice but to recognise all sites that pass the scientific criteria by which sites are evaluated as being SSSIs. The stock is then seen as a safe minimum standard, a threshold beyond which development must be prevented from venturing. Thus the agency responsible (until 1991) for this designation process could state its belief that the current level of notification and designation and the protection of individual sites should be seen as a minimum environmental safety standard for nature conservation, and therefore any damaging operations would take society below that minimum standard (Nature Conservancy Council 1990, section 4.17). Furthermore the agency stated (section 4.40):

> Many sites, notified as SSSIs or not, such as ancient woodland or ancient meadows, are considered to be irreplaceable and incapable of re-creation in any meaningful way. In such cases the site should act as a constraint on a project development at any cost.

A similar position of absolute constraints has been argued for by English Nature (1992, 1994) and the Council for the Protection of Rural England (Jacobs 1993) with regard to a range of environmental assets and their features.

However, the process of negotiating with landowners places the conservation agency in an awkward position, when supposed environmental management objectives have to be weighed against monetary resources, given the agency's budget constraints. In practice the agency was, and its descendants are, forced to trade the protection of various aspects of the environment, so reducing the minimum stock. The existence of flora and fauna is far from being regarded as an absolute constraint, to be maintained whatever benefits might be gained from developing the ecosystems they depend on. If there were such a constraint, there would be no potentially damaging operations and management agreements would be for increasing conservation values rather than preventing destructive actions.

The decision process can be thought of in the following general terms (see Spash and Simpson 1993, 1994). The agency may have a preference for, say, biodiversity and uniqueness which allows it to rank all sites according to conservation value. Thus, deciding what is an SSSI requires some decision criterion, but this is seen as scientific rather than economic, i.e. the efficiency goal is of little or no relevance. However, the decision is being forced into an economic framework because of the need to maximise conservation value subject to a budget constraint. That is, the agency has a limited amount of resources to use for the protection and maintenance of SSSIs; internally the agency has other goals and externally it must compete with other government departments. Thus, when faced with, say, the option of designating a new site versus improving the integrity of old ones the cost will become an integral part of the decision. The opportunity cost to landowners of lost development will then require actual compensation to be paid for lost production (note how this contrasts with the Hicks-Kaldor criterion, which only requires potential compensation and assumes redistributive payments would be made on other grounds, such as distributive justice). The landowner is in a strong position if the land can be withheld, potentially damaging operations threatened or the potential loss of earnings exaggerated (i.e. an asymmetry of information exists). Thus the agency is now confronted by the landowner's ability to extract rent and must spread its limited budget in a fundamentally utilitarian fashion. That is, scientists, or other experts in the conservation agency, are forced to form consequentialist preferences over sites so as to decide where the funds go.

6. ENVIRONMENT AND HUMAN CONTROL: LEARNING LESSONS

There are several conclusions to be drawn from the brief look at the two case-studies. Environmental economics is often regarded as unacceptable because of the way it seems to suggest that the optimal control of pollution can be determined via an environmental CBA. Environmental CBA is then contrasted with the cost-effectiveness approach, which is more acceptable because of the presumption that difficulties raised by benefit assessment can be avoided, and optimality is a theoretical irrelevance. However, cost effectiveness still requires benefit assessment, although the range may be restricted by the fact that one level of the decision process has already been undertaken. That is, the extent of control is decided and then the appropriate type of control is assessed. While optimisation is indeed normally practically unhelpful and misleadingly objective, determination of the extent of control is still fraught with difficulty in terms of scientific assessment, uncertainty, complexity and in the construction of an acceptable political process.

Craig *et al.* (1993) and Spash and Simpson (1993) both show how intrinsic value principles may be at the heart of environmental legislation, but the application of policy demonstrates a utilitarian or more generally consequentialist philosophy. The link of intrinsic value principles with scientific objectivism is an interesting possible explanation for the motivation behind supposedly 'fact'-based decisions, e.g. designation of protected areas. However, conservation agencies constrained by financial budgets must choose between preservation options. As a result planning proposals are approved which indicate the trade-off between preservation and development; examples include the Cardiff Bay barrage (Hanley *et al.* 1991), Gwenlais Valley SSSI (Dunn 1994) and peat extraction on Thorne Moors SSSI (Pearce 1992).

The economic argument implies that there is an opportunity cost to any action and this is the relevant value upon which to concentrate when making decisions. That is, if the loss of material wealth is accepted this is the trade-off made and it reflects the preferences of those involved. Unfortunately, at the extreme where individuals express what can only be described as infinite values, the language of trade-offs becomes meaningless. At this point reflection turns to other ways of describing human preferences, and concerns for justice, rights, compassion and freedoms are more easily understood expressions of what the economic model refers to as infinite valuations, and tends to regard as 'irrational' anomalies.

Environmental management appeals to constraints which seem to imply non-utilitarian values or at least goals outside of efficiency. If the constraints are a refusal to make trade-offs between, say, more material wealth and lower environmental quality then the underlying preference function can be described as lexicographic (see Spash and Hanley 1995). Under these circumstances compensation has no role to play because no amount of material wealth can compensate for the loss of environmental quality. The focus is then upon limiting activities which reduce environmental quality to the extent that they no longer occur.

Now, given this underlying concern for how the economic methodology approaches environmental valuation, cost effectiveness can be seen more clearly as only a constrained CBA. The appeal to trade-offs is an essential part of cost effectiveness and thus is accepted in the characterisation of environmental management as described in this paper. Furthermore, the appeal to facts based upon empiricism creates a false sense of freedom from moral and other value judgements. The overall requirement is for a political consensus upon environmental action, and this requires being fully aware of the political economy of decision-making. Scientific facts may help create a consensus more easily in the unmanaged environment such as wilderness areas, but still imply constraints upon action and value judgements. Economic values may lead to a consensus more easily in the human-built environment but still are bound within the constraints of a physical environment and a limited perspective given by the dominant paradigm's consequentialist philosophy.

In the exploration of where environmental economics fits into the overall management picture a key issue is the extent of human control over environmental systems. Mankind is seen as dominant over natural systems so that individual preferences are central to how economic decisions are made. These economic decisions feed into natural systems and influence their direction. The extent to which the flow of influence is two-way determines how far humans are seen to be in control of their own destiny. This underlies the old characterisation of policy positions with regard to the environment ranging from pessimist to optimist, as found in Lecomber (1979) for example. The view of environmentalists as pessimistic 'eco-doomsters' expresses a belief in the dominance of nature over humanity, and is clearly seen via negative feedbacks in Meadows *et al.* (1972, 1992). Technocentric optimists see man as supplanting the role formerly held by God and so placing himself in control of nature. A newer interpretation of the human condition is to avoid both extremes and see the interrelationship of humanity and environment. For example, Norgaard (1994) has argued in favour of coevolutionary development, which implies an indeterminate circularity of cause and effect.

The current movement away from the optimist/pessimist dichotomy implies some acceptance of this middle path. Thus environmental management can be taken as humans managing to survive within an environmental system of which they are an integral part. This 'management' can reject the technocentric view of survival 'without' nature, and the ecocentric view of survival 'without' human influence of nature. If environmental management is characterised in this manner the policy decisions required today appear to be unable to free themselves from environmental economics, even if, as some chapters in this book argue, the idea seems good. However, the economic paradigm required is fundamentally different from neo-classical optimisation of resilient, equilibrating systems and its characterisation of the 'rational' individual in an exclusively utilitarian world.

7. CONCLUSION: TOWARDS A MORE UNIFIED METHODOLOGY

The issues which come to the fore in discussing the role of economics in environmental management include the level and types of decisions which are regarded as within its province. The extent to which economics should play a role in environmental decision-making is undetermined. Effectively the argument is over the extent to which scientific and political constraints should operate over the goal of efficiency rather than the rejection of environmental economics for an alternative methodology. Those preferring the cost-effective approach emphasise a greater reliance on non-efficiency criteria but must realise this still means accepting a role for environmental valuation and the need to tackle the problems it poses. Cost effectiveness as a limited CBA uses all the same tools and suffers the same problems. Thus environmental management, by requiring cost effectiveness, accepts the valuation methodology of environmental economics. In addition, the enforcement of constraints implies opportunity costs due to the boundaries they create and must therefore face the economic and political consequences they imply.

However, the acceptance of the need for constraints requires a process whereby those constraints are determined and enforced. As shown in the land use section of this paper, actual compensation is in practice required to create and maintain a consensus for action, especially where cooperation is essential to successful environmental management. Determination of constraints as discussed in this paper can be viewed as scientifically based so as to control economic processes. However, the appeal to scientific facts to set the constraints is naïve in its belief that, in choices, fact and values are so easily separated. Similarly, the appeal to optimal economic solutions is misleading because these are unachievable neo-classical ideals giving a false sense of scientific objectivity. The recognition of human inability to control environmental systems and the subjectivity of 'factual' constraints implies a new methodology which emphasises choice of a path leading to potential scenarios rather than the selection of a specific equilibrium solution. A wider concept of environmental management requires disciplines which attempt to unify scientists and economists while acting through institutions which recognise the role of both in creating a consensus in developing dynamic approaches to environmental policy.[1]

NOTE

1 I am grateful to the participants at several meetings held at Lancaster University, organised by CSEC, where many ideas were discussed. I am particularly grateful to Michael Jacobs, Nick Hanley and Ian Simpson for comments on an early draft.

12

MULTI-CRITERIA MAPPING

Mitigating the problems of environmental valuation?

Andrew Stirling

1. ENVIRONMENTAL ECONOMICS IN A MARKET OF METHODS

In the early 1960s, the operations research and systems theorist C.W. Churchman lamented that 'probably the most startling feature of twentieth century culture is the fact that we have developed such elaborate ways of doing things and at the same time have developed no way of justifying any of the things we do' (Churchman 1961, cited in Shelley and Bryan 1964b: 8). Such are the rewards for finding a widely acceptable solution to this apparently modest requirement for justification, that it has exercised a dominating influence over many different disciplines, and spawned innumerable academic specialisms of its own. Technology assessment, decision analysis, policy analysis, systems analysis, operations research, life cycle analysis, multi-attribute utility theory, environmental impact assessment, comparative risk assessment, Bayesian statistics, portfolio theory, as well as the various forms of cost–benefit and cost-effectiveness analysis have all at different times (either individually or in combination) been proposed as aids to policy-making.[1] All offer a host of heuristic techniques and other methods for the assessment of past decisions. All prescribe normative approaches to investment, technology and policy appraisal.

Collectively, such techniques amount to what David Collingridge called 'justificationist' approaches to decision-making (1982). They are used to justify specific favoured strategies, policies or investment choices. In their more humble incarnations, such techniques are proposed as a complement to, rather than as a replacement for, political decision-making. However, in the terms set out by the historian of science, Thomas Kuhn, all such approaches have in common the ambition of turning large areas of policy-making into a 'normal science', where efforts at justification are subordinated to the institutional disciplines of a single paradigm (1970). In

186

other words, they seek to convert parts of fuzzy and controversial political *problems* into relatively tractable technical *puzzles.*

Irrespective of its particular analytical merits or shortcomings, any programmatic procedure which offers to simplify and discipline intractable and unruly political debate, or which provides a way of justifying past actions, will display pragmatic attractions to beleaguered decision makers. Accordingly, many of these techniques present lucrative opportunities for consultancy work, compelling justifications for research grants and attractive career options in themselves. As a consequence, there has been a tendency for the established 'market pull' of political demand to be augmented by a 'supply-push' effect arising from the institutional momentum acquired within the various specialisms.[2] As a result, though the particular techniques employed may vary over time and over different areas of policy, very little decision-making in fields concerned with the environment or with technology choice remains unaccompanied by elaborate attempts at justification through analysis.

Though it currently appears to be in the ascendant in several areas of analysis for policy-making,[3] neo-classical environmental economics is just one of many aspiring colonists of this tantalising but hazardous intellectual territory. Of course, as with each of its competitors, it presents a series of more or less specific idiosyncrasies and defects. Much criticism centres on the validity and acceptability of the fundamental philosophical and ethical underpinnings of environmental valuation in what has been dubbed the 'dubious theology' of neo-classical orthodoxy (Brown 1984).[4] On a more prosaic level, reviews of the published valuation literature in particular policy areas reveal enormous discrepancies between the results obtained by different valuation studies, thus seriously undermining the confidence that might be placed in any individual study (Stirling 1992). A further practical difficulty lies in what might be termed the price imperative: if environmental valuation is intended as a direct basis for policy intervention under a strict Pigovian tax rule, then, in order to be of any efficacy in practical policy-making, the results obtained must lie within a narrow region determined by prevailing market prices.[5]

A somewhat more generalised but no less recalcitrant series of problems are shared between neo-classical environmental economics and several of the other quantitative approaches.[6] Where attempts are made systematically to aggregate or compare the performance of different technological or policy options across a range of criteria (as is the case, for instance, in comparative risk assessment), a number of serious difficulties are invoked. First, how completely does the chosen set of yardsticks capture the full scope of the problem in all its many forms? Second, where some degree of circumscription is accepted on practical grounds, how consistent are the conventional boundaries of analysis adopted between studies and across the many disciplines involved? Third, how are we to deal with ignorance concerning the possibility of hitherto unforeseen effects or of synergistic interactions or non-linearities amongst those performance criteria that are thought to be well known?[7] Fourth, of course, there are the profound difficulties incurred in the prioritisation and reduction to a single metric of indices applied across a disparate range of incommensurable criteria (O'Neill 1993, Vatn and Bromley 1994).

A further series of even more fundamental problems is shared with an even wider range of techniques (such as environmental impact assessment) which seek simply to assess performance under an individual criterion, or under a disaggregated set of criteria. First, there are straightforward difficulties of resolution.[8] To what extent may even the most appropriate and finely specified index be seen to capture the full character of even a single, narrowly-defined environmental effect? Where comparisons are made across differing circumstances, there are difficulties with the fidelity of the chosen index. How well do the successive numerical measurement increments track what may often be discontinuous, irregular and even non-monotonic relationships between the precursors and manifestations of harm?[9] Attempts are often made to articulate measurements of overlapping or interdependent effects, or to combine approaches to different stages in the causal chain from emissions through ambient burdens to the magnitudes of final manifestations of harm. Here, we introduce difficulties with the coherence of the different methods and categories of effect.[10] How well do the pieces of the classificatory jigsaw fit together?

Simply in and of themselves, these various methodological problems constitute grounds for serious reservations about the analytical validity and policy utility of environmental valuation and other quantitative justificationist techniques. However, in seeking to develop an approach to the social appraisal of environmental performance which avoids or mitigates the deficiencies of environmental valuation, these particular difficulties are only the tip of the iceberg. Before exploring one possible means to deal with these problems, this chapter will take one or two steps back, and approach neo-classical environmental economics in a broader context, subsuming all justificationist approaches to social appraisal. Only by addressing the more general and fundamental issues raised in this wider field, may we hope satisfactorily to resolve the specific difficulties of environmental valuation.

2. THE QUEST FOR 'RATIONALITY' IN POLICY MAKING

Advocacy of 'rationality' in policy appraisal and decision-making is predicated on the possibility of demonstrating in a fashion which is beyond credible dispute that certain options are in some objective sense preferable to others. In order for their results to be credible, the various justificationist approaches tend tacitly to require assumptions that decision makers are capable of knowing in advance all relevant details and their respective degrees of importance.[11] They require an assumption that there exists a single definitive set of considerations that may be seen to have a bearing on any individual decision. This is accompanied by an (often tacit) understanding that there can be only one rational chain of inference from any single set of propositions. Where decisions are presented as reflecting democratically established principles and priorities, there is the implication that it is possible to reconcile and integrate diverse perspectives into a single coherent structure of social preferences. Finally, they require subscription to a deterministic conception of Nature and Society, such that the consequences of any action are held in principle to be predictable, given sufficient information concerning initial conditions. It is difficult to reconcile the widespread influence of justificationist approaches with the increasing recognition that each of these underlying foundations is seriously flawed.

First, we do not know the future. Prediction is a notoriously error-prone activity. Investments in large-scale plant, shifts in long-term technological strategies or the implementation of national policy programmes are all effectively unique events. They relate to conditions which are neither directly nor completely comparable with any that have gone before. Here, the well-rehearsed problem of *risk* is replaced by the far less tractable conditions of *uncertainty*[12] and *ignorance*.[13] Under these more formidable circumstances, orthodox probabilistic approaches amount to little more than the codified assertion of specialist opinions. They in no sense mitigate the essential subjectivity and unreliability of forecasting. Indeed, under the condition of ignorance we not only have no firm or credible basis for the assignment of probabilities, but no means even to identify a discrete set of possible outcomes, or permutations of outcomes. Even without attempts to derive the relative likelihoods of different possible eventualities, then, it is a heroic decision maker indeed who claims to have 'thought of everything' in identifying the possible eventualities themselves. In this light, by treating ignorance and uncertainty as if they were mere risk, well established techniques such as those provided by probability theory, are doubly deficient.[14]

Second, there is the question of the intrinsic comprehensibility of natural and social phenomena. By what causal links will different eventualities lead to different outcomes? The mechanistic worldview exported to other disciplines from classical physics over the past few centuries is now widely reported to be in retreat (e.g. Hofstadter 1979, Penrose 1989, Ruelle 1991, Woodcock and Davis 1978). Neo-classical economics seems to be particularly uncomfortably exposed to the demise of overly simplistic determinism (Faber and Proops 1994, Ormerod 1994). Indeed, such perspectives are being replaced in many areas with an understanding that, no matter how well understood they may be in principle, both natural and social processes are often highly sensitive to minute variations in initial conditions, non-linear in their dynamics or otherwise indeterminate.[15] The condition of ignorance is thus compounded. Not only are decision makers unable to compile a definitive list of all relevant considerations, they are also unable exhaustively to gather all the pertinent information relating to any individual consideration. This has important implications not only for the understanding of social and economic contexts, but also for technical understanding of engineered systems and their physical operating environments.

Third, it is well established both in social anthropology (Evans-Pritchard 1937, Hollis 1970, Wilson 1970) and the sociology and philosophy of science (Barnes and Bloor 1982, Bloor 1976 and 1983, Feyerabend 1975 and 1978) that, even if all considerations are known and agreed, it is manifestly possible to pursue alternative and equally rational chains of reasoning from a single set of propositions. For instance, in policy analysis a distinction is often drawn between the framework for the rationality of an individual decision maker and that of an organisation (Hogwood and Gunn 1984). Conversely, the history of science shows that it is equally possible for highly divergent modes of reasoning to converge at an effectively identical conclusion (Barnes and Shapin 1979). There thus seems no prior reason to believe that there can only ever be one 'rational' response, even where information and assumptions are held in common.

Finally, and perhaps of greatest importance in the highly politicised arena of environmental decision-making, there is the problem of reconciling the many disparate perspectives held by different constituencies throughout society. It was shown decades ago in formal mathematical terms by the economist Kenneth Arrow that it is impossible both democratically and consistently to aggregate individual preferences in a plural society (Arrow 1963). The derivation of any single social preference ordering (or aggregate social welfare function) will violate at least one of a minimal set of conditions. In formulating these conditions, Arrow applied the principle that social choice should display the same properties that neo-classicists routinely ascribe to individual choice. It is interesting that a condition imposing equity of weighting to the preferences of all individuals is absent from Arrow's list. Despite this, however, Arrow showed that it is *impossible* simultaneously to satisfy even this more permissive set of five conditions (see Pearce and Nash 1981). No matter how much information is available, and no matter how much consultation and consideration are involved, no purely analytical procedure can fulfil the role of a democratic political process. In other words, there is no uniquely 'rational' way to resolve contradictory perspectives, divergent values or conflicts of interest.

3. BEYOND THE 'ANALYTICAL FIX'

What is true in the macrocosm of social choice, is equally true in the microcosm of environmental appraisal. How then, may we go about seeking to improve the social appraisal of environmental effects? How might we go about accommodating the wide variability in perspectives adopted by different constituencies in a plural society? How might we hope to make the 'best' environmental policy choices (or even conceive of them) under these circumstances?

These are very large and complex questions to which there can certainly be no single complete prescriptive answer. However, it is possible to abstract a series of general features of the problem:[16]

1. Environmental policy choices are *path-dependent*. There exist many different possible channels of development, each one characterised by a different state of 'equilibrium' and its own internal logic, integrity and wider technological and environmental implications (cf. Arthur 1989, Cowan 1991, David 1985).

2. Environmental policy choices are *multi-dimensional* qualitative problems. The performance of the different options under appraisal is manifest across a wide range of mutually incommensurable (and often unquantifiable) appraisal criteria.

3. Environmental policy choices are *perspective-dependent*. The many different constituencies in a plural society assign different degrees of importance to different performance criteria.

4. Environmental policy choices are obscured by *incertitude*. There exists a pervasive state of ignorance concerning likely future performance under individual criteria and the intrinsic characters and interrelationships between different criteria.

5. Environmental policy choices are *processes* rather than discrete acts. The circumstances of decision makers and their perceptions concerning technical, social, economic, political and physical imperatives are all continually changing such that no analysis can ever be considered definitive and no appraisal is ever complete (Beck 1992, Schwartz and Thompson 1990).

6. Environmental policy choices are legitimate *social activities*. Where the activity of appraisal is largely confined to a particular industry and the associated public and academic bodies, there is a danger that wider social priorities might become subordinated to a narrower set of institutional perceptions and interests.[17]

Many established analytical approaches to environmental, and wider social, appraisal (such as neo-classical environmental economics and quantitative risk analysis) fail to address these aspects of the problem. Taking each of these difficulties in turn, such techniques are generally monolithic, in that they seek to identify single 'optimal' solutions rather than a range of subjective possibilities. They are usually simplistic, in that they seek to reduce a complex multi-dimensional reality to representation by means of a single uni-dimensional index. They often pretend at objectivity, although the results obtained are highly sensitive to subjective assumptions. They are synoptic, to the extent that they almost always ignore or marginalise the importance of incertitude. They tend to be misleadingly definitive, in that they are conceived and presented concretely as individual bounded projects rather than as permanent running themes in the political process. Finally, many of these approaches are inherently technocratic, to the extent that they are relatively opaque to critical scrutiny and inaccessible to wider participation.

If these problems are to be mitigated, then the procedures employed by society at large as a response to the challenge of social appraisal must display a number of opposing characteristics. Again, taking each issue in turn, alternative procedures should be pluralistic, in the sense that they permit the ready articulation of different methods and perspectives and allow the simultaneous contemplation of several alternative and equally potentially acceptable solutions. The models of performance which they develop should display greater realism in relation to the multi-dimensional nature of reality. They should openly acknowledge the subjectivity of the results obtained. They should adopt a position of more pragmatic humility in the face of uncertainty and ignorance. They should be open-ended and reflexive in allowing for continual appraisal and review, rather than sporadic intensive attempts at definitive analysis. Finally, they should be as transparent and accessible as possible to independent critical scrutiny and wider public participation.

Perhaps few would disagree with the desirability of such qualities in principle. However, the likely reaction of many will be one of scepticism over the realistic prospects for achieving such apparently ambitious goals. To this, it may be countered at the outset that there can be few goals *more* ambitious than the synoptic justificationist ideal of making final, definitive and objective decisions over what constitutes the single optimal choice of technology or policy irrespective of incertitude or the differing perspectives adopted throughout society. Although few conventional valuation studies would claim actually to have achieved this, such are often undoubtedly the implicit aspirations.[18] Against this background, the objectives set out above look distinctly modest! Ultimately, however, all that is audacious is the attempt at deliberate social choice itself. To the extent that this is an indispensable feature of political discourse, it is, for better or worse, non-negotiable. In this sense, then, and almost irrespective of the particular analytical techniques employed, all approaches to technology, policy or environmental appraisal are in the same boat.

If it is accepted that the qualities described here would be positive attributes of social choice, then the ambition of doing the job well should not be seen as a weakness, but as a strength. The question is, How might we go about building such qualities into the process of environmental decision-making?

4. MULTI-CRITERIA MAPPING

Where claims to 'objectivity' are made on behalf of the results of opaque analysis, they tend to succeed only in paralysing the process of social appraisal. Likewise, attempts to appropriate authority through the pretence at (or coercion of) 'consensus' may act still more effectively to sabotage this social process. However, when freed from vain aspirations to objectivity and spurious ambitions at consensus, social appraisal becomes a far more straightforward business. Thus unencumbered, interested parties and stake-holders may more easily identify those considerations which inform their individual judgement (at any particular moment) over the relative environmental merits of different technology or policy options.[19] Indeed, whether implicit or explicit, the forming and reforming of such positions is a prerequisite for any act of appraisal. If the appraisal process is iterative and reflexive, involving no requirement (or implication) that the perspectives adopted at any one moment are somehow irrevocable, then there can be a corresponding degree of trust that particular weightings will not become reified, manipulated, or taken by political adversaries as 'hostages to fortune'. Under such conditions, participants in an appraisal process may reflexively express the momentary relative subjective importance of their chosen appraisal criteria by means of numerical importance weightings. Where the appraisal criteria applied under each perspective are clearly defined and finely disaggregated, the representation of the performance of different options on some cardinal or ordinal scale under each separate criterion minimises problems of incommensurability.

For each individual subjective set of weightings, it is possible by this means to derive what might be termed an 'multi-criteria performance rank' for each of a range of technological or policy options. This is obtained by scoring the performance of each option under each individual criterion and summing the products of these scores and the weightings of each respective criterion. In mathematical terms, this simple linear additive operation may be represented as follows:

$$r_i = \Sigma_c s_{ic}.w_c \qquad [1]$$

where r_i is the multi-criteria performance rank of option i under a set of appraisal criteria, s_{ic} is the performance score of option i under criterion c and w_c is the importance weighting of criterion c. Where performance scores are subject to ambiguity, variability, ignorance or dispute, performance scores, and thus ranks, may be 'fuzzy' and so lie within a range (or across a stochastic distribution) of values.

As has already been noted, all justificationist techniques involve, to some extent or other, essentially similar procedures. The question is, How straightforward and how transparent are they? Some (like environmental valuation and comparative risk analysis), employ a single measure of performance (monetary value or human mortality) under a range of different criteria. Others (such as cost-effectiveness analysis), assign performance targets under each criterion and accept the option whose performance satisfies these constraints at lowest cost. However, the discipline which has elaborated these techniques to the most sophisticated (some would say baroque) degree, is multi-attribute utility theory (or multi-criteria analysis).[20] The procedures developed in this field are widely applied in areas such as decision analysis and operations research (e.g. Keeney 1982, Pinkus and Dixson 1981).

The problem comes with all such approaches when they attempt to resolve a unitary objective optimum. Orthodox multi-attribute analysis suffers no less from this deficiency than do other justificationist approaches such as neo-classical environmental economics. Different social, political and intellectual perspectives invoke different criteria, apply different importance weightings and assign different performance scores. This process involves essentially subjective value judgements which are irreducible features of political discourse, and which are not tractable to definitive analytical rationalisation. In a multi-criteria approach, the resulting variability in the ranking of options will compound (and probably greatly exceed) that arising from indeterminacy in the performance scores under individual criteria. Many of the possible permutations of political perspectives and scoring systems may yield different highest performing options. As a result, the use of a multi-attribute procedure to identify a single optimal option succeeds only in tacitly asserting an individual dominant perspective and performance data set, which for the purpose of analysis have been treated as 'objective'.

By contrast, the use of the same procedure simply to *map* the different possible *conditionally optimal* options against the different socio-political perspectives avoids this fundamental problem. In this sense, the multi-criteria technique is employed more as a kind of political sensitivity analysis than as a means to justify a particular decision. Such an approach offers a different way of articulating justification through analysis and the incrementalist 'muddling through' of political processes. It avoids the necessity of imposing *ad hoc* boundaries between the domains of Simon's 'rationalism' (1957 and 1960) and Lindblom's 'political market' (1957 and 1965). It negates the need to import exogenous 'rules for closure' (Gershuny 1978 and 1981). Indeed, the process is sufficiently straightforward that it may be repeated iteratively an indefinite number of times to allow the participant reflexively to explore the sensitivity of performance ranks to the setting of criteria, to weightings and to the scoring of options.[21] The technique may thus be used to construct a sensitivity map of the technology and policy choices preferred at any particular moment by different individuals, constituencies or agencies. This approach might be called *multi-criteria mapping*.

Insofar as they tend to confer spurious scientistic authority on what remain essentially political decisions, justificationist approaches to social appraisal are undoubtedly often expedient to decision makers. Multi-criteria mapping, by contrast, yields no convenient analytical fig-leaves or rhetorical smoke-screens. Instead, it offers to help structure and render more transparent, a discourse over the real issues in social choice. It presents a means explicitly to articulate the interpenetrating domains of analysis and political judgement. Conceived in this way, a 'multi-criteria mapping' method offers a number of important advantages over justificationist appraisal such as neo-classical environmental economics. Taking in turn each of the concerns raised in the criticisms of such techniques discussed in the last section, the principal advantages of a multi-criteria mapping approach may be set out as follows:

1 It is relatively *straightforward*, because the linear additive procedure governing the articulation of the different criteria is so briefly expressed and so readily reproduced.

2 It is more *transparent*, because the key variables (the criteria weightings and scores) are explicit rather than being buried in some elaborate technical procedure.

3 To this extent, the approach is quite *rigorous* in the sense that the results are determined exclusively and precisely by relatively few input variables (the criteria weightings and the option scores under each criterion).

4 Because of this transparency and rigour, the results of the exercise are readily subjected to critical review by simple sensitivity analysis. The approach might thus be thought more *accessible* and so less technocratic than are many synoptic justificationist techniques.

5 The lack of any necessity to reduce multi-dimensional appraisal problems to optimisation under a single index allows a greater degree of *realism* in relation to the complex and multi-faceted characteristics of the real world.

6 Likewise, the multi-criteria approach allows a greater *plurality* of appraisal methodologies, permitting the application by different participants of whatever are judged to be the most effective or appropriate techniques for each criterion, without methodological inhibitions concerning the aggregation of results with those obtained by disparate approaches under different criteria.

7 Perhaps most importantly, the approach acknowledges the fundamental *subjectivity* of technology appraisal, replacing unitary and ostensibly

'objective' results with a clear map of the sensitivities of individual 'conditionally optimal' solutions to starting assumptions and value systems.

8 If embedded in an appropriate institutional context,[22] these properties would allow multi-criteria mapping to play a role in a more *open-ended* approach to technology and policy choice and permit greater accessibility to wider participation.

A broad framework for the multi-criteria mapping approach is illustrated schematically in Figure 12.1. Each appraisal criterion might be conceived as a discrete dimension in a multi-dimensional social 'criteria space'. The performance of each possible 'conditionally optimal' policy option may be pictured as a single point in this criteria space. Differing perspectives over the relative importance of the different criteria and differing performance data will generate separate regions of this space, in which various of the different policy options may be considered conditionally optimal. Different social and political constituencies might employ the approach in an iterative and reflexive fashion to explore the implications of official performance appraisal results under their own particular perspectives.

At first sight, the enormous potential breadth and scope of what is being proposed here may seem somewhat daunting, if not prohibitive. This is all the more the case, since there is no reason in principle why this technique should be restricted to the appraisal of environmental performance alone. However, this is a general feature of the problem of technology and policy appraisal itself and not of the particular approaches that may be taken towards it. A multi-criteria mapping technique is not intrinsically limited by the circumscribed applicability of individual indices or theoretical frameworks. Far from being a problem, the relatively unbounded nature of multi-criteria mapping draws attention to the constrained utility of many alternative approaches such as environmental valuation or risk analysis. If, for reasons of expediency, limited time or limited resources, it is judged appropriate deliberately to circumscribe the scope of appraisal, such constraints may as easily be imposed in a multi-criteria mapping procedure as they are in other techniques. The difference is that the imposition of such boundaries will in these circumstances become a conscious and explicit act, rather than an implicit consequence of the hidden exclusion or under-emphasis of certain appraisal criteria by certain modes of analysis.

5. MULTICRITERIA MAPPING OF PORTFOLIOS

So far so good. However, two of the deficiencies of justificationist approaches to social choice described in the last section have thus far not been addressed. What of uncertainty and ignorance in appraisal? What of the need for plurality in accommodating a range of possible path-dependent channels of technological or policy development and

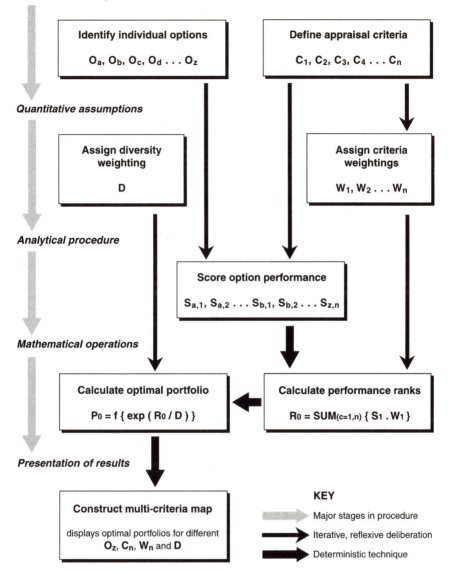

Figure 12.1 Schematic illustration of multi-criteria mapping

avoiding risks of long-run market 'lock-in' to unsatisfactory options (e.g.: Arthur 1989, Cowan 1990, David 1985, David and Bunn 1988)? For reasons I discuss in more detail elsewhere (Stirling 1994a, 1994b, 1995), an effective response to all these final difficulties may be found in one strategy: the deliberate pursuit of *diversity*.

Although the problems to which it is a response are highly intractable, diversity itself is a relatively straightforward notion. The starting point must be the adoption of a transparent and robust formal characterisation of the concept of diversity itself. Here, we may distinguish three necessary but individually insufficient subordinate properties of diversity: disparity, variety and balance.[23] Disparity reflects the degree to which the individual options are perceived to be different from each other. Variety is simply the number of options included in a portfolio. Balance is the degree to which reliance is placed on each of these different options.

Although rarely acknowledged as such, the complex, qualitative and intrinsically subjective concept of disparity is fundamental to all forms of appraisal, including environmental valuation. It is conventionally, if implicitly, addressed in analysis in terms of the disaggregation and definition of the various options themselves. In a multi-criteria mapping approach, the definition of options might best be treated as an exogenous input, lying entirely in the hands of the participants. Alternatively, a more formal multi-dimensional concept of disparity might be applied according to systematic consideration of the pertinent attributes of the candidate options under each subjective perspective, including their performance under the appraisal criteria applied in the mapping exercise. Either way, notions of disparity are captured in the definition and disaggregation of options.

The remaining properties of diversity (variety and balance) are simple numerical concepts. Variety is an integer. Balance is a set of fractions which sum to one. These two properties are fully articulated by a straightforward arithmetic algorithm derived for a directly analogous purpose from first mathematical principles in statistical mechanics and information theory.[24] It has been employed as an index of concentration in economics (Finkels and Friedman 1967), and as a measure of diversity in ecology, where it is known as the Shannon–Wiener Diversity index (H) (Pielou 1969 and 1975). For the purposes of the present discussion, it may be described as the positive value of the sum over all options of the proportional dependency on each option multiplied by the natural logarithm of this proportional dependency. In mathematical notation, this is written as:

$$H = - \Sigma_i p_i.\ln p_i \qquad\qquad [2]$$

where p_i is the proportional degree of dependence on each of i options included in a portfolio ($\Sigma_i p_i = 1$) and ln is the natural logarithm.

In short, diversification acts both to mitigate ignorance and accommodate plurality in appraisal. If the available options are sufficiently disparate under various criteria, the deliberate pursuit of diversity serves also to restrict the possibilities for commercial oligopoly or the domination of a particular sector by an individual technical or industrial complex. In this sense, rather than being seen as a quest for some single optimal (or even 'conditionally optimal') option, environmental policy choice might explicitly be conceived as a search for the best balance between performance and diversity across a *portfolio* of options. With recognition of the central importance of diversity and the identification of a robust measure, we have the makings of a potentially complete response to some of the general problems presented by neo-classical environmental economics.

A multi-criteria mapping approach is readily adapted to address the further criterion of portfolio diversity. All that is required is a single additional step in the procedure set out in the last section (and displayed in Figure 12.1). As has been described, a performance rank is calculated for each option under each perspective by summing the products of the scores and the criteria weightings over each criterion. The additional step is simply that participants each assign a weighting to express the relative priority which they attach to portfolio diversity. Just as is the case with the other criteria weightings, the weighting attached to diversity will be a matter for iteration and reflexive consideration of the results yielded. It will embody consideration of factors such as the nature of the chosen appraisal criteria, the degree of ignorance held to be associated with the assessment of option performance under these criteria and the perceived need for plurality in technological trajectories, as well as the composition of the portfolio of options yielded by the mapping exercise itself.[25]

Once this basic assumption has been adopted, the optimal composition of a portfolio of investment, technology or policy options may, somewhat ironically, be determined by a highly conventional neo-classical optimisation procedure. This is based on the notion that the overall utility of a particular mix of options represents a trade-off between the objectives of maximising, on the one hand, the performance of the individual options under an array of criteria and, on the other, the utility of portfolio diversity as a means to mitigate ignorance, accommodate plurality and avoid 'lock-in'. In formal terms, this trade-off may be expressed as follows:

$$\max(U); \ U = \Sigma_i r_i . p_i + \delta . H \qquad\qquad [3]$$

where max(U) is the maximum value taken by the total utility U of a portfolio of i options, r_i is the performance rank of option i derived in equation [1] above, p_i is the proportional degree of dependency on option i and H is the Shannon–Wiener function diversity index given in equation [2] above, multiplied by a coefficient (δ) which represents the weighting attached to portfolio diversity. It follows[26] that the solution to equation [3] is found where (using the notation given above):

$$p_i \propto \exp \frac{r_i}{\delta} \qquad\qquad [4]$$

In other words, the degree of reliance placed on option i in the optimal portfolio is proportional to the exponent of the ratio of the multi-criteria performance rank of option i (r_i) to the general weighting assigned to diversity (δ). This simple expression summarises the entire procedure described in this paper, an approach which might be termed *multi-criteria diversity mapping*.

Just like the multi-criteria mapping discussed in the last section, the multi-criteria diversity mapping technique yields a 'map' of different possibilities in social 'criteria space'. Each possibility identified on the sensitivity map represents a technology or policy choice which would be optimal with respect to a particular set of assumptions (or 'perspectives') concerning the relative importance of different criteria. However, instead of identifying a set of conditionally optimal *single* options, multi-criteria diversity mapping generates a set of conditionally optimal portfolios of such options. The degree to which the different options are represented in these portfolios will depend on their performance under the criteria and importance weightings assigned, and on the general weighting attached to diversity.[27]

6. A PRACTICAL ILLUSTRATION

So, what would a real exercise in environmental multi-criteria mapping actually look like in practice? The most important component of any full demonstration of this approach would necessarily be an open and reflexive consultation process. Unfortunately, such an undertaking lies beyond the scope of the present brief theoretical overview. For present purposes, then, it must suffice simply to illustrate the way that the procedure *might* work by considering a hypothetical schematic example. A certain degree of realism may be retained by taking care that the chosen criteria are representative of the key themes in a real environmental debate, by drawing empirical performance data from a wide range of established environmental appraisal sources and by ensuring that those hypothetical weighting schemes which are explored are plausible reflections of a wide range of divergent socio-political perspectives. The high political profile, environmental sensitivity and intensity of government and regulatory intervention make investment decisions in the electricity supply industry an obvious choice for such a demonstration.

The first step in the multi-criteria mapping procedure outlined in Figure 12.1 is to identify the individual policy options and define the set of appraisal criteria under which their performance is to be assessed. For the sake of brevity and ease of exposition, attention will here be confined to a conventionally recognised (and highly aggregated) set of options (fossil fuels, nuclear power and renewable energy) and a restricted but fairly representative range of criteria (financial cost, atmospheric pollution, land use and radioactivity). Being based on an extensive survey of academic, government and industry technology assessment studies (Stirling 1994b), Table 12.1 displays the performance of these three major classes of

Table 12.1 Environmental performance scores for UK electricity supply options

CRITERION / OPTION	Cost[4] p/kWh (normalised)	Air pollution[5] Kt_c/GWy (normalised)	Land use[6] km^2/GW_e (normalised)	Radiation issues[7] presence(1)/ absence (0) (normalised)
Fossil fuels[1]	2.9 (0.46)	10,000 (0.0009)	4.0 (0.09)	0 (0.5)
Nuclear power[2]	4.6 (0.29)	100 (0.09)	0.4 (0.9)	1 (0)
Renewable energy[3]	5.5 (0.24)	100 (0.9)	20 (0.02)	0 (0.5)

Notes

1 Includes coal, oil and natural gas from various sources presently available to UK markets using presently available plant.

2 Includes presently available magnox, advanced gas-cooled and pressurised water reactors.

3 Includes hydroelectricity (large, small), tidal, wave, wind, biomass (farm and forestry products) and wastes (wet, dry, municipal and industrial) and direct solar power. The options included under the category 'renewables' are significantly more mutually disparate than are the 'fossil fuels' or 'nuclear power'. As a conservative reflection of this proportionately greater diversity benefit from the renewables, the renewable performance ranks are in this simplified schematic exercise credited with a 5% premium under the medium diversity perspective and a 10% premium under the high diversity perspective. More detailed analysis (Stirling 1994a, 1995) addresses this factor by further disaggregation.

4 Levelised lifetime busbar costs at 1994 currency values assessed under UK Government availability and lifetime assumptions: median over 8% and 15% discount rates. All figures are subject to variability of +/ −20%. They reflect the costs for new investments at the margins of the existing system. The renewable figures represent marginal costs with respect to the UK supply curve (corresponding to a resource of some 100 TWh/y −30% of present UK electricity production). It is thus conservative with respect to the resource available at below this level, and optimistic with respect to the resource available above this level. A more detailed approach in terms of separate resource 'tranches' is outlined in Stirling (1994a, 1995). Principal sources for this data are: ETSU (1994) and DTI (1994, 1995).

5 Full fuel and life cycle CO_2 atmospheric emissions expressed as tonnes carbon. May be employed as crude first order proxy for other atmospheric emissions (such as SO_X, NO_X and particulates). Large variability, especially concerning emissions from combined cycle gas turbines which are typically an order of magnitude lower. The low value for the renewables is a conservative expression of the aggregate picture of a mix of options, with sustainably cultivated biomass often credited with negative net carbons emissions, though contributing certain other atmospheric pollutants. Principal reference: San Martin (1989).

6 Full fuel and life cycle land use figures provided. Very large variability, depending on assumptions concerning definition of 'affected land'. The assumptions adopted here yield particularly poor performance for renewable options such as wind power, which physically occupy far less land than that over which they are distributed. This somewhat conservative approach means that the resulting scores might also be seen as a crude first order proxy for effects which are contingent on land use, such as aesthetic landscape impacts. Literature reviewed in Stirling 1994b.

7 Addresses issues such as large scale long-term radioactive waste management, decommissioning of radioactive structures, catastrophic nuclear accident and terrorism risks and nuclear weapons proliferation issues, all of which are effectively confined to nuclear power.

electricity generating investment under these four chosen criteria. Although sufficing for the present illustrative purpose, it must be observed from the notes to the table that this presents a highly simplified expression of the full range and complexity of environmental performance.

To avoid misleading precision, the non-financial values are in Table 12.1 expressed to only one significant figure. In order to take account of the large degree of uncertainty and variability embodied in the published literature, the environmental performance figures given here represent the geometric means of a large sample of results. Although presenting a further dimension worthy of sensitivity testing, this empirical variability is, in practice, likely to be overshadowed by the even more pronounced variability in criteria weightings. The smaller italicised numbers in parentheses at the bottoms of the cells in the table are 'normalised' expressions of these same performance scores. Normalisation simply ensures that the various scoring systems are inter-comparable and free of inadvertent or hidden bias. It involves two steps. First, the figures are reciprocated where necessary in order consistently to represent performance on an ascending scale under all criteria. Second, the figures are scaled so as to preserve their ratios, whilst ensuring that the scores registered over all options under each criterion sum to one (subject to rounding errors). This corrects for the bias that would otherwise be introduced by the differing magnitudes of the various numerical performance indices.

Once the performance scores for each of the options identified under each of the defined criteria have been established, it remains to explore some of the divergent prioritisation schemes that might be applied to these criteria. Each of the sixty-three sections in Table 12.2 displays a weighting scheme reflecting a different hypothetical perspective concerning the relative importance (respectively in descending vertical order) of financial cost, atmospheric pollution, land use, radiation issues and diversity. The higher the weighting, the greater the relative importance. Although not constructed empirically through real consultation, this set of weighting schemes does accommodate a wide range of perspectives that we might plausibly expect to find expressed by various different constituencies in the energy debate.

Rather than being arrived at by the purely arbitrary picking of numbers, the matrix of weighting schemes in Table 12.2 represents a systematic permutation of views concerning three cross-cutting factors. The first factor might be described as the general level of environmental concern. This is expressed here in terms of the relative importance assigned to all environmental issues compared to financial costs. In orthodox neo-classical terms, the particular positions addressed here range between a view that the environmental externalities considered amount collectively to only one tenth of private costs, through a view that they are equal to private costs, to a view that all externalities together are ten times greater than private

Table 12.2 Prioritisation of criteria under various hypothetical perspectives

PRIORITY ASSIGNED TO DIFFERENT ISSUES	VIEW CONCERNING MARKET FAILURE								
	externalities > costs			externalities = costs			externalities < costs		
	Need for diversity			*Need for diversity*			*Need for diversity*		
	none	some	lots	none	some	lots	none	some	lots
Land use dominates									
Sceptical about pollution	1.5	1.5	1.5	15	15	15	150	150	150
	0	0	0	0	0	0	0	0	0
	10	10	10	10	10	10	10	10	10
	5	5	5	5	5	5	5	5	5
	0	5	10	0	5	10	0	5	10
Sceptical about nuclear risks	1.5	1.5	1.5	15	15	15	150	150	150
	5	5	5	5	5	5	5	5	5
	10	10	10	10	10	10	10	10	10
	0	0	0	0	0	0	0	0	0
	0	5	10	0	5	10	0	5	10
Nuclear risk dominates									
Sceptical about land use	1.5	1.5	1.5	15	15	15	150	150	150
	5	5	5	5	5	5	5	5	5
	10	10	10	10	10	10	10	10	10
	0	0	0	0	0	0	0	0	0
	0	5	10	0	5	10	0	5	10
Sceptical about pollution	1.5	1.5	1.5	15	15	15	150	150	150
	0	0	0	0	0	0	0	0	0
	5	5	5	5	5	5	5	5	5
	10	10	10	10	10	10	10	10	10
	0	5	10	0	5	10	0	5	10
Pollution dominates									
Sceptical about land use	1.5	1.5	1.5	15	15	15	150	150	150
	10	10	10	10	10	10	10	10	10
	0	0	0	0	0	0	0	0	0
	5	5	5	5	5	5	5	5	5
	0	5	10	0	5	10	0	5	10
Sceptical about nuclear risks	1.5	1.5	1.5	15	15	15	150	150	150
	10	10	10	10	10	10	10	10	10
	5	5	5	5	5	5	5	5	5
	0	0	0	0	0	0	0	0	0
	0	5	10	0	5	10	0	5	10
All issues of equal importance	1.5	1.5	1.5	15	15	15	150	150	150
	5	5	5	5	5	5	5	5	5
	5	5	5	5	5	5	5	5	5
	5	5	5	5	5	5	5	5	5
	0	5	10	0	5	10	0	5	10

KEY:

1.5	weightings attached to	financial costs
0		atmospheric pollution
10		land use issues
5		radiation issues
0		portfolio diversity

203

costs. Within each of these three perspectives, a further three permutations are generated by considering a trio of views concerning the importance of diversity. Where there is high confidence or strong consensus in appraisal, then diversity is assigned zero value. Successively greater perceptions of appraisal ignorance or social discord are in this case addressed by assigning weightings to diversity equivalent, respectively, to one third and two-thirds of all environmental issues put together. The third factor relates to the relative degrees of importance assigned to the different environmental issues themselves. Where a particular criterion is held to 'dominate' the others it is here assigned a weighting which is twice as great as the next most important issue. Where a particular criterion is described in the table as the subject of 'scepticism', its consequently negligible importance is reflected by assigning a weighting of zero. Although the particular ratios applied under each of these factors might easily be exchanged for other values, the overall set of sixty-three hypothetical perspectives generated by considering the permutations of these factors in Table 12.2 does provide the degree of transparency, coherence and internal consistency required for the present purely illustrative purpose.

Having adopted qualitative assumptions concerning the options and criteria under consideration, and having identified a set of alternative quantitative assumptions concerning the relative importance of the different appraisal criteria and diversity, the remaining steps in the multi-criteria mapping procedure are the straightforward mathematical operations described in equations [1] and [2] above and displayed in Figure 12.1. This procedure involves no extraneous assumptions beyond those deliberately addressed in the construction of the hypothetical perspectives above. The entire exercise may readily be performed using conventional spreadsheet software on an ordinary desktop computer. Accordingly, Table 12.3 displays as an array of pie charts the set of conditionally optimal electricity supply mixes which correspond with the performance scores given in Table 12.1 and the weightings schemes set out in Table 12.2.

Although efforts have been made to make the performance scores, the choice of criteria and the categories of option as realistic and as pertinent as possible, the hypothetical and simplistic nature of this present demonstration exercise means that the results should not be taken to have any direct bearing on real decision-making over electricity supply strategies. Instead, the purpose of this discussion has been schematically to illustrate the way that a multi-criteria mapping operation might be conducted, and the general form of the results that might be obtained. The final question that arises, then, concerns the practical use that might be made of a set of results such as those displayed in Table 12.3 and how they might help to mitigate the general difficulties with alternative approaches to environmental appraisal noted in this chapter.

The best way to answer this question is to imagine that the results

Table 12.3 Sensitivity of optimal electricity supply mix to differing perspectives

PRIORITY ASSIGNED TO DIFFERENT ISSUES	VIEW CONCERNING MARKET FAILURE								
	externalities > costs			externalities = costs			externalities < costs		
	View concerning need for diversity								
	none	some	lots	none	some	lots	none	some	lots
Land use dominates									
Sceptical about pollution	⬤	◕	◔	⬤	◕	◔	◕	◕	◔
Sceptical about nuclear risks	⬤	◕	◕	⬤	◕	◔	◕	◕	◔
Nuclear risk dominates									
Sceptical about land use	◔	◔	◑	◔	◑	◔	◕	◕	◕
Sceptical about pollution	◕	◔	◔	◔	◑	◑	◕	◕	◕
Pollution dominates									
Sceptical about land use	◔	◔	◑	◔	◔	◕	◕	◕	◕
Sceptical about nuclear risks	◔	◔	◔	◔	◔	◔	◕	◕	◕
All issues of equal importance	◔	◑	◑	◔	◑	◑	◕	◕	◕

KEY: ▨ fossil fuels ▨ nuclear power ▯ renewable energy

displayed in Table 12.3 *were* arrived at through an inclusive and wide-ranging participative consultation exercise, perhaps as part of a government Green Paper process, a Royal Commission, a Public Planning Inquiry or a major research programme. The first point to be made is that, rather than converging to a single precisely defined prescriptive conclusion, the multi-criteria mapping exercise yields a multitude of highly divergent signals. Far from being a perverse feature of the analysis, this is an indication of the fidelity with which the technique reproduces the degree of discord and aversion to ignorance in appraisal which remain so neglected in other approaches. Each of the different generating options are, under one perspective or another (and where no value is attributed to diversity), assigned the entirety of the system. Different perspectives yield every conceivable ordinal ranking sequence for the various options. Yet despite this initial apparent indeterminacy, a number of potentially useful regularities are also evident in this picture. It is on the basis of this type of regularity that multi-criteria mapping, although in itself transparently subjective and non-prescriptive, might nonetheless prove to be of very real value in arriving at practical decisions.

For instance, to the extent that the deliberate pursuit of diversity is a means to accommodate a plurality of social constituencies, the evident discrepancies between the optimal supply mixes yielded by different perspectives is itself a compelling indication that some degree of diversity is required. Despite the fact that certain individual perspectives reject a need for diversity, the evident degree of socio-political discord in the environmental appraisal of these options presents a very strong case, in and of itself, for policy intervention which deliberately fosters a degree of diversity in the supply mix. Beyond this, and slightly more specifically, it is clear that a supply mix dominated by the fossil fuel options is consistent only with a view that environmental issues are together significantly less important than financial issues, or where there is a combination of scepticism about the importance of atmospheric pollution and a perception that there is only minimal requirement for diversity. In other words, only by adopting perspectives such as these would it be possible to justify continuing to aim for an electricity supply mix on the lines of that of the present day.

Where land use issues are held to dominate other environmental concerns (perhaps under some of the more conservative of conservationist perspectives), nuclear power assumes a very high proportion of the supply mix – ameliorated only by the perception of a need for diversity. Under virtually all other circumstances, however, and except where there is scepticism over the importance of atmospheric pollution, the renewable energy options dominate the electricity supply mix. This is the case, despite the somewhat conservative assumptions adopted in this exercise about their costs (at low system penetrations), their land use characteristics and their diversity benefits. Indeed, in simple numerical terms, the renewables dominate as many of these hypothetical optimal supply mixes as do the fossil fuels. When it is taken into account that the renewable energy options presently comprise less than 3 per cent of the UK supply mix, it is clear that, under almost every single perspective where any value is assigned to diversity, the renewable contribution to the supply mix is substantially greater than it is at present. Furthermore, under more than one third of those circumstances where diversity is considered unimportant, renewables comprise the entire supply mix. The overall difference between the general prominence of the renewables and that of nuclear power is particularly striking. On the basis of a set of results such as these, and unless over-whelming weight were given to a small minority of perspectives, it would be difficult to justify any environmental regulatory intervention in electricity supply markets which acted to favour nuclear power over the renewables. Where they rely on the transparent display of regularities in a map of *real* subjective perspectives, conclusions such as this would be highly pertinent to decision-making. They would be all the more robust and specific since they are based on the explicit consideration of socio-political sensitivity, rather than on claims at some sort of transcendent objectivity in analysis.

The practical efficacy of a multi-criteria mapping exercise such as this, then, lies in identifying the broad-brush objectives of democratically accountable environmental regulatory intervention. If the energy sector is felt to offer a more easy field of application for such an approach than do many other areas, then it must be borne in mind that this industrial sector is, in itself, responsible for a disproportionate intensity of environmental concern. Moreover, if the approach were felt to be potentially useful in this field, possible applications in other policy areas are not difficult to envisage. Examples might include agriculture (for instance, the relative emphasis to give to promotion of organic, integrated pest management and input-intensive approaches) or transport (perhaps the overall proportions of passenger or freight-tonne miles serviced by rail, bus, private car, or urban mass transit systems). Indeed, applications need not be confined to those areas where a diverse portfolio of policy options are pursued in parallel. As can be seen by the columns giving zero weighting to diversity in Table 12.3, multi-criteria maps might as easily highlight single discrete options as diverse portfolios. However, it might be thought to be a distinct merit of this approach that it explicitly encourages a less monolithic attitude to the choice of options. This is particularly the case, when contrasted with the 'first past the post' results which tend to be yielded by justificationist techniques such as neo-classical environmental economics.

The actual pursuit of technology and policy options in the real world is a consequence of many complex, dynamic and historically contingent factors. If only for this reason, the conditionally optimal portfolios of policy options identified by multi-criteria mapping do not represent a simple yardstick against which to measure the status quo.[28] Instead, they generate a set of possible 'moving targets' towards which future strategies might deliberately be configured to aim. The targets for policy-making identified in this way are 'moving' both in the sense that they will be constantly changing with the availability of new empirical information and because of the shifting nature of the mix of social perspectives. Despite this inevitable dynamism, they offer a means to the consistent focusing of attention on the general objective of democratically informed and accountable policy intervention. For instance, in the example given above, it might reasonably be concluded that the active promotion of renewables to contribute considerably more than the present 3 per cent of the supply mix might offer a common denominator amongst virtually all the perspectives represented. With the targets for policy intervention thus identified, there is, of course, ample room for neo-classical economics in constructing an efficient and appropriate set of instruments for their implementation.

7. CONCLUSIONS

It is easy to criticise. In analysis, just as in policy-making, the real challenge lies in the construction of preferable concrete alternatives, in seeking practical tools for dealing with fundamental issues. This has been the goal of the present chapter. In proposing a framework based on multi-criteria mapping, one possible means to the mitigation of these problems has been discussed in general terms, with a specific concrete example of how such an approach might be applied in practice. It has not been possible to elaborate a fully developed research agenda, nor to resolve all the many questions that might be raised over the mode of implementation or institutional context for any operational multi-criteria mapping procedure. In these regards, as with so many other important analytical and policy issues, the devil will be in the detail. However, the discussion has been sufficiently specific to permit a judgement on the degree to which the central objectives of this account have been achieved; and it has been claimed that a procedure which employs a multi-criteria mapping technique such as that discussed here offers a better approach to democratic environmental policy intervention than that presently promised or delivered by neo-classical environmental economics.

Neo-classical environmental economists are often well aware of many of the difficulties that have been raised here. In such cases, persistent advocacy of a neo-classical approach tends not to be predicated on denial of the problems, but rather on a perception that the criticisms are somehow 'metaphysical' in nature, and thus beyond resolution by any practical analytical approach. At the very least, the present discussion of the characteristics and feasibility of multi-criteria mapping must cast serious doubt on such defensive advocacy of environmental valuation. It seems that the efforts of researchers and analysts might more fruitfully and more efficiently be directed at the exploration of the potential of alternative techniques, than they would at the further elaboration and extension of neo-classical environmental economics.

NOTES

1   Useful surveys of each of these areas are provided, respectively, in: Rip *et al.* 1995, von Winterfeldt and Edwards 1986, Hogwood and Gunn 1984, von Bertalanffy 1969, Pinkus and Dixson 1981, OECD 1993, Keeney *et al.* 1987, Lee 1989, IAEA 1991, Collingridge 1982, Chapman 1992, Cropper and Oates 1991, OECD 1989.

2   Cf: Freeman 1986, Mowery and Rosenberg 1979 and Nelson and Winter 1977 for pertinent reviews of the economic manifestations of the dichotomy between 'market push' and 'supply pull'.

3   Such as in the environmental regulation of the electricity supply industry in OECD countries, where, to judge by a plethora of analytical activity sponsored by the International Energy Agency of the OECD, the International Atomic Energy Agency, the European Commission, US Department of Energy and various US state regulatory commissions it appears to be inheriting the mantle of the largely discredited comparative risk assessment project (cf: references in Stirling 1992).

4   See also contributions in this volume, and Boulding and Lundstedt 1988, Brown 1992, Daly 1985, Daly and Cobb 1989, Jacobs 1991, Norton 1987, O'Neill 1993, Page 1991.

5   If the results are too low, then the incorporation of externalities in prices will have no significant impact on market behaviour. If the results are too high, internalisation is likely to be thought unfeasible due to the paralysing impact it would have on market activity. Empirical surveys of the results obtained in one area of prolific analytical activity are consistent with the tacit operation of a price imperative (Stirling 1992).

6   The two paragraphs following this one draw on more detailed discussion in Stirling 1994b.

7   The condition of ignorance is often neglected, but is variously defined and discussed in Collingridge 1982, Faber and Proops 1994, Loasby 1976, Wynne 1992 with further literature reviewed in Stirling 1994a, 1994b.

8   Discussed in the general context of environmental impact assessment in Bisset and Tomlinson 1984, Lee 1989, Wathern 1988.

9   The property which is called 'fidelity' here is discussed in terms of non-linearity by Granger-Morgan (1981) and non-monotonicity by Pool (1989) and West and Schlesinger (1990) and, for instance, in the specific empirical contexts of dose-response relationships in ionising radiation in Russell-Jones and Southwood 1987 and Lambert 1985 and of 'critical loads' for acid depositions by Chadwick and Kuylenstierna (1990).

10 This point is addressed by Holdren *et al.* 1979.

11 Collingridge (1982) discusses this as an aspect of what he terms 'synopticism'.

12 The term is used here in the widely accepted sense introduced by Knight (1921; cf. Bullard 1986, Funtowicz and Ravetz 1990, Luce and Raiffa 1957).

13 Cf. references cited under note 7 above.

14 Representing what F. von Hayek termed a 'pretence at knowledge' (1978). See: Stirling 1994a, 1994b and von Furstenberg 1990.

15 Useful popular reviews may be found in Gleick 1988, Lewin 1993, Prigogine and Stengers 1984, Waldrop 1992.

16 These issues are discussed in more detail in Stirling 1995.

17 This phenomenon is well established in the economic and sociological literature concerning 'socio-technical' or 'large technical' systems (cf. Hughes 1983, 1987, Winner 1977, 1981).

18 As evidenced in the frequent references to the 'real', 'full' or 'true' status of the results of external environmental cost studies (e.g. (respectively): Hubbard 1991, Hirata and Takahashi 1991, Hohmeyer 1992, Ottinger, 1990).

19 Examples of actual exercises of this sort may be found in Hope *et al.* 1988 and Keeney *et al.* 1987.

20 E.g.: Bell *et al.* 1977, Castellan and Sawyer 1990, Keeney 1977, Keeney and Raiffa 1976, von Winterfeldt and Fisher 1975. For ease of exposition, the particular approach described here employs a simple linear additive operation, though other multi-criteria approaches are employed in the literature.

21 Of course, the routine work of calculation and the display of results might best be handled by simple computer software, provided that the programme employed does not introduce any more elaborate procedures or extraneous variables beyond those discussed here.

22 Discussion of this important aspect lies beyond the scope of this chapter. However, such an approach might actually be quite readily accommodated by the existing inquisitorial frameworks such as the UK Public Inquiry system or the German Enquete Kommissions, being amenable to subsequent development in more specialised dedicated institutional or political structures.

23 The terminology is mine, which I explain and relate to usage in other areas of the literature in Stirling 1994a, 1995.

24 Discussed in more detail in Stirling (1994a) and derived from the properties of variety and balance and compared with alternative indices in Stirling (1994b).

25 For this reason, it is best regarded as an expression of the *marginal* utility of diversity (Stirling 1994a, 1994b).

26 Applying the method of indeterminate multipliers to solve equation [3].

27 In theory, all available options would be represented to some finite extent in any conditionally optimal portfolio. Those options with the least favourable performance under any given perspective would be assigned correspondingly low contributions. However, in the real world, the degree of dependency on different environmental policy options will display thresholds of magnitude below which each option is either not viable, or would display significantly diminished performance. For this reason, it might be reasonable to specify threshold dependencies for each option. If the dependency assigned by the diversity optimisation exercise is smaller than this minimum level, then that policy option will be entirely excluded from the diversity optimal portfolio. In this way, such portfolios will be confined to a discrete set of policy options, each making a viable contribution.

28 If, despite these difficulties, the technique were to be applied to this purpose, a different frame of reference would need to be adopted, including consideration of the performance of existing policy options in terms of their *avoidable* costs and disbenefits, rather than the average levelised figures over the duration of programmes or project lifetimes (Stirling 1994a, 1994b).

13

ENVIRONMENTAL VALUATION, DELIBERATIVE DEMOCRACY AND PUBLIC DECISION-MAKING INSTITUTIONS

Michael Jacobs

1. INTRODUCTION

Cost benefit analysis (CBA) and its ancillary practice of environmental valuation (EV) have been criticised, *inter alia*, on ethical, technical and practical-political grounds. The purpose of this chapter is to suggest some better and more appropriate decision-aiding institutions for use in public environmental policy. The basis of these suggestions is a criticism of the *normative political theory* underlying CBA and EV, and the description of a more appropriate theory of social choice.

2. PUBLIC GOODS

Most aspects of the environment that are subject to public policy are public goods, in three senses. The standard economic sense is that they are collectively consumed and indivisible. I share my enjoyment of the landscape and clean air (for example) with others; they cannot in general be made exclusively mine to purchase.

One consequence of this is the obvious one (long recognised by economists) that the total value of such goods cannot simply be an aggregation of each person's private valuation, made in isolation. Private valuations will be dependent, both upon other people's valuations, and – owing to the free rider problem – on the mechanism through which the good will be delivered. But in this context the more interesting consequence is that individual behaviour towards environmental goods has externalities. If I damage the landscape, or support damage done to it, this has consequences for other people in a way that damaging my own possessions (which are private goods) does not.

Causing such negative externalities may be represented not simply as being a matter of interest to others, but (because it damages them) wrong.

But environmental damage may be considered wrong even where it does not specifically hurt others. This is because – it may be felt – the environment has instrinsic value, or because living things have rights, and so on.

For many people, the environment is a public good in this second sense: it is an object of ethical concern. That is, what is done to it can be discussed in terms, not simply of costs and benefits (whether private or public), but of right and wrong. Public policy decisions about it therefore belong in the same category as decisions about (say) capital punishment and racism. This makes the environment a *public* good because ethics are a matter for argument, and argument requires a public arena in which to occur.

To see this, contrast public with private goods. Private goods are not, in general, ethical in nature. Whether you buy tomatoes or carrots, this sofa or that one, is a question of personal preference; not, in general, an issue of ethics. It is therefore basically none of my business. Most people accept that such preferences – when there are no externalities, and no ethical consequences – are not challengeable; they should be left to the individual. But where ethics are involved – as when externalities are involved – your preferences *are* my business. To call your preferences wrong is implicitly to bring them into the public arena for public argument.

The third and subtlest sense in which the environment is a public good is that it is an aspect of *the common good* (Jacobs 1995b). That is, valued parts of the natural world are widely regarded as goods to society, over and above the benefits they provide to individuals. Society is better for having them, even if the number of people who privately benefit from them is very small. It is this idea which underlies the concept of 'existence value': there are things which people want to exist, and to be publicly supported, irrespective of their own use for them.

3. THE POLITICAL THEORY OF COST–BENEFIT ANALYSIS

From the point of view of political theory the principal problem with CBA and EV is that they rest on the assumption that a model which may be appropriate, and which is in any case widely used, for *private goods*, is also appropriate for public ones.

Broadly speaking, the normative political theory in which CBA and EV can be said to be grounded has four principal axioms:

1 In social behaviour, human beings can be represented as separate, autonomous individuals seeking to satisfy their preferences.
2 These preferences are exogenously determined and ethically unchallengeable.
3 The role of social choice institutions is to discover these preferences and aggregate them to give the overall preference of society.

4 The optimal public decision is the one which maximises the total preference satisfaction (benefit over cost) of all individuals.

In practice, most advocates of CBA would modify (4). They would allow
that other values and considerations can legitimately influence the final
decision made by politicians. More radically, some would deny that CBA
and EV *require* this political theory at all. I shall return to both these
arguments, below. As a broad description of the *founding* theory of these
techniques, however, it seems fair.

This political theory is derived from a model of private choice in markets.
In markets individuals do – much of the time – act to satisfy their
preferences within budget and production constraints. The effect of the
market is to discover and aggregate these preferences and (given various
assumptions about competition) the result is assumed to be the maximisation of preference-satisfaction.

As environmental economists have been quick to point out, this model
does not exclude all non-self-interested motivations. Within their preferences, people may include concern for other people, for future generations,
for distributional justice, for the intrinsic value of nature, and even concern
for the common good (expressed as existence values). It incorporates these
motivations by turning them into types of 'preference', and by asking
people to state these preferences in the form of private choice. The
purpose of contingent valuation is to articulate these private choices so
that they can be made commensurable, in a cost–benefit analysis, with
other private choices expressed through actual or imputed markets.

4. PRIVATE CHOICE AND PUBLIC CHOICE

In this sense we may speak of contingent valuation and markets as being
types of *value-articulating institution*: they are arenas or mechanisms through
which people can articulate the different values they place on different
goods. Broadly speaking, it may be accepted that these two institutions are
appropriate for the valuation of private goods: that is, goods which people
consume individually and which provide essentially private benefits. In such
institutions, individuals, acting separately, spend their own money (real or
hypothetical) on goods which benefit them. The choices they make can be
taken as a plausible representation of the value they place on the goods in
question.

The point of 'EV-in-CBA', of course, is to find values for public goods,
not private ones. In this context, therefore, using these valuation institutions is essentially to treat choices about public goods as if they were
choices about private ones. But the problem with doing this is that these
kinds of choices are qualitatively different, and the differences are not
captured well by these institutions.

The principal difference concerns the frame of reference people employ when making choices about public goods. As we have seen, such goods have externalities, they are the subject of ethical concern, and in many cases they are themselves aspects of 'the common good'; that is, they are seen as having value to society over and above the value they give to individuals.

When people come to value public goods they therefore do not generally ask the question, How much is this worth to me? This is an appropriate question for private goods, because the consequences of my choice fall on me. In the case of public goods, however, the consequences fall not only – indeed, not primarily – upon me. They fall on others, on society in general, and they raise questions of right and wrong. In this context, many people will regard their own personal interest in the issue as relatively unimportant, especially if it is small in comparison with the other issues involved. They will try to value the good from a wider perspective, taking into account other people's interests, their own ethical values and their views on what is 'good for society as a whole'. In this sense they will act, not as a private 'consumer', but as a 'citizen' (Sagoff 1988b). The question they ask is, not, How much is this worth to me? but, What should happen? or, What should society do?

Now of course an individual's personal perspectives – whether they would gain or lose – is a relevant fact in answering this question. Indeed, their judgement of the public good or of the ethics of the matter may be influenced by it (for example, if they believe their rights have been violated). But it is not the only relevant fact; and in some cases it may be a rather minor consideration. Personally I may have no particular use for a rare wetland habitat, and building a road through it may reduce my daily journey time by twenty minutes. Rerouting the road to avoid the habitat may take ten minutes off my time saving, and add £20 to my tax bill. If the habitat were a private good, I would almost certainly say that it is not worth £20 and the loss of ten minutes per day. But it isn't a private good, it's a public one; and therefore other motivations enter the picture. In fact these personal considerations are far outweighed by other ones: by the observation that more houses will be destroyed by the proposed route than by the available alternative (externality argument), by my view that biodiversity has intrinsic value (ethical argument), and by my belief that it would not be good for society and our culture if we allowed another rare habitat to be lost (common good argument).

It is important to distinguish here between positive and normative claims. There is in fact considerable evidence that many people do adopt a wider perspective when considering environmental public goods (Blamey 1994b, Clark and Burgess 1994, Vadnjal and O'Connor 1994). This is backed up by studies of opinion formation on other public issues and in voting behaviour (Sears and Funk 1991). But of course not everyone may approach environmental issues in this way, and it certainly cannot be assumed that they do.

Indeed voting behaviour, at least in Britain since the late 1970s, would not seem to provide the required evidence: private self-interest, rather than the public good, seems to have been well to the fore in many people's voting choices.

But the fact that people do not always vote in pursuit of the public good is not an argument against the normative claim that they *should* do so; that thinking about public goods from a 'citizen' perspective is what membership of a political community – citizenship – ought primarily to be about. Cost–benefit analysis is founded on the normative political theory that public policy decisions should be made on the basis of aggregating private preference-based choices. The alternative theory being espoused here is that public policy decisions should be made on the basis of some conception of the public good, which is logically separate from the aggregation of individual private benefits and costs. The public good includes consideration of externalities, of ethical principles and of the common good.

5.   CONTINGENT VALUATION AS A VALUE-ARTICULATING INSTITUTION

I shall return to the positive claim about how people actually behave in a moment. For the normative theory, the crucial question is how 'the public good' should be decided. In practice there are two questions here. The first is how *decision makers* should judge what constitutes the public good. As noted, most advocates of CBA acknowledge that, while being an important part of it, CBA does not constitute the whole of the answer. But they do not presume to fill in the rest of it. Indeed, this is true of opponents of CBA as well (see for example Sagoff 1988b). It is simply assumed that politicians and environmental managers – those who take public policy decisions – have well-established and adequate (or perhaps simply unchallengeable) value systems, along with appropriate ways of making judgements when values conflict.

There seems no reason to accept this without argument, however, and we shall therefore explore this question (in two different contexts) further below. One dimension of it is the role that public opinion, broadly defined, should play in the decision makers' processes. This then raises the second question. How should *the public* be asked to judge what constitutes the public good?

Here, the advocates of CBA do have an answer. Environmental valuation, they argue, is the technique which provides decision makers with information on how much the public care about the environmental feature at issue. It is a superior instrument to an opinion poll because it forces people to 'put their money where their mouth is' (at least notionally). In opinion polls people can vote for anything because it does not come with a price tag attached; in valuation they are faced with the personal financial

215

consequence of their decisions. Moreover, by expressing these concerns in monetary terms, EV allows decision makers to weigh them against the financial costs and benefits of the policy or project.

Proponents of EV would go further than this. They would say that in contingent valuation (CV) the public have the opportunity not simply to express their self-interested preferences but to express their concern about externalities, their moral commitments and their existence values as well. This is why this technique is so important. It *does* get at the idea of 'the public good' – if this is how people want to regard the environment. The claim that EV-in-CBA is just about aggregation of self-interested private preferences is therefore simply mistaken.

Now if this is so it would be a strong argument. If it is true that CV can equally be used to articulate 'citizen' values of the public good, and CBA is *not* regarded as the only component of public decision-making (but only one contribution to it), the case against these techniques based on opposition to the political theory of private preference-aggregation would appear to collapse. This might have been the theory (as set out in the four axioms above) which originally bred EV-in-CBA, but it is not required by them, and can if necessary be abandoned. The techniques are just as usable within an alternative normative theory of citizenship and the public good. In other words, this argument goes, the valuation institutions are theory-neutral. Indeed, so far from biasing the results towards one type of value, they could even be used to *test* the positive hypothesis. They could reveal the relative weight of 'public good' and 'self-interest' motivations in public choices.

Unfortunately, this is not the case. It is certainly true that respondents to CV exercises do express 'citizen' motivations within them (Blamey 1994a, Blamey *et al.* 1994, Schkade and Payne 1994). This in fact poses problems for CV, since in many cases such responses cannot be interpreted as measures of consumer surplus in the way that the theory of EV-in-CBA requires (Blamey 1994a, Lockwood 1994, Spash and Hanley 1995).[1] But more importantly in this context, evidence has accumulated in the last few years that CV methods seriously *constrain* the articulation of 'public good' attitudes toward the environment.

First, the significant rate of 'protest' bids and refusals to participate in CV surveys suggests that many people do not accept the nature of the exercise. They do not wish to represent their valuations of the environment in the form of a private, monetary willingness to pay (Gregory 1986, Rowe *et al.* 1980, Stevens *et al.* 1991, Stone 1992). In some of these cases, it would appear that the respondents are expressing 'lexicographic' preferences, in which an environment-income trade-off is simply refused (Lockwood 1994, Stevens *et al.* 1991). Spash and Hanley (1995) found that 23 per cent of their sample, asked to value the biodiversity of an ancient woodland, exhibited such preference structures.

Second, several researchers have now sought to understand the responses to CV surveys by questioning the respondents afterwards. In one such quantitative study, Blamey (1994b) found that over 20 per cent of respondents 'didn't like the [CV] question', of whom 33 per cent said this was because they refused to make trade-offs and 63 per cent said that environmental protection (of forests) should not 'cost money in the way specified' (by private contributions to a trust fund). In even more revealing qualitative research studies, Clark and Burgess (1994) and Vadnjal and O'Connor (1994) found CV respondents to be seriously unhappy about the way in which the survey seemed to push them into private-good ways of thinking, and their disagreement with this approach to environmental valuation.

These results suggest that as a value-articulation institution CV is *not* theory-neutral. It encourages a particular approach to the valuation of environmental public goods, namely the 'consumer' one in which private income is exchanged for personal benefit. Although 'citizen' motivations *are* revealed in CV studies, the nature of the exercise – particularly when market-based 'open-ended' bidding formats are used[2] – is not conducive to this kind of value-articulation, and is likely to distort or misrepresent it. The method is closely tied, not surprisingly, to the normative theory of public decision-making from which it arose, namely that of private-preference aggregation.

6. THE PUBLIC GOOD QUESTION

From the point of view of the political theory of the public good, this is the first problem with CV as a value-articulating institution. It asks the wrong question. Asking the personal question, How much are you willing to pay? encourages people into a self-interested stance. This is the appropriate question in a market for a private good. But it is not the right question to elicit public good motivations in a situation where no market exists. Many people wish to express such motivations, and the normative theory suggests they should.

The question therefore needs to be the one which the public decision-making process is in fact required to answer, namely: What should be done, in the best interest of society as a whole? Asked impersonally, this question encourages respondents into a public good stance. It asks them not merely to consider their own private interest, but to take a wider perspective, making a judgement on what the government or other public authority *should* do – given everyone else's interest, ethical principles and a notion of the 'common good'. Now of course they may not respond in the required way; those who have a very large personal stake in the issue in particular may well not. But, as I discuss below, the majority are more likely to do so than with the quasi-market question.

It is important, of course, to retain the element of personal cost.

Advocates of CV are quite right to stress that this gives a realism to the questioning which is absent in many opinion polls. But in turn this requires that the payment vehicle is realistic. If the question is, What would be best for society?, the appropriate payment vehicle is a tax, which everyone in society is required to pay. The 'quasi-market' vehicle which is often used in CV surveys – that of a voluntary contribution to a trust fund – reinforces the idea that the environmental good is private: for your benefit, hence you pay. In practice, CV is generally used where government authorities must take decisions, choosing between environmental protection and development.[3]

Taxes are different from trust fund contributions in two important ways. Because they are compulsory, respondents know that everyone else will also have to pay. This significantly lowers the amount each individual will be required to pay. It also means – given a progressive tax system – that payments will depend on income.

These are crucial aspects of the question being asked. Knowing that other people will be required to pay is further encouragement to a public good stance: it protects against the possibility that others may free-ride on one's public-spiritedness. Knowing that payments will vary according to income (via progressive taxation) may do likewise: it increases the sense of fairness which likely is a precondition for citizen participation.

The 'What should be done?' question should also remind respondents that their choices will have costs. These might be personal costs, in higher taxation or higher prices. But they might simply be costs in terms of other areas of public spending. In practice, after all, it is unlikely that a single environmental project will lead to higher taxation; rather, some other area of public expenditure will be cut. Whatever the form of costs chosen, however, they should be included in the policy options between which respondents are asked to choose.

Now interestingly, this kind of question is precisely that which some contingent valuation practitioners are now using. The 'voting' format is an explicit attempt to move away from the original CV 'market' model in which private voluntary WTP bids were made for aspects of the environment itself. Many CV surveys now ask people to express their support or otherwise for public policy 'packages' to be paid for through taxes (Blamey 1994b, Carson 1994, Mitchell and Carson 1989). The growing use of such 'voting' techniques is a measure of how far the contingent valuation field has been influenced by criticism of the underlying theory.

Indeed, it is not clear that voting format surveys should simply be regarded as a technical improvement of the contingent valuation method. The basis of contingent valuation is the concept of consumer surplus: its aim is to reproduce market behaviour for non-market goods so that standard economic analysis can then be performed on the goods' costs and benefits. But voting format surveys do not generate information on preferences for the environment. They generate 'preferences' (though this term must be interpreted more widely than in the standard theory) for public policy packages. These packages include not only the environmental benefit, but various other costs and benefits arising as well, such as changes in employment, economic growth, and so on. Whether explicitly (in the description of the package given in the survey) or implicitly (in the way the package is perceived by respondents) it is impossible to isolate just the environmental benefit for 'valuation'. When asked to 'vote' on the package, respondents naturally consider the whole range of its costs and benefits.

But then the values given cannot be incorporated into a cost–benefit analysis. For the whole point of EV-in-CBA is to reveal just the environmental benefit; all the other costs and benefits are separately calculated in the CBA. To include these *and* the 'voted' values would be double-counting (Blamey *et al.* 1994). Voting format surveys therefore do not do what the theory of EV-in-CBA requires: they effectively substitute for the *entire* CBA exercise. The voting format appears to blow something of a hole in the theoretical task contingent valuation was intended to perform.

7. DELIBERATIVE DEMOCRACY

Voting format surveys go some of the way towards meeting the criticism of EV-in-CBA that is based on the political theory of citizenship and the public good. But they do not go all the way. They do not address the second problem with CV as a value articulating institution. This is that it is *private*. Respondents are asked to give their valuations in isolation. Indeed, in the original model of CV this was regarded as essential; it was said that if respondents were allowed to confer this would encourage 'strategic' behaviour (Cummings *et al.* 1986). In real markets, after all, people make consumption choices privately.

But public goods are not like private goods. As already noted, environmental features affect other people, they raise ethical questions which are of necessity public in character, and they often form part of the 'common good'. Forming attitudes towards them is therefore a different kind of process from forming attitudes (preferences) towards private goods. It involves reasoning about other people's interests and values (as well as one's own) and the weight which should be given to them; about the application of and conflict between ethical principles in particular circumstances; and about the nature of the society one wishes to create or sustain.[4] Such reasoning almost by definition requires an engagement with other people: to understand their interests and values, and to justify and test one's ethical and political arguments in debate.

Attitude formation towards public goods is therefore essentially a *public* not a private activity. It is an activity appropriate to a 'forum', not a 'market' (Elster 1986): to a public place where debate can be engaged in, arguments put on both sides, persuasion allied to tested facts. This is why democracy does not just consist in the provision of ballot boxes amid silence. Democracy is about public debate: the franchise is exercised only after citizens have heard all sides of the argument and discussed them with their family, friends and workmates.

This suggests that where public goods are at issue, the appropriate kind of value-articulating institution is not a private survey, but some kind of public forum in which people are brought together to debate before making their judgements. That is, the institution should be *deliberative* in character.

Debate cannot guarantee that participants *do* engage in 'public good thinking'. But deliberative institutions are likely to encourage this, for three main reasons. First, they require arguments to be put in terms of the public good. People who argue in debate simply on the grounds of what will benefit them personally do not persuade others; they have to express their position in terms of what will benefit society generally. Examination of the arguments of special interest lobby groups in public debates on legislation, etc., shows this clearly. Goodin (1986) describes this as the 'laundering of preferences'. But it is more than simply disguising one's real purposes in the cloak of acceptable argument. If it is to work it must be a genuine attempt to persuade others that what will benefit oneself *is* in the wider public interest, or can be justified in terms of general principles which can also apply to others. Such attempted persuasion is precisely what the deliberative model of value articulation seeks.

Second, deliberative institutions are likely to expose their participants to a wider range of points of view than is likely with private contemplation. Even if all these points of view are expressed in terms of self-interest, they will show the externalities involved in individual choice. In fact it is likely that ethical arguments and common good arguments will also be raised where applicable, because some people will hold these. This widening of the factors under consideration will encourage a shift from the entirely personal point of view to one at least influenced by a wider perspective.

Third, the act of deliberation with others tends to create a 'community' amongst the participants. Human contact, under conditions of equality and respect, encourages not merely understanding of others' positions, but mutual trust and recognition of common bonds. This is likely to strengthen public good motivations, because it generates sympathy and concern for others, because trust reduces free-riding, and because the recognition of commonality helps to engender the idea of the common good in a shared society.

There is evidence on this. Although they have not generally ended up with valuations, and so we have no direct means of comparison with CV exercises, focus and 'in-depth' discussion groups conducted on environmental issues reveal the kinds of reasoning and argumentation processes which occur in 'public', deliberative fora (Burgess *et al.* 1988, Clark and Burgess 1994 and forthcoming, Harrison and Burgess 1994). In almost all cases, the issues raised and the considerations which affect opinion are clearly related to conceptions of the public good, as well as to personal and self-interested concerns.[5]

The experience of such groups shows that people's attitudes and positions *change* through the deliberative process. The political theory underlying EV-in-CBA regards 'preferences' as essentially given within each person; they simply need to be 'revealed'. But this is not how public good values and attitudes are constituted. They do not come fully formed into the world from within the breast of each individual: they are articulated through the public processes of debate and argument. In these processes people's positions can alter, as new arguments are heard and perspectives appreciated.

Underlying this conception of deliberative value articulation is the normative political theory of *deliberative democracy* (Cohen 1989, Dryzek 1990a, Fishkin 1991, Miller 1992). It is the view that democratic public decision-making should consist, not in the utilitarian aggregation of individual preferences, but in public debate on the public good. It presupposes – and demands – the existence of what Habermas called the 'public sphere': a civil space, between economy and state, in which uncoerced, reasoned political argument among citizens can occur. Such argument in turn requires and expresses a shared 'communicative rationality' (Habermas 1984, 1989).

The purpose of deliberation is to reach agreement on what should be done by or on behalf of society as a whole. This does not require that 'unanimity' or 'consensus' be reached. In complex, pluralistic societies where interests and values conflict, this is impossible. But the theory of deliberative democracy does presume (against the standard liberal democratic view) that something more than compromise between fixed positions is possible (Miller 1992). By exposing participants' initial views to one another and to reasoned debate, they may change, and in this way be brought together. This may not result in complete convergence: compromise and (if a collective decision must be made) majority votes may still be necessary. But as the result of a debate on the public good, the compromise should still be between competing judgements of what should be done in the best interests of society as a whole, not an algorithmic computation of maximum personal preference-satisfaction.

8. DELIBERATIVE VALUE-ARTICULATING INSTITUTIONS

If the deliberative model of value-formation on public issues is accepted, this suggests that public attitudes towards environmental goods should not be gathered through private processes in which respondents are asked their choices in isolation. The value-articulation institution should be 'public' and deliberative in character.

Two specific institutions may be proposed. The first is what we might call a 'group CV'. A voting format CV survey would be conducted, but not through private questioning. Rather, respondents would be brought together in groups to deliberate on the question before being asked for their valuation or opinion. Such groups could be randomly chosen, or a number of different groups could be organised, each of people in a particular social category. The groups could meet just once, or several times.[6] They could simply be given written and pictorial information, as in a CV, or they could be empowered to call 'witnesses' to present arguments to them and be questioned. At the end participants would be asked to give their individual 'valuation'. But this would not be their private voluntary willingness to pay. It would be their judgement on whether it was right for the public authority to spend or reallocate the amount of money – or to accept the foregone national income or higher product prices – required to protect the given environmental feature. The estimated personal cost to each person from the decision would be specified.

If the calling of witnesses is permitted, the group CV would become more like the second type of deliberative institution, the 'citizens' jury' (Schrader-Frechette 1985). Citizens' juries are small groups of (usually) between twelve and twenty-five people, selected to represent the general public rather than any interest or sector, who meet to deliberate on a particular issue of public concern. Such groups have been used in the United States, Germany and Spain (Armour 1995, Stewart *et al.* 1994) covering a range of subject areas including planning and environmental issues. A moderator assists the discussion, and information and argument is presented both by 'neutral' officials and by interested (and interest group) witnesses. Citizens' juries generally conclude with a vote; in this there is no requirement for consensus or unanimity. Jury members may also be asked to explain their votes: the arguments that swayed them and the values or social objectives they brought to their choice.

Whereas in a group CV the 'valuation' asked for at the end will generally be judgements of one or more pre-defined policy options, the longer duration of a jury group and its ability to question expert witnesses offers the potential for constructing new policy options as well.

In the present context, the purpose of conducting a group CV or convening citizens' juries would be to provide a means of articulating public opinion about a public policy decision concerning the environment (Brown *et al.* 1995). But of course a standard CV exercise doesn't just articulate public opinion. It does so in a way which can then be used in a cost–benefit analysis to produce a 'recommendation' (in its own terms) for decision makers to consider; and the number of people involved in standard

CV exercises and their selection ensures that they are 'representative' of the population in which the decision is to be made. But deliberative institutions do not provide figures for a CBA: as already discussed, they cannot do this without double-counting. Rather, they provide decision makers with information about public opinion which can contribute to their decision.

This information is of two kinds. First, there are the votes themselves, conducted at the end of either the group CV or citizens' jury exercise. These give specific information about public opinion on the policy options, including the acceptability of their costs. The significance of the votes will partly depend on the degree of unanimity of the opinions given. A unanimous verdict or one with a very large majority is likely to influence decision makers – rightly – more than where opinion is divided.

Second, qualitative information on the debate itself is made available.[7] That is, decision makers can listen to the sorts of *meanings, reasons, values* and *arguments* which the participants brought to the subject matter and expressed in the debate, as well as their final opinion on the policy choice under debate. As focus and in-depth groups have shown, this reveals the rich complexity of attitudes and perspectives which people hold about environmental issues (Burgess *et al.* 1988, Clark and Burgess 1994, Harrison and Burgess 1994, Macnaghten *et al.* 1995). Awareness of this should also inform the decision-making process.

As to 'representativeness', deliberative institutions inevitably involve much smaller numbers of people than CV surveys, though there is no reason (apart from cost constraints) why several groups or juries should not be convened. Indeed with groups this is a requirement: in market and sociological research typical focus group studies of 'the general public' use eight to twelve groups of between six and ten people (Macnaghten *et al.* 1995). But the point of deliberative institutions is to dig deeper into people's values and beliefs than private surveys can do. It is to *explore* public opinion, not just to 'reveal' surface choices. It can therefore be argued that even though smaller numbers are involved, the people are actually being better represented. There is a trade-off here in the quantitative and qualitative dimensions of 'representativeness'.

9. DELIBERATIVE DECISION-RECOMMENDING INSTITUTIONS

How is the information provided by the group CV or the citizens' jury used to make or recommend decisions? That is, in the theory of deliberative democracy, what takes the place of the CBA? There are two contexts in which public environmental decisions are made.

The first is the large-scale decision, usually involving substantial development or other changes in land use, which affects a number of significant interests. Such decisions are made by politicians, either at local or at national level. They often involve considerable public debate. In the UK, Department of Transport road-building projects through areas of valued landscape and habitat offer typical examples.

For such decisions, the abstract theory of deliberative democracy might simply argue that politicians should engage in deliberation in the same way that the citizens were expected to do in the value-articulation institution. They should seek the public good through public debate in legislative chambers such as local councils or parliaments. One factor in their deliberation – a very important one – should be the conclusions and content of the 'citizen' deliberative value-articulation process.

Now to some extent this *is* what is required. Deliberative democracy seeks a more open, public debate among politicians: the theory supports a trenchant criticism of the actually-existing institutions of liberal parliamentary democracy (Dryzek 1990a, Fishkin 1991). But this is not an adequate position in the real, present-day world in which these institutions continue to exist. This is because, first, decisions are almost always made by governments, not legislatures, and therefore the decisive debate takes place behind the closed doors of the ruling party. Second, politicians and parties, particularly at national level, are frequently captured by special interest groups. And third, many of the development proposals which threaten the environment and are the subject of public controversy are themselves proposed or supported by the state and by the politicians representing or constituting it.

In these circumstances, deliberative democracy requires an intermediate stage between the articulation of public opinion and the decision. A number of what we might call *decision-recommending institutions* are possible: institutions which create a space for, and provide the conditions of, a genuinely 'public sphere' in which deliberation is possible. They can be divided into two broad categories.

First, there are *indirect deliberation* institutions. These use a group of impartial enquirers (that is, people who are not directly involved in the issue) to consider an issue and recommend a decision to the government or legislature. An example of such an institution (until its unfortunate demise) was the Resource Assessment Commission in Australia (Stewart *et al.* 1991). In the UK the nearest equivalent would probably be the Royal Commission on Environmental Pollution, although its studies are generally less focused on specific policy or project decisions.

Planning enquiries as currently structured in the UK do not meet the appropriate criteria: they generally operate within narrow terms of reference (excluding from consideration the wider policy which generates the given project), start from a presumption in favour of development, and adopt an adversarial approach in which different interest groups have different access to resources to present their case. They are frequently perceived as 'captive', structured to arrive at the outcome the government desires

(Nuffield Foundation 1986). By contrast, deliberative enquiries should be imbued with the philosophy of deliberative democracy: of citizenship, communicative rationality, open argument, persuasion and the public good.

Within the theory of deliberative democracy, the purpose and activity of a public enquiry is obviously *not* to attempt to estimate individual preferences and aggregate them to arrive at the optimal decision. It is to determine the best possible decision in terms of the public good, through argument and practical judgement. Factors to be assessed would include genuinely marketed costs and benefits (which could be brought together in a CBA – though it will often be more helpful to disaggregate net present value between different social groups and over time). They would also include the consequences and impacts for ecology, culture and community, as identified and expressed by expert witnesses and interests groups; and ethical and other values arising, similarly. And of course the quantitative and qualitative results of the deliberative value-articulation institutions should also be taken into account as an expression of overall 'public opinion'.

The second type of decision-recommending institution involves *direct deliberation*: not by the members or inspector of a public enquiry but directly by the participants in the controversy. An example here is the Commission on Resources and the Environment in British Columbia (CORE 1993). CORE sets up direct negotiations between the interest groups and communities concerned with land use planning issues. If agreement can be reached through deliberation, the provincial government agrees to abide by the decision. If agreement cannot be reached, the decision-making power reverts back to the government planning department. Since it is not known what decision the planning authority will make, the participants have a strong incentive to reach agreement if they can. The philosophy and intention behind the negotiating process – which is facilitated by CORE staff – is that of deliberation towards the public good, rather than simply compromise between fixed positions.

Of course, ultimately, and rightly, all political decisions are made by politicians and governments. They are elected and are accountable; they can be removed. Politicians and governments can of course ignore the recommendations even of independent public enquiries and negotiating fora. However part of the creation of a more deliberative democracy will be a political culture in which this is difficult – *unless* overriding reasons can be given in terms of the public good.

10. ENVIRONMENTAL MANAGEMENT AND PROFESSIONAL CULTURES

The second type of environmental decision is concerned with alternative ways of 'managing nature', rather than with major development. It involves

225

issues such as whether to plant one species or another, to go for more recreation, more restricted access land or more commercial forestry, how much subsidy to pay for particular conservation practices, and so on. Such decisions are not usually 'public' in the sense of being publicly debated, and they are made by professional environmental managers rather than politicians.

For some of these decisions, where alternative ecological, recreational and commercial options for large areas of land are involved, the institutions just discussed will be appropriate. But for smaller decisions they will be too expensive and time-consuming – as, of course, will CV and CBA. How should such decisions be made? The answer is that environmental managers should use their professional judgement. There is simply no other way: where complex choices must be made, balancing many different variables, there is no algorithm or 'rational method' which can remove the requirement for practical judgement (O'Neill 1993).

But the problem with this, of course, is that the existing professional culture among environmental managers, through which they make judgements, is under challenge, both from new public environmental concerns and from Treasury and audit departments requiring justifications for public expenditure. We therefore need to begin to develop a new professional culture.

This process should not be undertaken by professionals alone. It should be guided by arms-length, deliberative commissions of enquiry made up of elected politicians, interest group representatives and lay (citizen) representatives as well as professionals. Their role would be to create a new framework for making small-scale management decisions. They would do this by making 'sample' decisions: looking at a series of case-studies typical of the sorts of decisions that environmental managers face and then deciding what to do in those cases. They would reach their judgements after deliberation, reflecting in their consensus both 'expert' and 'lay public' values. Their sample decisions would then be used as benchmarks, models or guidance from which the environmental management professions could begin to derive a 'new' cultural tradition. Its policy makers and managers would be expected to apply analogous judgements in their everyday decisions.

In this way professional cultures and management decisions would themselves be subject to deliberative procedures, though at one remove. National agencies should obviously generate policy coherence within and between the different scales, so that decisions in one place relate to (for example, balance out) decisions made in another. All decisions should of course still be open to public scrutiny, with rights of participation and appeal by those affected.

11. SUSTAINABILITY AND OTHER OUTCOME ETHICS

So far we have discussed the deliberative process purely in terms of *procedure*. It has been assumed that, in both types of deliberative institution (value-articulation and decision-recommending), and in the actual decision-making process of environmental management, an agreement can be reached, at least in principle, on what should be done, on what best approximates to or represents the public good. But surely this involves more than just a shared commitment to a procedure, to a communicative rationality? Does it not also require a sharing, at least at some level, of end-values? How can a citizen group, commission of enquiry or manager reach a consensus or a decision without reference to values and objectives, to a common sense of what is good or better?

This argument is of particular relevance to the environmental debate, since many environmentalists have very strong end-values. They believe that the environment, broadly speaking, should be protected: whether on grounds of intergenerational justice, the rights of living things, the intrinsic value of nature, to preserve cultural integrity or some combination of these. The term 'sustainability' is now widely used to express the environmental objective: while open to interpretation, this can broadly be taken to mean that the quality and quantity of the valued environment should not decline, with particular elements of 'critical natural capital' requiring specific preservation (Collis *et al.* 1992, Jacobs 1991).

How could the outcome ethic or end-value of sustainability be incorporated into the deliberative process (in any of the given institutions)? There would appear to be three ways. First, it could simply be introduced into the deliberative debate by its advocates. It would then have to stand or fall by their persuasive powers and the judgement of the participants or enquiry.

Second, it could be imposed on the process as one positive end-value among others. The institutions could be asked to reach decisions in pursuit of sustainability (along with other values as well, such as equity and economic growth). In circumstances where sustainability has already been adopted as a policy objective by government, for example through the setting of environmental targets, this might be appropriate.

Third, it could be imposed on the process as a negative end-value or constraint. That is, some possible decisions could be ruled out of court on the grounds that they contravened the principle of sustainability. Sustainability would act like human rights do in general democratic debate: as a 'trump' which overrides contrary outcomes.[8] Here environmental targets would act as primary objectives, which must be achieved before other objectives are met.

Which one of these roles sustainability plays will no doubt depend on the prevalence of this value in society at large. Many of its advocates might see themselves as trying, currently, to move it from the first role to the second, and eventually to the third.

A final point may be made here. So long as sustainability is *not* generally regarded as a binding constraint on public policy decisions, one must acknowledge the potential conflict between the procedural ethic of deliberative democracy and the outcome ethic of sustainability (see for example Goodin 1992, Saward 1993). There are good grounds for believing that, owing to discounting, the bias towards self-interested motivations and lack of knowledge about environmental harms, EV-in-CBA will not generate sustainable outcomes (Jacobs 1991, 1995a). There is no guarantee, however, that deliberative procedures will do so either. One can regard them as the most likely procedures to do so, and one may consider that they are good in themselves. One can hold both types of value, procedural and outcome. But the potential that the favoured procedure will not generate the favoured outcome remains. This might be called the paradox of democratic sustainability.

12. CONCLUSION: NORMATIVE THEORY AND INSTITUTIONAL DESIGN

The institutions proposed here are based on a normative political theory, that of deliberative democracy. But the contention being made is not simply that these are (in my opinion) good institutions, based on a good theory. It is that *all* institutions for articulating public opinion and for recommending or making decisions are normative in character.

The political theory underlying EV-in-CBA sees 'preferences' as given, ready simply to be 'revealed' by an appropriate value-articulating institution. But we noted earlier that public good attitudes and values can (and are intended to) change in deliberative institutions. What goes on in such institutions is therefore not the 'revelation' of pre-existing values, but their active *construction*. In fact, as some practitioners have now noted, the social construction of preferences is also what happens in CV exercises (Gregory *et al.* 1993).

The crucial point, however, is that the construction process is different in different value-articulating institutions (see for example Brown and Slovic 1988 and Payne *et al.* 1992). As we have seen, contingent valuation exercises constrain or inhibit 'citizen' motivations, encouraging respondents into a 'consumer' stance. Deliberative processes do exactly the opposite.

But if different institutions cause different values to be articulated, then the apparently positive or descriptive task of EV-in-CBA – to reveal the public's preferences for environmental goods – is no longer possible. People don't have a single set of preferences; the attitudes they articulate depend on the institution in which they are asked to articulate them. If it is a traditional market-based CV exercise they will tend to articulate private-good, self-interested values; if it is a deliberative exercise what will tend to emerge are public-good, 'other-regarding' and ethical values.[9]

But then this in turn means that there are no theory-neutral institutions. CV does not 'reveal' preferences; it constructs them in a certain way. Deliberative institutions construct them in a different way. The outcomes from each will be different. Decision makers and practitioners cannot simply ask, 'What value does the public place on this environmental good?' and design a neutral institution to discover this. They must ask, 'what are the *kind* of values which we wish people to articulate?', and then design a particular institution to encourage these. That is, they must choose their normative political theory first, and this will determine their institutional design. In turn the institution will help to construct the preferences.[10]

There is thus no avoiding the normative task. Contrary to the claims of most of its advocates, EV-in-CBA is as much a normative choice as that of deliberative democracy. Like the latter, it expresses one possible idea of how decisions should be made in society, and assumes a particular view of human beings and the environment.

We set out above the axioms of the normative political theory underpinning EV-in-CBA. For comparison, we can now do the same for the theory of 'environmental deliberative democracy':

1 People are not isolated individuals making choices separate from others; their social identity is governed by the community or public realm in which they live, and their well-being is made up of a plurality of non-commensurable goods. These include public goods and the common good as well as individual consumption.
2 Individuals' preferences, attitudes and values are transformable rather than given. They are formed out of social processes, including debate and argument. Such processes – those involved in citizenship – are a form of education which is constitutive of human flourishing.
3 The process of public decision-making is one of searching for agreement on what constitutes or approximates closest to the public good, possibly within a set of given end-values. This is done through deliberation and practical judgement in the public sphere.
4 The environment is not a commodity like produced goods and services; as the context within which all life occurs, it is part of what constitutes the common human good, and as such (as well as for its intrinsic value) it is the subject of ethical consideration.

It is clear, I think, that these axioms are very different from those underpinning the institutions of environmental valuation and cost–benefit analysis. They concern some of the deepest questions of what human beings are like and what constitutes a good society. It is not surprising that debate over the institutions which embody them has generated so much heat.[11]

NOTES

1 This is also true if the valuations given do not actually refer to the environmental feature in question at all, but instead reflect 'warm glow' or 'symbolic' responses to the environment in general. Such responses are not the same as – though they may be mixed up in – 'public good' valuations of the feature itself. For a discussion see Blamey and Common 1994, Kahnemann and Knetsch 1992, Kahnemann and Ritov 1994, Plott 1993.

2 'Market-based' formats ask respondents to contribute to a trust fund or similar voluntary payment vehicle; 'voting' formats use a compulsory tax as the payment vehicle. 'Open-ended' bidding formats ask respondents to nominate their own willingness to pay or willingness to accept figure. In 'dichotomous choice' (DC) formats respondents are presented with a figure and asked for a Yes or No response, with the figure offered being varied among the sample. DC formats sometimes then offer higher or lower figures depending on whether a Yes or No answer has been given ('iterative bidding'). These differences are discussed further later in the chapter.

3 Of course, in some circumstances the contribution to a voluntary trust fund *is* a realistic payment vehicle, for example when a non-profit conservation organisation must buy an area of natural habitat to preserve it from development. But then the CV exercise is in effect a form of market research, discovering if there are enough people prepared to pay. This is quite different from *justifying* a decision to preserve the habitat on the grounds that the general public values it. There may be many people prepared to pay a tax to preserve it, thereby ensuring that others do not free-ride on their public-spiritedness, who would not be prepared to pay into a voluntary fund – on the very grounds that this 'privatises' the protection of a public good. For evidence of such positions, see Clark and Burgess 1994, Vadnjal and O'Connor 1994.

4 It does not require, as some have supposed, the taking of an 'impartial' view in which one's own personal perspective is abstracted: what Nagel (1986) calls 'the view from nowhere'. It merely requires an attempt to understand and to take into consideration the needs, values and interests of others, as well as one's own, and to consider non-egoistic ethical principles. For a discussion see Young 1990.

5 Such groups also conclusively refute the idea, sometimes expressed by economists and other experts, that 'ordinary people' (for which read 'non-middle class people') are unable to engage in sufficiently reasoned argument on public issues.

6 The use of 'in-depth' groups, which meet four or five times and which therefore generate a different dynamic and reveal more deeply-considered values, has been pioneered by Burgess and Harrison; see Burgess *et al.* 1988, Clark and Burgess 1994, Harrison and Burgess 1994.

7 This is important. One of the objections made to deliberative processes, both in theory and practice, is that they can be over-influenced by particularly articulate or forceful individuals, and can prevent the expression of opinions or values by those whose natural discourse does not follow that of the majority in the group (Young 1990, 1994). This can be reduced by appropriate differentiation of groups, by use of modes of discourse and expression appropriate to the groups, and by skilful moderation (Burgess *et al.* 1988). But it can also be *audited* by examination of the transcripts, in which dominance, manipulation and coercive power relations should be evident if they have occurred.

8 Eckersley (forthcoming) suggests that the development of 'environmental rights' could serve this purpose.

9 It is important to recognise that this is not the same as saying that the

'information' given to respondents is different. It is a standard result in the CV literature that the amount and type of information given to respondents affects their valuations, as does the payment vehicle (Mitchell and Carson 1989). But those forms of so-called 'bias' relate to the good being valued itself: if the description of the good (including the payment vehicle) differs, so will the valuation. The argument here is not that a different description of the *good* will generate different values, but that the nature of the value-articulating *institution* changes the values. In fact, of course, the structure of the institution changes the nature of the information with which respondents are faced. One might go so far as to say that deliberation improves the 'information' available, since a wider range of perspectives is brought to bear upon it. This is why, one must suppose, juries in trials are sent into the jury room to debate the evidence they have heard, and not simply asked to vote immediately after it has been presented in court.

10 This is of course merely to echo Aristotle (1948), who argued that certain institutions in society help to develop the virtues (while others don't); therefore society should develop those institutions. For a discussion in relation to the institutionalist tradition in political economy, see O'Neill 1994. For a similar argument within a different tradition (that of cultural theory) see Wildavsky 1987.

11 This chapter has benefited greatly from comments made on an earlier draft by Simon Bilsborough, Jacqui Burgess, John Cameron, Marc Carter, Robyn Eckersley, Jack Knetsch, Michael Lockwood, John Mulberg, Mark Peacock, Colin Price, Peter Soderbaum and Clive Spash. None of them is, however, responsible for any errors which remain.

14

ENVIRONMENT AND CREATIVE VALUE

John Foster

1. ECONOMICS AND THE STRUCTURE OF VALUE

The economistic thinking about environment which this book has been largely engaged in criticising is founded in a certain way of approaching questions of value: a way which nevertheless answers clearly to something very important in the idea of value itself. The difficulties with such thinking which become prominent from the environmental perspective are unlikely, therefore, to reveal merely the contours of a *mistake*; rather, they may help to shape our understanding of the nature of value-judgement, considered as a human practice of engagement with the world at large.

To what central characteristics of this practice does economistic thinking respond? Consider a claim such as, 'We should, all things considered, prevent the further extinction of species': one which environmentalists from a variety of camps would certainly be happy to make. The line of thinking which can lead (though it need not) to neo-classical environmental economics takes such a claim as equivalent to:

[W] The benefits of preventing further extinctions outweigh the costs of so doing.

What we have here is the assumption that practical claims have an essentially meliorist ethical structure; our motivation for action arises as our impulse to pursue perceived goods, to want the good is necessarily to prefer the better, and therefore to judge of the good to be pursued in action is to weigh the available options in some scale of betterness.[1]

It is crucial to see that the language of 'costs and benefits', just as used in [W], need not commit us to any more than this; in particular, it need not commit us to any view implying that cost–benefit *analysis* within a utilitarian framework offers an appropriate form of decision-procedure to institutionalise such judgement.

For one thing, the term 'benefit' carries no necessary implication that such claims as [W] are reducible to expressions of self-interest, still less to expressions of differentially-forceful subjective preference. We might

232

equally have said, in objective mode, that the good involved in or associated with preventing further extinctions outweighs that involved in or associated with the alternative. Nor need the good in question even be thought of as somebody's good (necessarily it will be perceived from someone's perspective, but that is a rather different matter); it could perfectly well be a general, impersonal good such as we all – or at least, many of us – disinterestedly acknowledge in the preservation of things like species.

Of course, many of the concerns which lead us to make such claims as [W] will indeed be, in a fairly loose and unpejorative sense, self-interested: we want to maintain our credit in the gene bank, we want to avoid blundering into ecosystem catastrophe through the ignorant destruction of keystone species, we want a world delightful with dolphins and abounding in koala bears. But it seems at least *prima facie* that [W] leaves room for another general kind of concern, of the sort which environmental economics tries to capture with the notion of 'existence value': concern for species as in themselves or intrinsically worth saving.

By the same token, it is not necessary to read [W] in any flatly consequentialist spirit, with benefits and costs seen as distinguishable results or products of the possible actions under review. All that is so far at stake is that our assessment of the comparative goodness or rightness of acts has the particular structure implied in the idea of 'weighing'. Aspects of the relevant benefits – such as the strong positive value of respecting rights or moral standing where these are recognisable – can perfectly well belong intrinsically to the acts under consideration.

Most importantly, such statements about the comparative weight of benefit as against cost need not be seen as giving or anticipating the result of any calculation; rather, they represent an eminently natural way of embodying and conveying a judgement. The evaluative claim that the benefits of doing A outweigh the costs is not, in fact, typically a claim of the form: 'The benefits sum to x, the costs to y, therefore . . .'. Instead, it constitutes, as it were, a single interpretive move by which the various relevant aspects confronting us are brought into a unitary motivating relation. These aspects we realise to ourselves, as we consider them, not quantitatively but in terms of a very wide-ranging normative-descriptive vocabulary; to do A would (say) be decent and honourable, but would have consequences B and C which would be respectively uncomfortable and anti-social, while a good many people would take it as implying D which would seem pretentious . . . and so on. All these terms carry for us their distinctively different vibrations of pleasure and distaste, appeal and recoil, requirement and prohibition. Needing to act, or not, on the basis of what we take A to involve, we resolve all these various qualitative perceptions together into a single pattern of *these outweighing those* which the judgement or evaluative claim expresses.

It should be noted that this process of deliberation has an inherently collaborative structure, deriving from its dependence on the various significances attending different uses of this normative-descriptive *language*. Even asking oneself '*Is* this the right term?' is collaborative in this sense, though the collaborator is only oneself stepping back and looking again; but evidently the process as it leads to a comparative weighing ideally completes itself in actual dialogue, the attempt to meet real others in a commonly-established meaning.

To see practical judgement as a process of weighing options in quest of the better is thus at least to see this process as one of what we might call *cost–benefit synthesis*: the consolidation of ethical multiplicity as it actually challenges us into a structure of comparison conformable to the demands of deliberation and directed towards rational action. It is the idea of weighing which gives this structure its characteristic shape, and from which the associated paired terms for countervailing forces take their significance. Our example [W] above, that is, might without essential alteration have been expressed in terms of the outweighing of cons by pros, losses by gains, or simply (as noted) of bad by good. All these pairs have their advantages and disadvantages (yet another possible pair, of course); they each lend their own rather different flavour to the kind and style of deliberation taken to be in question. 'Costs and benefits', in particular, might be supposed to lend a somewhat individualistic and monetary flavour – though there can also seem to be a certain inevitability about the description, from the perspective of the person making a judgement, of what is to be shunned as a cost and what is to be sought as a benefit. (After all, costs do not have to be quantifiable: we can say 'It cost him a great deal to admit that', without being tempted to enquire precisely how much.) No doubt the economistic thinking which looks to formalise the interpretive process of judgement in a social decision procedure, and comes out with cost–benefit *analysis* as a way of standardising the synthesis which such judgement achieves, may be said to have run away with the monetary analogy suggested by 'costs'; preceding chapters have supplied a range of arguments for taking this to be so.[2] But there is undeniably something in the core of practical judgement itself waiting to be run away with.

2. RATIONAL VALUE-COMPARISON

It can, accordingly, seem irresistible to represent in this melioristic fashion our judgement that (for example) we should prevent the further extinguishing of species. And indeed, unless we do so, any prospect of a rational environmental policy for a modern society looks rather remote. For one certainty about any such policy is that it will have to turn on the central role of the *deliberated trade-off*: the agreement, capable of being generalised in some sense across society as a whole, that since there are limits and we cannot have as much as we want of both *A* and *B*, so much of *A* is worth giving up in order to have so much more of *B*. No such conclusion is going to be defensible in a complex and highly differentiated society without recourse to well-grounded general agreement about comparative values: the sort of collective agreement that, situation by situation, 'these costs are outweighed by these benefits', which environmental CBA, for all its manifest deficiencies, has at least been trying to establish as the basis of policy. And I take it for granted that if our kind of society can't make coherent and comprehensive environmental policy, the human future will be bleak indeed.

This suggests all that we need to say (here, at any rate) about pluralism and value-commensurabilty. Of course values are plural, in the sense that lots of things matter, and they matter in lots of different ways even to the same people, never mind as between different people. Of course there is no single implicit ordering out there which some sudden improvement in our ethical instrumentation would permit us at last to register. And equally clearly it is not the case that in order to make practical judgements among these values for ourselves, we must buy into some single master-value which we can use as a measuring rod; as Bernard Williams famously said, any assumption 'to the effect that two considerations cannot be weighed against each other unless there is a common consideration in terms of which they can be compared' is 'utterly baseless':

> aesthetic considerations can be weighed against economic ones (for instance) without being an application of them, and without their both being an example of a third kind of consideration . . . If one compares one job, holiday or companion with another, judgement does not need a particular set of weights.
>
> (Williams 1985: 17)

But while the idea of value-pluralism is all very well when it serves to remind us of these important meta-ethical points, our eagerness to emphasise the pluralism must not lead us to overlook the fact that what are taken to be plural are still *values*. If the idea of 'weighing' contributes anything at all to our understanding of what goes on in judgement, it does so by capturing our awareness of the possibility that comparing, to take Williams's example, an aesthetic with an economic consideration, can at least yield us reasons *for* acting on the one kind of consideration which are, at the same time and by the same token, reasons *against* acting on the other – and vice versa – however disparate these considerations may be within some more generally-conceived plurality of evaluative concerns. Indeed, if a decision has to be made, as in this fallen world it so often does, between two mutually incompatible real options, then the reasons for one *must* be reasons against the other.[3] Values, as it were, can be left to disport themselves in happy plurality when off-duty, but the need for a decision calls at least the relevant ones rather sharply into line. And it is hard to see how this engagement between reasons in (as it were) the same plane of justification, an engagement which seems a minimum requirement for any rational choice, could fail to translate into at least *weak* commensurability, if one expresses the issue for such a choice in terms of the values embodied respectively by each consideration. At minimum, that is, there must be the formal 'common consideration' underpinning the idea of value itself. To represent rational choice in terms of value is to imply that, when we choose, we do so by constituting one set of considerations as having greater value than another; and values in *this* sense seem to be weakly commensurable necessarily.

3.   ENVIRONMENT AND THE DISCOVERY OF VALUE

By now, however, something very odd appears to be happening to the central idea of 'weighing'. It is as if we were claiming that the value-commensurability of the objects of judgement is grounded in our capacity and rational need to weigh them comparatively; that what we weigh has weight because we can weigh it, and insofar as we need to weigh it. But is this the kind of meaning that anything purporting – even metaphorically – to be our idea of weighing, can have?

Well, we certainly seem to be able to say that, in weighing up alternative options, we are not registering evaluative weights which the objects of our deliberation possess independently of us: rather, we are *weighting* some aspects on the one hand, others on the other, and some more heavily than others. We weigh considerations not as we measure lengths, but as we stress various key points in an exposition – a matter of actively constituting what is there. And the dynamics of deliberation – the shifting tensions as we move consideringly among provisional characterisations of general values and particular instances, consult our feelings and those of others, look again at what is there, review, revise, and converge (typically) on a resolution of these tensions in judgement – contribute powerfully to this sense of our 'weighing and balancing' our reasons as an active process. But still: *weighing*. We can indeed 'give things weight', but only because (so to speak) there is weight around to give. Just as the possibility of generosity depends, irritatingly, on the existence of property rights (I cannot give anybody anything where all is held in common), so the possibility of giving things weight depends on the existence of (relevant) 'weights' which we can actually discover. The whole idea-complex associated with weighing strikes in so aptly to our thoughts about value because it expresses the sense of our choices being *guided*, and that means: influenced from beyond the will. (The psycho-sensitive compass which always points in the direction which I *think* is North cannot guide me, however carefully I have thought, and however exhaustively we have all discussed it.)

It is this conviction, that value cannot arise as (ultimately) an assertion of

236

the individual or collective will, which our encounter with environmental value serves so importantly to reinforce. The value of other living things, to take an obvious instance, is simply denatured if we do not think of it as something which we discover. Nor is it just something discoverable by individuals, who might thus encounter in their dealings with nature the embodied values of a culture which in some sense precedes them; but it is something discoverable, too, in any such collective practice of evaluation. That non-human lives matter in themselves is something that human beings, together, find out – and find out about *the world*, not about themselves and their more-or-less shared feelings. To suppose otherwise is just to mistake our role within the drama of life, a habit of miscasting ourselves with which the new growth of ecological and environmental consciousness has ensured that we can no longer remain comfortable, if we ever were. Here as in other major shifts in the climate of opinion (one might compare the Enlightenment's emerging recognition of human rights) a change in structure of feeling and cast of mind is a change in the sense of the world which we can make with our key concepts; and already we can no longer make much sense of the idea that non-human life has only the value we care to accord it.

If so, then is the mattering of some parts of independent living nature *more* than others, and more or less than particular human concerns, also something which we discover? How, indeed, can we discover value in the world without also discovering there the differences in value to which evaluation responds, and by which judgement should be guided? The trouble is that environmental value palpably can't be like this either – and paradoxically, it might seem, for the same general kind of reason. To suppose that the grizzly bear really is objectively and intrinsically more valuable than the Wyoming bighorn sheep (or that it is less valuable, or that they just happen to be objectively and intrinsically equal in value) is to read back into the very constitution of the natural world an adventitious structure of human reason. It is adventitious, in the sense that grizzly and bighorn might have lived the lives they live now in this world, had humans never arisen, and their supposed differential value would have had (as it were) *absolutely* no purchase on the shape of these lives.[4] To imagine that in themselves the lives of such creatures could have this kind of relation to one another would in fact be no less ridiculous – and, given changed beliefs, a good deal more hubristic – than the claim attributed by Keith Thomas (1983: 19) to the physician George Cheyne, who in 1705 said that the Creator had made the horse's excrement smell sweet because He knew that men would often be in its vicinity.

'Are values in Nature subjective or objective?', asked Holmes Rolston in a well-known paper (1983), and the answer (though rather brisker than Rolston's thirty pages) can only be: neither, if they are taken as alternatives

– but actually, both. That is the real importance both for meta-ethics and for rational practical choice of our evaluative encounter with environment.

4. THE CREATIVITY OF VALUE-JUDGEMENT

To give this answer, however, we need to be able to make sense of how judgement can genuinely discover value which it also and at the same time genuinely constructs. And this sense clearly needs to be made out not just for environmental value, but in respect of value generally. For what we are confronting here – led up to it irresistibly by consideration of our place as valuers in nature – are the conditions under which the fundamental paradox of value is habitable.

I want to sketch these conditions in terms of the creativity of judgement. In judging we make a creative self-commitment – something to which *value*, the whole intricate and subtly-differentiated language of practical comparison which we inherit and develop, stands less as an index of individual motivating reason (whether internal or external) than as the essential medium in which we each have to move and act. While for the purposes of argument I shall try to establish this by showing how the criteria and processes of judgement closely parallel those of more familiarly creative expression, what I am offering is not intended to be mere expository analogy. The ordinary business of valuing, radically collaborative and socially embodied as it necessarily is, lies on a continuum of creative human action, elsewhere on which we find the specific originating creativity of the artist (pre-eminently of the artist in *words*, which is why literature is the pre-eminently ethical art, but also recognisably in other media): that is the substantive claim.[5]

I claim, too, that once we have seen into this dimension of our general creativity and recognised what it requires of us, we shall understand its exercise in the environmental domain much better. In particular, we shall be better placed to see both why environmental values must be centred on human beings (or perhaps, centred *in* the human world), and why this need imply neither hubris nor an instrumentalising stance towards nature at large. And seeing things in this light, with our theme of deliberative institutions for environmental policy choice also in mind, will lead me to some concluding suggestions of a broadly educational character.

What are the criteria of good judgement in matters of evaluation? – criteria inherent to the practice, arising out of the idea of judgement itself, and of its due exercise. In the first place, such a judgement has to be made by an individual and cannot be taken over from others. If, faced with the need to judge values, I simply adopt your view, I have not really made any judgement about the matter directly in hand. (I may have judged that your views on such questions are reliable, but that is a different matter.) Call this the criterion of authenticity. Note, too, that it is not necessarily a question of originality; my judgement does not have to break fresh ground or startle with its novelty to be a real judgement; it just has to be mine, to issue at first hand from me. I must judge values *for myself*.

But not *to suit myself* – this is the second criterion. A value-judgement arrived at with half an eye to how I should like things to stack up, is equally a failure in judgement. Genuine judgement is about a kind of honesty and responsibility towards the common sense we can make, for which 'keeping my thumb out of the pan' is a natural metaphor – though it is a vastly more difficult business than this perhaps suggests, given the insistence and insidious pervasiveness of ego. Call this the criterion of disinterestedness.

(Obviously there are many kinds of claim naturally expressed in terms of better and worse, benefits and costs, where what I, or we, want or don't want is precisely to the point. Here, it seems to me, is the use, at least in ethics, of the distinction between values and preferences. The latter, we might say, are typically expressed by statements which have the form and some of the functions of value-judgements, but which are not seeking to meet the criterion of disinterestedness. The perception that preferences answer ultimately to values and not vice versa – the denial of ethical subjectivism – is then the perception that this criterion of disinterestedness must be attended to somewhere.)

These criteria of authenticity and disinterestedness are, as I say, parallelled by equally inherent criteria for the deployment of creativity in art. Work which we are prepared to recognise, in any artistic medium, as creative must carry the stamp of its author's unique identity, borrowing neither in life-thrust nor in essential form from others. Here, as well as authenticity, we do tend to talk of originality, in the sense of the innovation required of each creative talent to find its own voice. It is not, though, the Romantic form of this struggle, the lone defiant figure, so much as the artist whose individuality is realised within a widely shared and socially-established tradition of expressive conventions, who shows best what the undramatic authenticity of ordinary judgement aspires to be like. But this emphasises by the same token how creative work, even the most original, cannot issue from or answer to the merely individual psychology of the artist as *ego*; necessarily personal, it must not be limitingly personal. In it, the artist is grappling with painfully real pressures of lived experience, but not just by way of a private struggle conducted, for one reason or another, in public; the creative artist makes a *shared order* out of experience which is sharply and perhaps still unresolvedly his.[6]

These criteria, then, define an often exacting *impersonality* as internal to the idea of value-judgement, just as it is to that of artistic creativity. Exacting, because it will be apparent that their demands are in deep tension, and in any situation where the need for judgement presses on us – where issues are unclear, and of personal or public moment – these tensions can readily become acute. Trying to realise implications

239

authentically, to see for myself, I find myself looking through the distorting glass of self*hood*, drawn towards that subjectivity which distorts values into an expression of merely personal concern. Striving, against that temptation, back towards disinterestedness, I can slip into the safe conventionality of perception which absolves me from self-committal. Value-judgement is always threatening to fail in due impersonality at this least manageable of levels (the conflict between poles of attraction, or nodes of force, with its corresponding sense of the outcome as an achieved equipoise, clearly having something to do with the felicity of metaphors drawn from weighing and balancing to characterise our activity of evaluative thought).

What is at issue here, in fact, is the way in which value-judgements can claim an appropriate *objectivity*: deriving, that is, not from some independently existing envalued reality, but from the purity of the process whereby what is envisaged as valuable is made real for judgement. That process is purified in part by a commitment to its collaborative nature, to the essentially open place for endorsement through constructive revision by real others which each individual value-judgement ('This is so, isn't it?') contains. But that in turn derives from a commitment to direct our evaluative thinking towards a world taken to be a field of common access; judgement depends on what Murdoch (1970: 34) calls 'a just and loving gaze directed upon an individual reality'.

This further or second-order criterion – call it, in Murdoch's own borrowing from Simone Weil, a criterion of attention – is again paralleled in what we expect of artistic creativity. This does not, of course, mean anything to do with representationalism in art. Much more demandingly for criticism, it means that though good or even great art can be lighthearted (think of Mozart), it cannot be gratuitous or frivolous; it must address the real. That is, it must take itself seriously without solemnity, and have some bearing on what can be made of human life in its actual, generally experienced conditions and circumstances.

I have identified authenticity, disinterestedness and attention as criteria of *good* evaluative judgement, or perhaps as ideal characteristics to which such judgement aspires. It is all in keeping with the nature of these criteria that judgement should be liable to a particular kind of *failure*: a kind importantly different from that to which belief is liable. Belief has to be neither an authentic self-commitment nor disinterested: if I believe something just because I am told to, or because I badly want it to be true, I still believe it, and it can actually *be* true. Much, no doubt, will be amiss with my doxastic strategy if all or even many of my beliefs arise in those ways; but what I will then have will be an unreliably-formed set of beliefs, some of which may nevertheless encounter truth and indeed help me to discover further truth. But if value-judgements are not authentic, disinterested and attentive, they fail essentially: there is nothing really *there*. A value-judgement which is entirely conventional, thoroughly self-regarding or based just on impulse has the same vacuity and futility as a poem or a painting produced on a similar basis. Judgements, like such empty art, are deficient typically not by being false, but by failing to raise the issue of their truth.

The issue of truth is raised in judgement because its proper attention to the world encounters *as discovered* the value with which it also endows its objects. A judgement reflecting an open, collaborative commitment (no simple matter, often, but a difficult lived heuristic) is not made true by anything *else* ('how things are'). The relation of the achieved 'just and loving gaze' to the reality on which it is directed is not in that way external; but nevertheless what is envisaged is, precisely, a reality. As such, it can surprise us while we recognise ourselves in it; and towards it we can have the same kind of responsibility as we have towards a discovery. Nor could there at all generally be a question of illusion or false analogy here: such reality can stand *finally* firm as the ground of action, as certain as anything empirically known.

These formulations, of course, could be said merely to recapitulate what I called above the fundamental paradox of value. But acknowledgement of the process as creative enables us to move beyond paradox (though not, finally, beyond mystery). For we are readier, at any rate, to recognise what is involved here as it manifests itself in the realm of artistic creation. The artist in shaping his material explores towards a structured organisation originating with him, but one which at the same time reveals itself as a significance which his labours are realising and bringing out. This is not just an 'aesthetic' phenomenon, indeed, but a process with which anyone who ever tries, for instance, to put an apprehension of any complexity into words, is intimately familiar: the emerging meaning, a creature of my developing intention, takes shape as requirement, a call on my expressive skills, a challenge to attentive self-discipline and self-submission if I am to 'get it right'. The demands of impersonality in creation, the sensed claim of an achievable objectivity, reflect more than the necessarily interpersonal existence of any available medium, and the radically collaborative nature, therefore, of any significant construction; they register the self-recognition of an individual creative will actively responsible *for* that which it is also finally responsible *to*. When we see that discovery, truth and responsibility come into the enterprise of evaluation in essentially the same way, the paradox of our investing the world with requirement may begin to seem a more tolerable, if still a disturbing, habitation.

How does all this bear on 'environment'? What I am arguing, in sum, is that the attitude or posture of spirit towards value in the world which we find deep environmental concern demanding of us, is actually the only posture of spirit in terms of which any valuing at all is ontologically coherent. Only in creative humility can we value. But the corollary is that in creative humility we *can* value; and we can value environmental goods among the rest; and moreover, we can value them in that unevadable full sense of 'value' which brings with it what I have called the 'cost–benefit synthesis': the judgement for this and that practical purpose that these goods do really and reliably outweigh those. (If we are properly circumspect, indeed, we may be able legitimately to give *some* dimensions of judgements like this a quantitative framing of one kind or another for relevant policy situations.)

There are really two points here. One is basically institutional, and concerns the way in which something as systematised and rationally bureaucratic as the policy process in our kind of society might plausibly be brought into relation with what I am gesturing at in the phrase 'creative humility'; I try to say a little about this very knotty problem in the final section. The other point is more philosophical: it has to do with the bearing of the creativity of value on what Bernard Williams (1992: 68) notes as a characteristic paradox of conservation:

> What many conservation interests want to preserve is a nature that is not controlled, shaped or willed by us, a nature which, as against culture, can be thought of as just *there*. But a nature which is preserved by us is no longer a nature that is simply not controlled. A natural park is not nature, but a park; a wilderness that is preserved is a definite, delimited wilderness. The paradox is that we have to use our power to preserve a sense of what is not in our power. Anything we leave untouched we have already touched. It will no doubt be best for us not to forget this, if we are to avoid self-deception and eventual despair. It is the final expression of the inescapable truth that our refusal of the anthropocentric must itself be a human refusal.

My claim has been that when the valuing which informs and guides our uses of power in environmental protection is rightly seen as creative, it is revealed as a process where we, the collaborative community of valuers, are generating something which is, at the same time and radically, 'not in our power'. Certainly we are now obliged to make judgements about the various values of species, of ancient woodlands, of biodiversity, of undisturbed systems and cycles in general. But the discipline of attention subserving authentic and disinterested judgement about these matters is a discipline of openness and unwilled seeing, an essentially shared receptiveness towards a natural world which we expect to declare itself to us *in* our valuing of it.

Very importantly, values constructed in the acknowledgement that this must be their spirit and logical mode do seem thereby subject to broad restrictions on their substantive content. If *this* is what valuing nature is, it would seem that it cannot without profound self-frustration issue in any systematic, calculative setting of core natural values *below* those arising from human interests. Justifying the deliberate elimination of species, for instance, on such an understanding of what justification involves looks as unpromising an enterprise as using discourse ethics to justify tyranny. This is a crucial theme, but one which I can't pursue here. For present purposes it is enough to note that, in general, the valuing which conserves nature on this understanding can both discharge our human responsibilities and leave us with something which is *not*, ultimately, 'controlled, shaped or willed by us'. We can find ourselves, on human terms and from the human centre, at home in a world charged with value from beyond the circles of human concern, and neither self-deception nor despair is then to the point.

5. ENVIRONMENTAL JUDGEMENT, EDUCATION AND INSTITUTIONS

In the paper from which I quoted just above, Bernard Williams identifies our deeper valuing of nature as grounded in 'Promethean fear', a fear of taking too lightly or inconsiderately our relations to a nature which is 'independent of us, something not made, and not adequately controlled' (1992: 67). This is certainly one way of highlighting the real problem which he then goes on to point out:

> There is no simple way to put such values into a political sum . . . It may well be that our ways of honouring such values cannot take an economic form . . . It can only be the mobilisation, encouragement and expression of these attitudes, their manifest connection with things that people care about, that can give them an adequate place on the agenda.
>
> (1992: 68)

Nor is the difficulty with honouring such values in an economic form just a contingent one. As Williams's mythological recourse elegantly makes clear, it is of the *essence* of our deep environmental values that they should resist any approximation to economic value. Prometheus as rational calculator would be just a contradiction.

The trouble is that the 'mobilisation' of concern which Williams seems content to offer as an alternative has so very often, in our kind of society, itself to take an economic form. It is not just that our judgement must confront environmental issues both as specialised by scientific knowledge, and in their wider cultural and ethical context – so that 'the environmentally literate citizen . . . will have a blend of ecological sensitivity, moral maturity and informed awareness of natural processes that would make her or him unlikely to contribute to further degradation of natural processes at either individual or corporate levels' (Brennan 1994). The judgement exercised by such a citizen must acknowledge, further, the diverse plurality of perspectives, interests and constituencies clustering around such issues in contemporary society, yet if it is to address real problems in such a context it cannot rest in mere plurality; its aim must be the constant creative achievement of reasoned convergence. And reason, in very many cases, will have to converge on action with particular economic implications, say on the restriction of productive processes or the diversion of limited resources to preservation or restoration.

Here, evidently, we are grappling with those basic difficulties of relating the economic to the meta-economic through the social exercise of judgement, which I was exploring in the Introduction, and to which much in the book has responded. But at this point I should like to bring into the equation another, and at first sight a rather different, problem with environmental judgement. This is connected with the fact that the capacity to judge well by the criteria which we have been examining must be learnt and nurtured, both by individuals and in its institutional forms. Such judgement, depending as does any creative form on an accumulated but constantly revised practical wisdom, cannot float free of an embodied tradition: it needs to be seen as itself embedded in an appropriately non-specialist practice, something into which its practitioners need to be initiated. Recent interest in the theory of discursive or deliberative democracy – redeploying the lessons of the Aristotelian *polis* for modern conditions[7] – clearly seeks to meet this need. But understanding practical judgement in this way, and contemplating at the same time the highly complex value-profile of typical environmental choices, we cannot avoid recognising the difficult but central issue of discursive competence. A uniquely exacting delicacy of attention must be at the heart of adequacy in environmental valuation, if this enterprise is at all as I have tried to describe it. Such attention is very far from being something which just comes naturally, or at which all citizens can be expected, with perhaps a little facilitation, to be equally adept. It involves, indeed, a deliberately cultivated range of experience, richness of information, habit of essential logic, fineness of sensibility and athleticism of imagination: capacities and achievements which only a small minority can realistically be expected to combine. There is, in other words, a major problem of reconciling democracy and authority within the practice of environmental judgement itself.

Now while there are obviously important political and administrative dimensions to this problem, a principal resource for addressing it will have to be educational. Moreover, given the complexity of the demands on judgement, it seems clear that a major element in that resource will have to be education at the university level[8] – at the level where the environmental awareness and judgement of the most energetic minds and sensibilities in each generation are in question. I want to end by suggesting (in merest outline) that, actually, any hope of resolving either of these two crucial problems for democratic environmental valuation (call them, as a shorthand, Promethean value and discursive authority) lies in the same response: the redevelopment of a living practice of humane general education at this level, centred on our new environmental responsibilities.

The focus here is on *humane* education, because this follows from the whole thrust of my argument in section 4 above. Value in general, but

244

Promethean value pre-eminently, can only come to bear on our judgement to the extent that we construct it creatively. As far as environmental value goes, this demands much more than Brennan's 'ecological sensitivity, moral maturity and informed awareness of natural processes'. It demands that we inhabit, and conduct our valuing from within, a real and potent tradition of relevant creative activity. This requirement only the humane modes of thought can begin to meet. As some recent official dicussion has recognised (Toyne Report 1993), the humanities disciplines in education have an obvious contribution to make to environmental *understanding*; they cultivate an awareness of the context of environmental problems in terms both of past causes and of changing concepts and attitudes. When the focus of concern shifts to *judgement*, however, their relevance lies in the relation which their practice bears to our consciously reflective dwelling in value. The idea of environmental responsibility envisages nature as a structure of significance; human judgement is responsible for creating this structure and continuously maintaining it in existence; and what we need is a living sense, continuously recruited and refreshed, of how the culture can create the significances of environment responsibly. No such sense is available which is not kept in close vital touch with the humane disciplines of thought as they bear on environmental concerns: in the first place, with the study of imaginative literature, with first-hand philosophical investigation and with historical interpretation. For in these modes of thought we come to full active consciousness of the creative-interpretive judgement which sustains the human world of value. And in their inclusion as key elements within the comprehensive discourse established by a generalist environmental education, we can begin to see how responsible judgement, aware of its Promethean inheritance, may also hope to be shaped by an awareness of economic and other practical constraints.

It should be clear, too, that the relation between, on the one hand, the cultural engagement thus generating and refining environmental value, and on the other the wider social institutions of an environmentally-literate democracy, could not be the merely external relation between 'education' and economic life which has lately been accepted as the norm. Centres of such discourse could not possibly be seen as existing to produce citizens appropriately trained in environmental value-judgement, or to supply research findings as 'management information' to the real protagonists of social decision-making. Rather they would be crucial protagonists themselves, essential parts of the institutional structure of judgement: loci of the necessary reintegration of intelligence. Such reintegration could not, in the nature of differential competence, be a general condition of the exercise of judgement – at its fullest it would be sustained by the work of a statistically small minority. It would achieve existence where a vital creative deference to Promethean value could inform and be informed by, for instance, a properly skilled attention to economic and policy implications, and these places would feed an appropriately-grounded discursive authority through the intellectual life of the whole deliberative community.

How this could work in institutional reality needs to be the subject of much further thought, though not in these pages. How, for instance, could the discursive institutions sketched so intriguingly by Michael Jacobs in the previous chapter, and the creative centres of environmental value which I am envisaging, be set in plausible conjunction so that they interanimated one another? It would certainly be more than a matter of having humanists among other specialists from the local university on some of the deliberative panels, and more than regular 'continuing environmental education' opportunities for those engaged in environmental policy-making – though both these ideas seem to point to small steps in the right general direction. The future development (both conceptual and practical) of environmental education, and its whole relation to environmental judgement, are indeed huge and pressing issues. But they are only two among the many challenges which this book has suggested that we must now confront, if our new commitment to valuing nature is seriously to be honoured.[9]

NOTES

1 For a clear recent account of this structure, see the early part of Broome 1991, though his development of the idea is thoroughly, even aggressively, economistic.

2 See especially chapters by O'Neill, Stirling and Jacobs.

3 Compare Nagel (1979) on the 'disparity between the fragmentation of value and the unity of decision'

4 This is of course to make yet another point against the environmental economists' concept of 'existence value'. See Pearce and Moran 1994, where survey evidence is claimed to support an existence value of US $18.5 per capita per annum for the grizzly as against only $8.6 for the bighorn, and these values are treated as somehow capturing for economic analysis the intrinsic value which people recognise in the continued existence of these two species respectively. The obvious response (and compare Roxbee Cox, this volume) is that whatever a differential expressible in these terms may be said to capture, it cannot be a relation between values which we recognise in these independent lives 'in themselves'.

5 Anything persuasive in this line of argument is very largely owing to the English literary critic F. R. Leavis, who developed out of his critical practice the leading ideas which I am trying to take over for a new context. See in particular Leavis 1969, ch.1, Leavis and Leavis 1970, ch.5, and Leavis 1986: 285–97.

6 I have no space here to defend these offered parallels, which will therefore appear dogmatic; the test must lie in their suggestiveness for the issue at hand.

7 See Michael Jacobs, this volume.

8 Or rather, it has to be said, at the level of some among those many and diverse institutions which are presently called universities in the UK.

9 An earlier version of some of the material in this chapter appeared as Foster (1994); I am grateful to the editors of *Analyse & Kritik* for permission to re-use it here.

BIBLIOGRAPHY

Adams, J. (1979) *Transport planning: Vision and Practice*, London: Routledge.
—— (1994) 'The role of cost–benefit analysis in environmental debates', draft report to Green College, Oxford.
Aldred, J. (1993) 'Does a definition of rational self-interest that seeks to incorporate altruism lead to tautology?', submitted to *Economics and Philosophy*.
—— (1994) 'Existence value, welfare and altruism', *Environmental Values* 3.
Anderson, I. (1991) 'Gold rush threatens Australia's green dreams', *New Scientist* 130, 1766, 27 April.
Aquinas (1963) *Summa Theologiae*, London: Eyre and Spottiswoode.
Aristotle (1948) *Politics*, trans. E. Barker, Oxford: Oxford University Press.
—— (1934) *Nicomachean Ethics*, trans. H. Rackham, London: Heinemann.
Armour, A. (1995) 'The citizens' jury as model of public participation: a critical evaluation', in O. Renn, T. Webler and P. Wiedemann (eds) *Fairness and Competence in Citizen Participation*, Dordrecht: Kluwer.
Arrow, K. J. (1963) *Social Choice and Individual Values*, 2nd edn, New York: Wiley.
—— (1974) *The Limits of Organization*, New York: Norton.
Arthur, B. (1989) 'Competing technologies, increasing returns and lock-in by historical events', *Economic Journal* 99.
Atiyah, P. S. (1979) *The Rise and Fall of Freedom of Contract*, Oxford: Clarendon Press.
Attfield, R. (1983) *The Ethics of Environmental Concern*, Oxford: Blackwell Publishers.
—— (1987) *A Theory of Value and Obligation*, London: Croom Helm.
Attfield, R. and Dell, K. (eds) (1989) *Values, Conflict and the Environment*, Oxford: Ian Ramsey Centre.
Axelrod, R. M. (1984) *The Evolution of Cooperation*, New York: Basic Books.
Ayres R. U. and Walters, J. (1991) 'The greenhouse effect: damages, costs and abatement', *Environmental and Resource Economics* 1, 3.
Baehr, P. and Whittrock, B. (eds) (1981) *Policy Analysis and Policy Innovation: Patterns, Problems and Potentials*, London: Sage.
Barbier, E. B. (1993) 'Introduction: economics and ecology – the next frontier', in E. B. Barbier (ed.) *Economics and Ecology: New Frontiers and Sustainable Development*, London: Chapman and Hall.
Barnes, B. and Bloor, D. (1982) 'Relativism, rationalism and the sociology of knowledge', in Hollis and Lukes.
Barnes, B. and Shapin, S. (eds) (1979) *Natural Order: Historical Studies of Scientific Culture*, London: Sage.
Bateman, I. and Bryan, F. (1994) 'Recent advances in the monetary evaluation of environmental preferences', in R. Wood (ed.) 'Environmental economics,

sustainable management and the countryside', proceedings of a workshop held on 25 April 1994, Countryside Recreation Network, University of Wales, Cardiff.

Bauman, Z. (1991) *Intimations of Past Modernity*, London: Routledge.

Baumol, W. J. and Oates, W. E. (1988) *The Theory of Environmental Policy*, 2nd edn, Cambridge and New York: Cambridge University Press.

Beck, U. (1992) *Risk Society*, London: Sage.

Becker, Gary S. (1974) 'A theory of social interactions', *Journal of Political Economy* 82, 6.

—— (1976a) 'Altruism, egoism, and genetic fitness: Economics and sociobiology', *Journal of Economic Literature* 14, 2.

—— (1976b), *The Economic Approach to Human Behaviour*, Chicago: University of Chicago Press.

Beckerman, W. (1994) 'Sustainable development: is it a useful concept?', *Environmental Values* 3, 3.

—— (1995) 'How would you like your sustainability, sir? Weak or strong? A reply to my critics', *Environmental Values* 4, 2.

Bell, D., Keeney, R. and Raiffa, H. (1977) *Conflicting Objectives in Decisions*, Chichester: Wiley.

Bergström, S. (1993) 'Value standards in sub-sustainable development: on limits of ecological economics', *Ecological Economics* 7, 1.

Bhaskar, R. (1975) *A Realist Theory of Science*, Leeds: Leeds Books (2nd edn 1978, Brighton: Harvester).

—— (1979) *The Possibility of Naturalism: A Philosophic Critique of the Contemporary Human Sciences*, Brighton: Harvester.

Bijker, W., Hughes, T. and Pinch, T. (1987) *The Social Construction of Large Technical Systems: New Directions in the Sociology and History of Technology*, Cambridge, Mass.: MIT Press.

Bisset, R. and Tomlinson, P. (eds) (1984) *Perspectives on Environmental Impact Assessment*, Boston: Reidel.

Blamey, R. (1994a) 'Consumer versus citizen responses in environmental valuation surveys: Clarification and empirical evidence', mimeo, Centre for Resource and Environmental Studies, Australian National University, Canberra.

—— (1994b) 'Citizens, consumers and contingent valuation: clarification and comparison of market and referendum response formats', paper presented to the 3rd biennial meeting of the International Society for Ecological Economics, San José, Costa Rica, October.

Blamey, R. and Common, M. (1994) 'Symbolic responses in contingent valuation studies', mimeo, Centre for Resource and Environmental Studies, Australian National University, Canberra.

Blamey, R., Common, M. and Quiggin, J. (1994) 'Respondents to contingent valuation surveys: consumers or citizens?', mimeo, Centre for Resource and Environmental Studies, Australian National University, Canberra.

Block, W. (ed.) (1989) *Economics and the Environment: A Reconciliation*, Vancouver, BC: Fraser Institute.

Bloor, D. (1976) *Knowledge and Social Imagery*, London: Routledge.

—— (1983) *Wittgenstein: A Social Theory of Knowledge*, London: Macmillan.

Boulding, K. E. and Lundstedt, S. E. (1988) 'Value concepts and justification', in Peterson *et al.*.

Bowers, J. B. (1993) 'Pricing the environment: a critique', *International Review of Applied Economics* 7.

Boyce, R. R., Brown, T. C., McClelland, G. H., Peterson, G. L. and Schulze, W. D.

(1992) 'An experimental examination of intrinsic values as a source of the WTA–WTP disparity', *American Economic Review* 82, 5.

Boyle, K. J. and Bishop, R. (1987) 'Valuing wildlife in benefit cost analyses', *Water Resource Research* 23, 5.

Boyle, K. J., Desvouges, W. H., Johnson, F. R., Dunford, R. W. and Hudson, S. P. (1994) 'An investigation of part–whole biases in contingent valuation studies', *Journal of Environmental Economics and Management* 27.

Brandt, R. E. (1979) *A Theory of the Good and the Right*, Oxford: Oxford University Press.

Brennan, A. (1984) 'The moral standing of natural objects', *Environmental Ethics* 6.

—— (1992) 'Moral pluralism and the environment', *Environmental Values* 1.

—— (1994) 'Environmental literacy and educational ideal', *Environmental Values* 3.

Brookshire, D., Eubanks, L. and Sorg, C. (1986) 'Existence values and normative economics: implications for valuing water resources', *Water Resources Research* 22, 11.

Brookshire, D. and Smith, V. (1987) 'Measuring recreation benefits: Conceptual and empirical issues', *Water Resources Research* 23, 5.

Broome, J. (1991) *Weighing Goods*, Oxford: Blackwell Publishers.

Brown, J. (ed.) (1989) *Environmental Threats: Perception, Analysis and Management*, London: Belhaven.

Brown, P. G. (1992) 'Climate change and the planetary trust', *Energy Policy* 20, 3.

Brown, T. C. (1984) 'The concept of value in resource allocation', *Land Economics* 60.

Brown, T. C. and Slovic, P. (1988) 'Effects of context on economic measures of value', in G. L. Peterson, B. L. Driver and R. Gregory (eds) *Amenity Resource Valuation: Integrating Economics with Other Disciplines*, State College, Philadelphia, Pa.: Venture.

Brown, T. C., Peterson, G. L. and Tonn, B. E. (1995) 'The values jury to aid natural resource decisions', *Land Economics* 71.

Buchanan, A. (1985) *Ethics, Efficiency and the Market*, Oxford: Clarendon Press.

Buckley, P. J. and Casson, M. C. (1993) 'Economics as an imperialist social science', *Human Relations* 46, 9.

Bullard, J. (1986) *Rethinking Rational Expectations*, in von Winterfeldt and Edwards.

Burgess, J., Harrison, C. and Maiteny, P. (1991) 'Contested meanings: The consumption of news about nature conservation', *Media, Culture and Society* 13.

Burgess, J., Limb, M. and Harrison, C. M. (1988) 'Exploring environmental values through the medium of small groups: parts 1 and 2', *Environment and Planning A* 20.

Burke, E. (1968) [1790] *Reflections on the Revolution in France*, Harmondsworth: Penguin.

Callicott, J. (1986) 'The intrinsic value of non-human species', in B. Norton (ed.) *The Preservation of Species*, Princeton, NJ: Princeton University Press.

Carson, R. T. (1994) 'Valuation of tropical rainforests: philosophical and practical issues in the use of contingent valuation', paper presented to the 3rd biennial meeting of the International Society for Ecological Economics, San José, Costa Rica, October.

Castellan, N. and Sawyer, T. (1990) 'Multi-attribute decision models: Task order and group effects', in von Furstenberg.

Castle, E. N., Berrens, R. P. and Adams, R. M. (1994) 'Natural resource damage assessment: speculations about a missing perspective', *Land Economics* 70.

Chadwick, M. and Kuylenstiernia, J. (1990) *The Relative Sensitivity of Soils in Europe to*

Acid Depositions: A Preliminary Assessment of the Sensitivity of Aquatic and Terrestrial Ecosystems, York: Stockholm Environment Institute.

Chapman, C. (1992) 'Risk management: prediciting and dealing with an uncertain future', submission to Ontario Environmental Assessment Board, University of Southampton.

Charlton, W. (ed.) (1970) *Aristotle's Physics*, Book I and II, Oxford: Clarendon Press.

Christensen, P. P. (1991) 'Driving forces, increasing returns and ecological sustainability', in Constanza.

Churchman, C. W. (1961) *Prediction and Optimal Decision*, New York: Prentice Hall.

—— (1968) *The Systems Approach*, New York: Delacorte Press.

Clark, J. and Burgess, J. (1994) 'The Pevensey Levels residents' group: a summary report', mimeo, Department of Geography, University College London.

—— (forthcoming) 'Asking questions about answering questions: a case study of public understanding of a contingent valuation survey', in P. Lowe (ed.) *Environmental Valuation and Public Policy*, Reading: CAB International,.

Cline, W. R. (1992) *The Economics of Global Warming*, Harlow: Longman.

Coase, R. H. (1960) 'The problem of social cost', *Journal of Law and Economics* 3.

Cobbing, P. and Slee, B. (1992), 'The application of contingent valuation to the economic valuation of environmental resources', report to the Nature Conservancy Council for Scotland and Grampian Regional Council.

Cohen, J. (1989) 'Deliberation and democratic legitimacy', in A. Hamlin and P. Pettit (eds) *The Good Polity*, Oxford: Blackwell Publishers.

Coleman, J. S. (1991) *Foundations of Social Theory*, Cambridge Mass.: Harvard University Press.

Collier, A. (1994) 'Value, rationality and the environment', *Radical Philosophy* 66.

Collingridge, D. (1982) *Critical Decision Theory: A New Theory of Social Choice*, London: Frances Pinter.

Collis, I., Jacobs, M. and Heap, J. (1992) *Strategic Planning and Sustainable Development*, Peterborough: English Nature.

Common, M. and Perring, C. (1992), 'Towards an ecological economics of sustainability', *Ecological Economics* 6.

Conrad, J. (ed.) (1980) *Society, Technology, and Risk*, New York: Academic Press.

Constanza, R. (ed.) (1991) *Ecological Economics: The Science and Management of Sustainability*, New York: Columbia University Press.

Cooper, D. (1992) 'The idea of environment', in Cooper and Palmer.

Cooper, D. and Palmer, J. (1992) *The Environment in Question*, London: Routledge.

CORE (1993) *1992–93 Annual Report to the British Columbia Legislative Assembly*, Victoria, BC: Commission on Resources and Environment.

Cowan, R. (1990) 'Nuclear power reactors: a study in technological lock-in', *Journal of Economic History* 50, 3.

—— (1991) 'Tortoises and hares: choice among technologies of unknown merit', *Economic Journal* 101.

Craig, P., Glasse, H. and Kempton, W. (1993) 'Ethics and values in environmental policy', *Environmental Values* 2, 2.

Cropper, M. L. and Oates, W. E. (1991) *Environmental Economics: A Survey*, Washington, DC: Resources for the Future, Discussion Paper QE90–12–REV.

Crouch, E. A. and Wilson, R. (1982) *Risk Benefit Analysis*, Cambridge Mass.: Ballinger.

Crowley, B. L. (1987) *The Self, the Individual, and the Community: Liberalism in the Political Thought of F. A. Hayek and Sidney and Beatrice Webb*, Oxford: Clarendon Press.

Cummings, R. G., Brookshire, D. S. and Schulze, W. D. (1986) *Valuing Environmental*

Goods: An Assessment of the Contingent Valuation Method, Totowa, NJ: Rowman and Allanheld.

Curran, J. (1991) 'Mass media and democracy', in J. Curran and M. Gurevitch (eds) *Mass Media and Society*, London: Edward Arnold.

Daily, G. C., Ehrlich, P. R., Mooney, H. A. and Ehrlich, A. H. (1991) 'Greenhouse economics: learn before you leap', *Ecological Economics* 4, 1.

Daly, H. E. (1985) 'The circular flow of exchange value and the linear throughput of matter-energy: a case of misplaced concreteness', *Review of Social Economy*.

—— (1991) 'Population and economics: a bioeconomic analysis', *Population and Environment* 12.

—— (1992), 'Allocation, distribution and scale: towards an economics that is efficient, just and sustainable', *Ecological Economics* 6.

—— (1995) 'On Wilfred Beckerman's critique of sustainable development', *Environmental Values* 4, 1.

Daly, H. E. and Cobb, J. B. (1989) *For the Common Good: Redirecting the Economy towards Community, the Environment and a Sustainable Future*, London: Greenprint.

Dasgupta, Partha (1991) 'The environment as a commodity', in Helm.

David, P. (1985) 'Clio and the economics of QWERTY', *Economics* 75, 2.

David, P. and Bunn, J. (1988) 'The economics of gateway technologies and the evolution of network industries', *Information, Economics and Policy* 4, 2.

Demsetz, H. (1967) 'Toward a theory of property rights', *American Economics Review (Papers and Proceedings)* 57, 2: 347–59.

Department of the Environment (1995) *A Guide to Risk Assessment and Risk Management for Environmental Protection*, London: HMSO.

Diamond, P. A. and Hausman, J. A. (1993) 'Contingent valuation: is some number better than no number?', mimeo, Massachusetts Institute of Technology, Dept of Economics.

Doering, R. (1993) 'Canadian Round Tables on the environment and the economy: their history, form and function', Ottawa: National Round Table on the Environment and the Economy.

Douglas, M. (1970) *Implicit Meanings*, London: Routledge and Kegan Paul.

Doyal, L. and Gough, I. (1991) *A Theory of Human Need*, London: Macmillan.

Dryzek, J. (1990a) *Discursive Democracy*, Cambridge: Cambridge University Press.

—— (1990b) 'Green reason: communicative ethics for the biosphere', *Environmental Ethics* 12.

DTI (1993) UK Government Department of Trade and Industry, *The Prospects for Coal: Conclusions of the Government's Coal Review*, Command 2235, London: HMSO.

—— (1994) UK Government Department of Trade and Industry, *New and Renewable Energy: Future Prospects for the UK*, Energy Paper 62, London: HMSO.

—— (1995) UK Government Department of Trade and Industry, *The Prospects for Nuclear Power: Conclusions of the Government's Nuclear Review*, London: HMSO.

Dunn, P. (1994) 'A setback for Green lobby over valley', *The Independent*.

Durkheim, E. (1933) *The Division of Labour in Society*, trans. G. Simpson, Illinois: Free Press.

Eckersley, R. (forthcoming) 'Greening liberal democracy: the rights discourse revisited', in B. Doherty and M. de Geus (eds) *Democracy and Green Political Thought*, London: Routledge.

Edwards, R. (1979) *Pleasures and Pains*, New York: Cornell University Press.

Elliot, R. (1982) 'Faking nature', *Inquiry* 25.

Elliot, R. and Gare, A. (eds) (1983) *Environmental Philosophy*, Milton Keynes: Open University Press.

Ellsberg, D. (1961) 'Risk, ambiguity and the Savage axioms', *Quarterly Journal of Economics* 75.

El Serafy, S. (1995) 'In defence of weak sustainability: a response to Beckerman', *Environmental Values* 4, 4.

Elster, J. (1986) 'The market and the forum: three varieties of political theory', in J. Elster and A. Hylland (eds) *Foundations of Social Choice Theory*, Cambridge: Cambridge University Press.

Emery, F. E. (ed.) (1969) *Systems Thinking*, Harmondsworth: Penguin.

English Nature (1992) *Strategic Planning and Sustainable Development*, Peterborough: English Nature.

—— (1994) *Planning for Environmental Sustainability*, Peterborough: English Nature.

ETSU (1994) UK Government Energy Technology Support Unit, *An Assessment of Renewable Energy for the UK*, ETSU-R-82, London: HMSO.

Etzioni, A. (1988) *The Moral Dimension: Toward a New Economics*, New York: Free Press.

Evans-Pritchard, E. (1937) *Witchcraft, Oracles and Magic Among the Azande*, Oxford: Oxford University Press.

Eyerman, R. and Jamison, A. (1991) *Social Movements: A Cognitive Approach*, London: Polity Press.

Faber, M. and Proops, J. (1994) *Evolution, Time Production and the Environment*, 2nd edn, Berlin: Springer.

Fankhauser, S. (1995) *Valuing Climate Change: The Economics of the Greenhouse*, London: Earthscan.

Feyerabend, P. (1975) *Against Method*, London: Verso.

—— (1978) *Science in a Free Society*, London: Verso.

Finkels, M. and Friedman, R. (1967) 'The application of an entropy theory of concentration', *Yale Law Journal* 76.

Fischoff, B., Watson, S. and Hope, C. (1984) 'Defining risk', *Policy Sciences* 17.

Fischoff, B. and Furby, L. (1988) 'Measuring values', *Journal of Risk and Uncertainity* 1.

Fishkin, J. (1991) *Democracy and Deliberation: New Directions for Democratic Reform*, New Haven, Conn.: Yale University Press.

Foster, J. (1994) 'Beyond costs and benefits: weighing environmental goods', *Analyse & Kritik*, 16.

Frank, R. H., Gilovich, T. and Regan, D. T. (1993) 'Does studying economics inhibit cooperation?', *Journal of Economic Perspectives* 7, 2.

Freeden, M. (ed.) (1988) *J. A. Hobson: A Reader*, London and Boston: Unwin Hyman.

Freeman, C. (1986) 'The case for technological determinism', paper presented at ESRC Conference, Cambridge.

Fremlin, J. H. (1985) *The Risks of Power Production*, London: Macmillan.

Friedman, M. (1953) 'The methodology of positive economics', in M. Friedman, *Essays in Positive Economics*, Chicago: University of Chicago Press.

Friends of the Earth Scotland (1995) 'The environmental space for Scotland: interim summary', Friends of the Earth Scotland, Edinburgh.

Funtowicz, S. O. and Ravetz, J. R. (1990) *Uncertainty and Quality in Science for Policy*, Dordrecht: Kluwer.

Gadamer, H. G. (1989) *Truth and Method*, 2nd rev. edn, trans. W. Glen-Doepel, revised by J. Weinsheimer and D. G. Marshall, London: Sheed and Ward.

Galbraith, J. K. (1969) *The New Industrial State*, Harmondsworth: Penguin.

—— (1970) *The Affluent Society*, 2nd edn, Harmondsworth: Penguin.

Garfinkel, H. (1963) 'A conception of, and experiments with, trust as a condition

BIBLIOGRAPHY

for stable concerted action', in O. J. Harvey (ed.) *Motivation and Social Interaction*, New York: Ronald Press.

—— (1967) *Studies in Ethnomethodology*, Englewood Cliffs, NJ: Prentice Hall.

Garrod, G. D., and Willis, K. G. (1994) 'Valuing biodiversity and nature conservation at a local level', *Biodiversity and Conservation* 3.

Geach, P. (1967) 'Good and evil', in P. Foot (ed.) *Theories of Ethics*, Oxford: Oxford University Press.

—— (1977) *The Virtues*, Cambridge: Cambridge University Press.

Georgescu-Roegen, N. (1971) *The Entropy Law and the Economic Process*, Cambridge, Mass.: Harvard University Press.

Gershuny, J. (1978) 'Policy making rationality: a reformulation', *Policy Sciences* 9.

—— (1981) 'What should forecasters do? A pessimistic view', in Baehr and Whittrock.

Giddens, A. (1990) *The Consequences of Modernity*, London: Polity Press

Gleick, J. (1988) *Chaos: Making a New Science*, London: Sphere.

Goodin, R. (1986) 'Laundering preferences', in J. Elster and A. Hylland (eds) *Foundations of Social Choice Theory*, Cambridge: Cambridge University Press.

—— (1992) *Green Political Theory*, Cambridge: Polity Press.

Goodpaster, K. (1978) 'On being morally considerable', *Journal of Philosophy* 75.

Goodstein, E. B. (1994) 'In defence of health-based standards', *Ecological Economics* 10.

Gordon, J. (1994) *Canadian Round Tables and Other Mechanisms for Sustainable Development in Canada*, Luton: Local Government Management Board.

Gordon, S. (1991) *The History and Philosophy of Social Science*, London: Routledge.

Gosling, J. C. B. (1969) *Pleasure and Desire*, Oxford: Clarendon Press.

Gough, I. (1993) 'Need, concept of', in Hodgson *et al.*, vol. 2.

Granger-Morgan, M. (1981) 'Probing the question of technology-induced risk', *IEEE Spectrum* 18, 11.

Green, C. H. and Tunstall, S. M. (1993), *The Non-use Value of Sites of Environmental Value: What, Why and Who?*, Flood Hazard Research Centre, Middlesex University.

Green, C. J. *et al.* (1990) *Project Appraisal* 5, 2.

Gregory, R. (1986) 'Interpreting measures of economic loss: evidence of contingent valuation and experimental studies', *Journal of Environmental Economics and Management* 13, 4.

Gregory, R., Lichtenstein, S. and Slovic, P. (1993) 'Valuing environmental resources: a constructivist approach', *Journal of Risk and Uncertainty* 7, 4.

Griffin, J. (1986) *Well-Being*, Oxford: Clarendon Press.

Grove-White, R. (1993) 'Environmentalism: a new moral discourse for technological society', in K. Milton (ed.) *Environmentalism: The View from Anthropology*, London: Routledge.

Habermas, J. (1984) *The Theory of Communicative Action*; vol. 1: *Reason and the Rationalisation of Society*, trans. T. McCarthy, Boston, Mass.: Beacon Press.

—— (1989) *The Structural Transformation of the Public Sphere*, Cambridge: Polity Press.

Hagstrom, W. O. (1965) *The Scientific Community*, New York: Basic Books.

Hahn, R. W. (1989) 'Economic prescriptions for environmental problems: how the patient followed the doctors orders', *Journal of Economic Perspectives* 3, 2.

Hanley, N., Munro, A. and Jamieson, D. (1991) 'Environmental economics and sustainable development in nature conservation', unpublished report to Nature Conservancy Council, Economics Department, University of Stirling.

Hardin, R. (1988) *Morality within the Limits of Reason*, Chicago: University of Chicago Press.

253

Hare, R. M. (1987) 'Moral reasoning about the environment', *Journal of Applied Philosophy* 4.

Harrison, C. M. and Burgess, J. (1994) 'Social constructions of nature: a case study of conflicts over the development of Rainham Marshes SSSI', *Transactions of the Institute of British Geographers* 19, 3.

Hausman, J. A. (ed.) (1993) *Contingent Valuation: a Critical Assessment*, Amsterdam: North Holland Press.

Hayek, F. (ed.) (1935) *Collectivist Economic Planning*, London: Routledge and Kegan Paul.

—— (1978) *New Studies in Philosophy, Politics, Economics and the History of Ideas*, Chicago: University of Chicago Press.

Hayer, M. (1995) *The Politics of Environmental Discourse*, Oxford: Clarendon Press.

Helm, D. (ed.) (1991) *Economic Policy Towards the Environment*, Oxford: Blackwell Publishers.

Helm, D. and Pearce, D. (1991) 'Economic policy towards the environment: an overview', in Helm.

Hinterberger, F., Luks, F. and Schmidt-Bleek, F. (1995) 'What is natural capital?', *Wuppertal Papers* No. 29, Wuppertal: Institute for Climate, Environment, Energy.

Hirata, G. N. and Takahashi, P. K. (1991) *Assessing the Real Cost of Energy*, Honolulu: Hawaii Natural Energy Institute.

Hirsch, F. (1977) *Social Limits to Growth*, London: Routledge.

Hirshleifer, J. (1977) 'Economics from a biological viewpoint', *Journal of Law and Economics* 20.

—— (1978) 'Natural economy versus political economy', *Journal of Social and Biological Structures* 1.

Hobson, J. A. (1914) *Work and Wealth: A Human Valuation*, London: Macmillan.

Hodge, I. D., Adams, W. M., and Bourn, N. A. D. (1994) 'Conservation policy in the wider countryside: agency competition and innovation', *Journal of Environmental Planning and Management* 37.

Hodgson, G. M. (1988) *Economics and Institutions: A Manifesto for a Modern Institutional Economics*, Cambridge and Philadelphia, Pa.: Polity Press and University of Pennsylvania Press.

—— (1993a) 'Institutional economics: surveying the old and the new', *Metroeconomica* 44, 1. Reprinted in G. M. Hodgson (ed.) *The Economics of Institutions*, Aldershot: Edward Elgar.

—— (1993b) *Economics and Evolution: Bringing Life back into Economics*, Cambridge and Ann Arbor, Mich.: Polity Press and University of Michigan Press.

Hodgson, G. M., Samuels, W. J. and Tool, M. R. (eds) (1993) *The Elgar Companion to Institutional and Evolutionary Economics*, 2 vols, Aldershot: Edward Elgar.

Hofstadter, D. (1979) *Goedel, Escher, Bach: An Eternal Golden Braid*, London: Vintage.

Hogwood, B. W. and Gunn, L. A. (1984) *Policy Analysis for the Real World*, Oxford: Oxford University Press.

Hohmeyer, O. (1992) 'Renewables and the full costs of energy', *Energy Policy* 10, 4.

Holdren, J. *et al.* (1979) 'Energy: calculating the risks', *Science* 204.

Holland, A. (1994) 'Natural capital', in R. Attfield and A. Belsey (eds) *Philosophy and the Natural Environment*, Cambridge: Cambridge University Press.

—— (1995) 'The assumptions of cost–benefit analysis: a philosopher's view', in K. Willis and J. Corkindale (eds) *Environmental Valuation: New Perspectives*, Wallingford: CAB International.

—— (forthcoming) 'Failing to get the measure of sustainability', in P. Lowe (ed.) *Environmental Valuation and Policy Appraisal*, Reading: CAB International.

Holland, A. and O'Neill, J. (1996) 'The ecological integrity of nature over time: some problems', *Global Bioethics* 11, 1.

Holland, A. and Roxbee-Cox, J. (1992) 'The valuing of environmental goods: a modest proposal', in A. Coker and C. Richards (eds) *Valuing the Environment*, Aldershot: Edward Elgar.

Hollis, M. (1970) 'Reason and ritual', in Wilson.

Hollis, M. and Lukes, S. (1982) *Rationality and Relativism*, Oxford: Blackwell Publishers.

Hope, C., Jones, M. and Hughes, R. (1988) *A Multi-Attribute Model for the Study of UK Energy Strategies*, Cambridge: Cambridge University Department of Management Studies.

HSE (1988) UK Health and Safety Executive, *The Tolerability of Risk from Nuclear Power Stations*, London: HMSO (revised and reprinted 1992).

Hubbard, H. M. (1991) 'The real cost of energy', *Scientific American* 264, 4.

Huggett, R. J. (1993) *Modelling the Human Impact on Nature*, Oxford: Oxford University Press.

Hughes, T. (1983) *Networks of Power*, Baltimore, Md.: Johns Hopkins University Press.

—— (1987) 'The evolution of large technical systems', in Bijker *et al.*.

Hurka, T. (1987) 'Good and good for', *Mind* 96.

Hutchinson, T. W. (1938) *The Significance and Basic Postulates of Economic Theory*, London: Macmillan.

IAEA (1991) International Atomic Energy Agency, *Electricity and the Environment: Background Papers for a Senior Expert Symposium Held in Helsinki, 13–17 May 1991*, Vienna: IAEA–TECDOC–624.

Idso, S. B. (1984) 'A review of recent reports dealing with the greenhouse effect of atmospheric carbon dioxide', *Journal of Air Pollution Control Association* 34, 5.

IEA (1989) International Energy Agency, *Energy Technologies for Reducing Emissions of Greenhouse Gases*, Paris: IEA.

Ives, D., Kemp, R. and Thieme, M. (1991) *The Statistical Value of Life and Safety Investment*, Norwich: University of East Anglia Environmental Risk Assessment Unit, Research report 13.

Jacobs, M. (1991) *The Green Economy: Environment, Sustainable Development and the Politics of the Future*, London: Pluto Press.

—— (1993) *Sense and Sustainability: Land Use Planning and Environmentally Sustainable Development*, London: Council for the Protection of Rural England.

—— (1994) 'The limits of neoclassicism: towards an institutional environmental economics', in M. Redclift and T. Benton (eds) *Social Theory and the Global Environment*, London: Routledge.

—— (1995a) 'Sustainability and the market: a typology of environmental economics', in R. Eckersley (ed.) *Markets, Bureaucracy and the Environment: New Directions in Environmental Governance*, London: Macmillan.

—— (1995b) 'Common goods: wellbeing, identity and constitutive value', mimeo, Centre for the Study of Environmental Change, Lancaster University.

—— (1995c) 'Sustainable development, capital substitution and economic humility: a response to Beckerman', *Environmental Values* 4, 1.

Jasanoff, S. (1990) *The Fifth Branch: Scientist Advisers as Policy Makers*, Cambridge, Mass.: Harvard University Press.

Johannson, P. O. (1990) 'Valuing environmental damage', *Oxford Review of Economic Policy* 6.

Jones-Lee, M. (1989) *The Economics of Safety and Physical Risk*, Oxford: Blackwell Publishers.

Kahneman, D. and Knetsch, J. L. (1992) 'Valuing public goods: the purchase of moral satisfaction', *Journal of Environmental Economics and Management* 22, 1.

Kahnemann, D. and Ritov, I. (1994) 'Determinants of stated willingness to pay for public goods: a study in the headline method', *Journal of Risk and Uncertainty* 9, 1.

Kant, I. (1991a) 'On the common saying: This may be true in theory but it does not apply in practice', in H. Reiss (ed.) *Political Writings*, Cambridge: Cambridge University Press.

—— (1991b) 'An answer to the question What is enlightenment?', in H. Reiss (ed.) *Political Writings*, Cambridge: Cambridge University Press.

Kapp, K. W. (1976) 'The nature and significance of institutional economics', *Kyklos* 29, Fasc. 2. Reprinted in W. J. Samuels (ed.) (1988) *Institutional Economics* 1, Aldershot: Edward Elgar.

—— (1978) *The Social Costs of Business Enterprise*, 3rd edn (first published 1950), Nottingham: Spokesman.

Keat, R. N. (1981) *The Politics of Social Theory*, Oxford: Blackwell Publishers.

—— (1993) 'Scepticism, authority and the market', in R. Keat, N. Whiteley and N. Abercrombie (eds) *The Authority of the Consumer*, London: Routledge.

—— (1994) 'Citizens, consumers and the environment: reflections on *The Economy of the Earth*', *Environmental Values* 3.

Keeney, R. L. (1977) 'The art of assessing multi-attribute utility functions', *Organisational Behaviour and Human Performance* 28.

—— (1982) 'Decision analysis: an overview', *Operations Research* 30, 5.

Keeney, R. L. and Raiffa, H. (1976) *Decisions with Multiple Objectives: Preferences and Value Trade-offs*, New York: Wiley.

Keeney, R., Renn, O. and von Winterfeldt, D. (1987) 'Structuring West Germany's energy objectives', *Energy Policy.*

Keynes, J. M. (1933) *Essays in Biography*, London: Macmillan.

Khalil, E. L. (1990) 'Entropy law and exhaustion of natural resources: is Nicholas Georgescu-Roegen's paradigm defensible?', *Ecological Economics* 2.

—— (1993) 'Trust', in Hodgson *et al.*, vol. 2.

Knetsch, J. L. (1994) 'Environmental valuation: some problems of wrong questions and misleading answers', *Environmental Values* 3, 4.

Knight, F. (1921) *Risk, Uncertainty and Profit*, Boston, Mass.: Houghton Mifflin.

Krimsky, S. and Golding, D. (1992) (eds) *Social Theories of Risk*, Westport, Conn.: Praeger.

Kuhn, T. (1970) *The Structure of Scientific Revolutions*, Chicago: University of Chicago Press.

Lambert, B. (1985) *How Safe is Safe: Radiation Controversies Explained*, London: Unwin Hyman.

Lange, O. (1970) *Introduction to Economic Cybernetics*, Oxford: Pergamon Press.

Lasch, C. (1979) *The Culture of Narcissism*, New York: Norton.

Lash, S., Szerszinski, B. and Wynne, B. (1996) *Risk, Environment and Modernity: Towards a New Ecology*, London: Sage.

Lavoie, D. (1985) *Rivalry and Central Planning: The Socialist Calculation Debate Reconsidered*, Cambridge: Cambridge University Press.

Leavis, F. R. (1969) *English Literature in Our Time and the University*, London: Chatto and Windus.

—— (1986) (ed. G. Singh) *Valuation in Criticism*, Cambridge: Cambridge University Press.

Leavis, F. R. and Leavis, Q. D. (1970) *Dickens the Novelist*, London: Chatto and Windus.

Lecomber, R. (1979) *The Economics of Natural Resources*, London: Macmillan.

Lee, N. (1989) 'Environmental impact assessment: a training guide', Occasional Paper 18, EIA Centre, University of Manchester.

Leopold, A. (1989) *A Sand County Almanac*, Oxford: Oxford University Press.

Levi, I. (1986) *Hard Choices*, Cambridge: Cambridge University Press.

Levin, P. (1979) 'Highway inquiries: a study in governmental responsiveness', *Public Administration* 57.

Lewin, R. (1993) *Complexity: Life at the Edge of Chaos*, London: Dent.

Lindblom, C. E. (1957) 'The science of muddling through', *Public Administration Review* 19.

—— (1965) *The Intelligence of Democracy*, New York: Free Press.

—— (1977) *Politics and Markets: The World's Political-Economic Systems*, New York: Basic Books.

Loasby, B. (1976) *Choice, Complexity and Ignorance: An Enquiry into Economic Theory and the Practice of Decision Making*, Cambridge: Cambridge University Press.

Lockwood, M. (1994) 'Noncompensatory preference structures in nonmarket valuation', mimeo, Johnstone Centre of Parks, Recreation and Heritage, Charles Sturt University, Albury, New South Wales.

Lowe, P., Clark, J. and Cox, G. (1993), 'Reasonable creatures: rights and rationalities in valuing the countryside', *Journal of Environmental Planning and Management* 36.

Luce, R. and Raiffa, H. (1957) *Games and Decisions: Introduction and Critical Survey*, New York: Wiley.

Lukes, S. (1985) *Marxism and Morality*, Oxford: Oxford University Press.

Lutz, M. A. and Lux, K. (1979) *The Challenge of Humanistic Economics*, Menlo Park, Calif.: Benjamin/Cummings.

—— (1988) *Humanistic Economics: The New Challenge*, New York: Bootstrap Press.

Machlup, F. (1972) 'The universal bogey: economic man', in M. Peston and B. Corry (eds) *Essays in Honour of Lord Robbins*, London: Weidenfeld and Nicolson.

MacIntyre, A. (1985) *After Virtue: A Study in Moral Theory*, 2nd edn (first published 1981), London: Duckworth.

Macnaghten, P., Grove-White, R., Jacobs, M. and Wynne, B. (1995) *Public Perceptions and Sustainability in Lancashire*, Lancaster: Centre for the Study of Environmental Change, Lancaster University and Lancashire County Council.

Madariaga, B. and McConnell, K. (1987) 'Exploring existence value', *Water Resources Research* 23, 5.

Malthus, T. R. (1820) *Principles of Political Economy* 1st edn, London: John Murray.

Margolis, H. (1982) *Selfishness, Altruism and Rationality*, Cambridge: Cambridge University Press.

Marin, A. (1992) 'Costs and benefits of risk reduction', appendix to ch. 6, *Risk: Analysis, Perception, Management*, London: Royal Society.

Marshall, A. (1920) *Principle of Economics*, 8th edn, Books I and II, London: Macmillan.

Martinez-Alier, J. (1987) *Ecological Economics*, Oxford: Blackwell Publishers.

—— (1991) 'Ecological perception, environmental policy and distributional conflicts: some lessons from history', in Constanza.

Martinez-Alier, J., with Schlupmann, K. (1987) *Ecological Economics: Energy, Environment and Society*, Oxford: Blackwell Publishers.

Maxwell, S. (1994), 'Valuation of rural environmental improvements using contingent valuation methodology: a case study of the Marston Vale community forest project', *Journal of Environmental Management* 41.

Meadows, D. H., Meadows, D. L. and Randers, J. (1992) *Beyond the Limits: Global Collapse or a Sustainable Future*, London: Earthscan.

Meadows, D. H., Meadows, D. L., Randers, J. and Behrens W. W. (1972) *The Limits to Growth*, London: Pan Books.

Melucci, A. (1989) *Nomads of the Present*, Philadelphia, Pa.: Temple University Press.

Meyer, A. and Cooper, A. (1995) *A Recalculation of the Social Costs of Environmental Change*, Sturminster Newton: Global Commons Institute/Ecologist.

Milbrath, L. (1989) *Envisioning a Sustainable Society: Learning Our Way Out*, Albany, NY: State University of New York Press.

Mill, J. S. (1844) *Essays on Some Unsettled Questions of Political Economy*, London: Longman, Green, Reader and Dyer. Reprinted 1948 by the London School of Economics.

—— (1874) 'Nature', in *Three Essays on Religion*, London: Longmans.

Miller, D. (1992) 'Deliberative democracy and social choice', *Political Studies* 40.

Mitchell, R. C. and Carson, R. T. (1989) *Using Surveys to Value Public Goods*, Washington DC: Resources for the Future.

Moore, G. E. (1903) *Principia Ethica*, Cambridge: Cambridge University Press.

Mowery, D. and Rosenberg, N. (1979) 'The influence of market demand upon innovation', *Research Policy* 8.

Murdoch, I. (1970) *The Sovereignty of Good*, London: Routledge.

Nagel, T. (1979) *Mortal Questions*, Cambridge: Cambridge University Press.

—— (1986) *The View From Nowhere*, Oxford: Oxford University Press.

Nature Conservancy Council (1990) *The Treatment of Nature Conservation in the Appraisal of Trunk Roads* (submission to the Standing Committee on Trunk Road Assessment), P. G. Hopkinson, J. Bowers and C. A. Nash, Institute for Transport Studies, University of Leeds.

Nelson, R. and Winter, S. (1977) 'In search of a useful theory of innovation', *Research Policy* 6.

NOAA Panel (1993) National Oceanic and Atmospheric Administration 'Report of the NOAA Panel on contingent valuation', *US Federal Register* 58.

Nordhaus, R. (1991) 'To slow or not to slow: the economics of the greenhouse effect', *Economic Journal* 101.

Norgaard, R. B. (1990) 'Economic indicators of resource scarcity: a critical essay', *Journal of Environmental Economics and Management* 18.

—— (1994) *Development Betrayed: The End of Progress and a Coevolutionary Revisioning of the Future*, London: Routledge.

North, R. D. (1995) *Life on a Modern Planet*, Manchester: Manchester University Press.

Norton, B. (1986) *The Preservation of Species*, Princeton, NJ: Princeton University Press.

—— (1987) *Why Preserve Natural Variety?* Princeton, NJ: Princeton, University Press.

—— (1994) 'Economists' preferences and the preferences of economists', *Environmental Values* 3.

Nuffield Foundation (1986) *Town and Country Planning*, London: Nuffield Foundation.

O'Connor, M. (1993) 'On the misadventures of capitalist nature', *Capitalism, Nature and Society*, September.

OECD (1989) *Environmental Policy Benefits: Monetary Valuation*, Pearce, D. and Markandya, A., Paris: OECD.

—— (1993) *Expert Workshop on Life Cycle Analysis of Energy Systems*, Paris: OECD.

258

O'Neill, J. (1993) *Ecology, Policy and Politics: Human Well-being and the Natural World,* London: Routledge.

—— (1994) 'Preferences, virtues and institutions', *Analyse & Kritik* 16, 2.

—— (1995) 'In partial praise of a positivist', *Radical Philosophy* 74.

—— (forthcoming) 'Public choice, institutional economics, environmental goods', *Environmental Politics.*

—— (forthcoming) 'Economy, polity, neutrality', *Political Studies.*

Ormerod, P. (1994) *The Death of Economics,* London: Faber.

Ottinger, R. (1990) 'Getting at the true cost of electric power', *The Electricity Journal.*

Page, T. (1991) 'Sustainability and the problem of valuation', in Constanza.

Parfit, D. (1984) *Reasons and Persons,* Oxford: Clarendon Press.

Parsons, T. (1937) *The Structure of Social Action,* vol. 2, New York: McGraw-Hill.

—— (1968) *The Structure of Social Action,* New York: Free Press.

Payne, J. W., Bettman, J. R. and Johnson, E. J. (1992) 'Behavioural decision research: a constructive processing perspective', *Annual Review of Psychology* 43.

Pearce, D. (1993) *Economic Values and the Natural World,* London: Earthscan.

Pearce, D. and Markandya, A. (1989) *Environmental Policy Benefits: Monetary valuation,* Paris: OECD.

Pearce, D. and Moran, D. (1994) *The Economic Value of Biodiversity,* London: Earthscan.

Pearce, D. and Nash, C. A. (1981) *The Social Appraisal of Projects: A Text in Cost–benefit Analysis,* London: Methuen.

Pearce, D., Markandya, A. and Barbier, E. (1989) *Blueprint for a Green Economy,* London: Earthscan.

Pearce, D. *et al.* (1991) *Blueprint 2: Greening the World Economy,* London: Earthscan.

Pearce, D. W. and Turner, R. K. (1990) *Economics of Natural Resources and the Environment,* New York and London: Harvester.

Pearce, F. (1992) 'The Battle for Britain's bogs', *New Scientist* 136, 1849, 28 November.

Peirce, C. S. (1893) 'Evolutionary love', reprinted in C. W. Peirce (1923) *Chance, Love and Logic,* ed. M. R. Cohen, New York: Harcourt, Brace.

—— (1934) *Collected Papers of Charles Sanders Peirce,* vol. V, *Pragmatism and Pragmaticism,* ed. C. Hartshorne and P. Weiss, Cambridge, Mass.: Harvard University Press.

Penrose, R. (1989) *The Emperor's New Mind: Concerning Computers, Minds and the Laws of Physics,* London: Vintage.

Peterson, G. L., Driver, B. L. and Gregory R. (eds) (1988) *Amenity Resource Valuation: Integrating Economics with Other Disciplines,* Philadelphia, Pa.: Venture.

Pielou, E. (1969) *An Introduction to Mathematical Ecology,* New York: Wiley.

—— (1975) *Ecological Diversity,* New York: Wiley.

Pigou, A. C. (1920) *The Economics of Welfare,* 4th edn, London: Macmillan.

Pinkus, C. E. and Dixson, A. (1981) *Solving Local Government Problems,* London: Allen and Unwin.

Pitkin, H. (1981) 'Justice: on relating public and private', *Political Theory* 9.

Plant, R. (1989) 'Socialism, markets and end states', in J. Le Grand and S. Estrin (eds) *Market Socialism,* Oxford: Oxford University Press.

Plott, C. R. (1993) 'Contingent valuation: a view of the conference and associated research', in J. A. Hausman (ed.) *Contingent Valuation: A Critical Assessment,* Amsterdam: North Holland.

Polanyi, K. (1944) *The Great Transformation,* New York: Rinehart.

Poole, R. (1985) 'Morality, masculinity and the market', in P. Osborne and S. Sayers (eds) *Socialism, Feminism and Philosophy,* London: Routledge.

Poole, R. (1989) 'Is it chaos or is it just noise?', *Science* 243.

Porter, T. (1995) *Trust in Numbers*, Princeton NJ: Princeton University Press.

Power, M. (1995) *The Audit Explosion*, London: Demos.

Prigogine, I. and Stengers, I. (1984) *Order out of Chaos: Man's New Dialogue with Nature*, London: Flamingo.

Raiffa, H. (1985) 'Back from prospect theory to utility theory', in Thompson, Wierzbicki and Grauer.

Randall, A. (1987) *Resource Economics: An Economic Approach to Natural Resource and Environmental Policy*, Chichester: Wiley.

Ratcliffe, D. (1977) *A Nature Conservation Review*, Cambridge: Cambridge University Press.

Rawles, K. and Holland, A. (1993) 'The ethics of conservation', *ECOS* 14.

Raz, J. (1986) *The Morality of Freedom*, Oxford: Clarendon Press.

Regan, T. (1981) 'The nature and possibility of an environmental ethic', *Environmental Ethics* 3.

—— (1984) *The Case for Animal Rights*, London: Routledge.

Rip, A., Misa, T. and Schot, J. (1995) *Managing Technology in Society*, Frances Pinter.

Rizvi, S. A. T. (1994a) 'The microfoundations project in general equilibrium theory', *Cambridge Journal of Economics* 18, 4.

—— (1994b) 'Game theory to the rescue?', *Contributions to Political Economy* 13.

Robbins, L. (1932) *An Essay on the Nature and Significance of Economic Science*, London: Macmillan.

Roberts, L., Haynes, M. and O'Riordan, T. (eds) (1986) *Nuclear Power and Public Acceptance*, Norwich: University of East Anglia.

Rolston, H. (1983) 'Are values in Nature subjective or objective?', in Elliott and Gare.

—— (1988) *Environmental Ethics*, Philadelphia, Pa.: Temple University Press.

Rosenthal, D. and Nelson, R. (1992) 'Why existence value should not be used in cost–benefit analysis', *Journal of Policy Analysis and Management* 11.

Roskill (1971) *Report of the Roskill Commission of Inquiry on the Third London Airport*, London: HMSO.

Routley, R. and Routley, V. (1979) 'Against the inevitability of human chauvanism', in K. E. Goodpaster and J. Sayre (eds) *Ethics and the Problems of the 21st Century*, Notre Dame, Ind.: University of Notre Dame Press.

Rowe, R. D., d'Arge, R. C. and Brookshire, D. S. (1980) 'An experiment on the economic value of visibility', *Journal of Environmental Economics and Management* 7, 1.

Roy, S. (1989) *Philosophy of Economics*, London: Routledge.

Royal Society (1992) *Risk: Analysis, Perception and Management*, London: Royal Society of London.

Rubin, J., Helfand, G. and Loomis, J. (1991) 'A benefit–cost analysis of the northern spotted owl. Results from a contingent valuation study', *Journal of Forestry* 89.

Ruelle, D. (1991) *Chance and Chaos*, Harmondsworth: Penguin.

Ruskin, J. (1866) *Unto This Last: Four Essays on the First Principles of Political Economy*, London: John Wiley.

Russell-Jones, R. and Southwood, R. (1987) *Radiation and Health: the Biological Effects of Low Level Exposure to Ionising Radiation*, Chichester: Wiley.

Sagoff, M. (1988a) 'Some problems with environmental economics', *Environmental Ethics*, 10, 1.

—— (1988b) *The Economy of the Earth*, Cambridge: Cambridge University Press.

Salt, H. S. (1928) *Our Vanishing Wildflowers*, London: Watts and Co.

Samples, K. C., Dixon, J. A. and Gowen, M. M. (1986) 'Information disclosure and endangered species valuation', *Land Economics* 62.

Samuelson, P. A. (1961) *Foundations of Economic Analysis*, Cambridge, Mass.: Harvard University Press.

San Martin, R. (1989) *Environmental Emissions from Energy Technology Systems: The Total Fuel Cycle*, in IEA.

Saward, M. (1993) 'Green democracy?', in A. Dobson and P. Lucardie (eds) *The Politics of Nature*, London: Routledge.

Schkade, D. O. and Payne, J. (1994) 'How people respond to contingent valuation questions: a verbal protocol analysis of willingness to pay for an environmental regulation', *Journal of Environmental Economics and Management* 26, 1.

Schrader-Frechette, K. (1985) *Science Policy, Ethics and Economic Methodology*, Dordrecht: Reidel.

Schumacher, E.F. (1974) *Small is Beautiful*, London: Abacus.

Schumpeter, J. A. (1976) *Capitalism, Socialism and Democracy*, 5th edn (first published 1942), London: George Allen and Unwin.

Schwartz, M. and Thompson, M. (1990) *Divided We Stand: Redefining Politics, Technology and Social Choice*, Brighton: Harvester.

Sears, D. O. and Funk, C. L. (1991) 'The role of self-interest in social and political attitudes', *Advances in Experimental Social Psycology* 24.

Sen, A. (1977) 'Rational fools: a critique of the behavioural foundations of economic theory', *Philosophy and Public Affairs* 6.

—— (1986) 'Foundations of social choice theory: an epilogue', in J. Elster and A. Hylland (eds) *Foundations of Social Choice Theory*, Cambridge: Cambridge University Press.

—— (1987) *On Ethics and Economics*, Oxford and New York: Basil Blackwell Publishers.

—— (1990) 'Is the idea of purely internal consistency of choice bizarre?', Harvard Institute of Economic Research discussion paper no. 1477.

Sheffrin, S. (1978) 'Habermas, depoliticization and consumer theory', *Journal of Economic Issues* 12.

Shelley, M. W. and Bryan, G. L. (1964a) 'Judgements and the language of decisions', in Shelley and Bryan 1964b.

Shelley, M. W. and Bryan, G. L. (eds) (1964b) *Human Judgements and Optimality*, New York: Wiley.

Shiva, V. (1992) 'The real meaning of sustainability', in Cooper and Palmer.

Simon, H. (1957) *Administrative Behaviour*, 2nd edn, New York: Macmillan.

—— (1960) *The New Science of Management Decision*, Englewood Cliffs, NJ: Prentice Hall

Singer, P. (1979) *Practical Ethics*, Cambridge: Cambridge University Press.

Slovic, P. (1992) 'Perceptions of risk: reflections on the psychometric paradigm', in Krimsky and Golding.

Smith, P. G. R. and Theberge, J. B. (1986) 'A review of criteria for evaluation of natural areas', *Environmental Management* 10.

Söderbaum, P. (1992) 'Neoclassical and institutional approaches to development and the environment', *Ecological Economics* 5, 2.

—— (1994) 'Environmental policy', in Hodgson *et al.*, vol.. 1.

Solow, R. M. (1974) 'The economics of resources or the resources of economics', *American Economic Review* 64.

Spash, C. L. (1993) 'Estimating the importance of inviolable rights: the case of long term damages and future generations', unpublished report to the Scottish Economic Society.

—— (1994a) 'Double CO_2 and beyond: benefits, costs and compensation', *Ecological Economics* 10.

—— (1994b) 'Trying to find the right approach to greenhouse economics: some reflections upon the role of cost–benefit analysis', *Analyze & Kritik* 16.

—— (1995) 'The political economy of Nature', *Review of Political Economy* 7, 3.

Spash, C. L. and Hanley, N. D. (1995) 'Preferences, information and biodiversity preservation', *Ecological Economics* 12, 3.

Spash, C. L. and Simpson, I. A. (1993) 'Protecting sites of special scientific interest', *Journal of Environmental Management* 39.

—— (1994) 'Utilitarian and rights based alternatives for protecting sites of special scientific interest', *Journal of Agricultural Economics* 45, 1.

Steele, D. (1992) *From Marx to Mises: Post-capitalist Society and the Challenge of Economic Calculation*, La Salle, Ill.: Open Court.

Steppacher, R. (1994) 'Kapp, K. William', in Hodgson *et al.*, vol. 1.

Stevens, T. H., More, T. A. and Glass, R. J. (1994) 'Interpretation and temporal stability of CV bids for wildlife existence: A panel study', *Land Economics* 70.

Stevens, T. H., Echevarria, J., Glass, R. J., Hager, T. and More, T. A. (1991) 'Measuring the existence value of wildlife: What do CVM estimates really show?', *Land Economics* 67, 4.

Stewart, Justice D. G., Mills, R. and Hamilton, C. (1991) *Perspectives on the RAC*, Occasional Paper No. 2, Canberra: Resource Assessment Commission.

Stewart, J., Kendall, E. and Coote, A. (1994) *Citizens' Juries*, London: Institute for Public Policy Research.

Stirling, A. (1992) 'Regulating the electricity supply industry by valuing environmental effects', *Futures* 24, 10.

—— (1994a) 'Diversity and ignorance in electricity supply investment: addressing the solution rather than the problem', *Energy Policy* 22, 3.

—— (1994b) 'Technology choice for electricity supply: putting the money where the mouth is?', D.Phil thesis, Science Policy Research Unit, University of Sussex.

—— (1995) 'Diversity in electricity supply portfolios: an alternative to probabilistic approaches', Sussex: *Bulletin of the European Network for Energy Economics Research* 16.

Stone, A. (1992) 'Contingent valuation of the Bamah Wetlands, Victoria', in M. Lockwood and T. De Lacy (eds) *Valuing Natural Areas: Applications and Problems of the Contingent Valuation Method*, Albury, NSW: Johnstone Centre of Parks, Recreation and Heritage.

Taylor, P. (1986) *Respect for Nature*, Princeton, NJ: Princeton University Press.

Thomas, K. (1983) *Man and the Natural World*, Harmondsworth: Allen Lane.

Thompson, E. P. (1991) [1971] 'The moral economy of the English crowd in the eighteenth century', in *Customs in Common*, London: Merlin Press.

Thompson, M., Wierzbicki, A. and Grauer, M. (eds) (1985) *Plural Rationalities and Interactive Decision Processes*, Berlin: Springer.

Toman, M.A. (1994) 'Economics and sustainability: balancing trade-offs and imperatives', *Land Economics* 70.

Tool, M. R. (1979) *The Discretionary Economy*, Santa Monica, Calif.: Goodyear.

Toyne Report (1993) *Environmental Responsibility: An Agenda for Further and Higher Education*, London: HMSO.

Turner, R. K. (1988a) 'Wetland conservation: Economics and ethics', in D. Collard, D. Pearce and D. Ulph (eds) *Economics, Growth and Sustainable Environments*, London: Macmillan.

Turner, R. K. (ed.) (1988b) *Sustainable Environmental Management: Principles and Practice*, London: Belhaven.

Turner, R. K. and Pearce, D. (1993) 'Sustainable economic development: economic and ethical principles', in E. Barbier (ed.) *Economics and Ecology: New Frontiers and Sustainable Development*, London: Chapman and Hall.

UKHMG (1995) 'The economics of safety regulation in the UK: an initial report', UK Government Interdepartmental Working Party on the Setting on Safety Standards, chaired by M. Spackman (Treasury); subgroup of Standing Interdepartmental Group on Economic Appraisal and Evalution.

Vadnjal, D. and O'Connor, M. (1994) 'What is the value of Rangitoto Island?', *Environmental Values* 3, 4.

van De Veer, D. and Pierce, C. (1986) *People, Penguins and Plastic Trees: Basic Issues in Environmental Ethics*, Wadsworth.

Vatn, A. and Bromley, D. (1994) 'Choices without prices without apologies', *Journal of Environmental Economics and Management* 26.

Veblen, T. B. (1919) *The Place of Science in Modern Civilisation and Other Essays*, New York: Huebsch. Reprinted 1990 with a new introduction by W. J. Samuels, New Brunswick, NJ: Transaction.

von Bertalanffy, L. (1969) 'The theory of open systems in physics and biology', in Emery.

von Furstenberg, G. (ed.) (1990) *Acting Under Uncertainty: Multidisciplinary Conceptions*, Boston: Kluwer.

von Mises, L. (1949) *Human Action: A Treatise on Economics*, London: William Hodge.

—— (1981) *Socialism*, trans. J. Kahane, Indianapolis, Ind.: Liberty Press.

von Winterfeldt, D. and Edwards, W. (1986) *Decisions Analysis and Behavioural Research*, Cambridge: Cambridge University Press.

von Winterfeldt, D. and Fischer, G. (1975) 'Multi-attribute utility theory: models and assessment procedures', in Wendt and Vlek.

Waldrop, M. (1992) *Complexity: The Emerging Science at the Edge of Order and Chaos*, London: Viking.

Waller, W. J. (1994) 'The Veblenian dichotomy and its critics', in Hodgson *et al.*, vol. 2.

Walsh, R. G., Loomis, J. B. and Gilman, R. A. (1984) 'Valuing option, existence and bequest demands for wilderness', *Land Economics* 60.

Wathern, P. (ed.) (1988) *Environmental Impact Assessment: Theory and Practice*, London: Unwin Hyman.

Weale, A. (1992) 'Nature versus the state? Markets, states, and environmental protection', *Critical Review* 6, 2–3: 153–70.

Wendt, D. and Vlek, C. A. J. (eds) (1975) *Utility, Probability and Human Decision Making*, Dordrecht: Reidel.

West, B. and Schlesinger, M. (1990) 'The noise in natural phenomena', *American Scientist* 78.

Wiggins, D. (1980) 'Weakness of will, commensurability and the objects of deliberation and desire', in A. Rorty (ed.) *Essays on Aristotle's Ethics*, Berkeley, Calif.: University of California Press.

Wildavsky, A. (1987) 'Choosing preferences by constructing institutions: a cultural theory of preference formation', *American Political Science Review* 81, 1.

Williams, B. (1985) *Ethics and the Limits of Philosophy*, London: Fontana.

—— (1992) 'Must a concern for the environment be centred on human beings?', in C. C. W. Taylor (ed.) *Ethics and the Environment*, Oxford: Corpus Christi College.

Williams, R. (1961) *The Long Revolution*, London: Chatto and Windus.

Willis, K. (1995) 'Contingent valuation in a policy context: the NOAA report and its implications for the use of contingent valuation methods in policy analysis in Britain', in K. Willis and J. Corkindale (eds) *Environmental Valuation: New Perspectives*, Wallingford: CAB International.

Willis K. G. and Benson, J. F. (1988) 'Valuation and wildlife' in R. K. Turner (ed.) *Sustainable Environmental Management: Principles and Practice*, Boulder, Colo.: Westview Press.

Wilson, B. (ed.) (1970) *Rationality*, Oxford: Blackwell Publishers.

Winner, L. (1977) 'Autonomous technology: technics out of control as a theme in political thought', Boston, Mass.: MIT Press.

—— (1983) 'Techne and politeia: the technical constitution of society', in Durbin, P. and Rapp, F., *Philosophy and Technology*, Dordrecht: Reidel.

Winpenny, J. (1991) *Values for the Environment: A Guide to Economic Appraisal*, London: HMSO.

Wittgenstein, L. (1958) *Philosophical Investigations*, 2nd edn, trans. G. E. M. Anscombe, Oxford: Blackwell.

—— (1969) *On Certainty*, trans. G. E. M. Anscombe and D. Paul, Oxford: Blackwell Publishers.

Wood, C. (1995) *Painting By Numbers*, Witham Park: Royal Society for Nature Conservation.

Woodcock, A. and Davis, M. (1978) *Catastrophe Theory: A Revolutionary New Way of Understanding How Things Change*, Harmondsworth: Penguin.

Wynne, B. (1975) 'The rhetoric of consensus politics: a critical review of technology assessment', *Research Policy* 4.

—— (1980) 'Technology, risk and participation: on the social treatment of uncertainty', in Conrad.

—— (1982) *Rationality and Ritual: The Windscale Inquiry and Nuclear Decisions in Britain*, Chalfont St Giles: British Society for the History of Science.

—— (1986) 'Public perceptions of nuclear risks: institutional development or technological treadmill?', in L. E. Roberts, M. Haynes and T. O'Riordan.

—— (1987) 'Risk perception, decision analysis, and the public acceptance problem', in *Risk Management and Hazardous Wastes: Implementation and the Dialectics of Credibility*, Berlin: Springer.

—— (1989) 'Building public concern into risk management', in J. Brown.

—— (1992) 'Uncertainty and environmental learning: Reconceiving science and policy in the preventive paradigm', *Global Environmental Change* 2, 2.

Wynne, B. and Mayer, S. (1993) 'How science fails the environment', *New Scientist* 138, 1876, 5 June.

Yearley, S. (1991) *The Green Case*, London: Harper Collins.

Young, I. M. (1990) *Justice and the Politics of Difference*, Princeton, NJ: Princeton University Press.

—— (1994) 'Communication and the other: beyond deliberative democracy', in M. Wilson and A. Yeatman (eds) *Justice, Biculturalism and Difference*, Wellington, NZ: Bridget Williams Books.

INDEX